Honoré de Balzac

Father Goriot and M. Gobseck

Honoré de Balzac

Father Goriot and M. Gobseck

ISBN/EAN: 9783337303501

Printed in Europe, USA, Canada, Australia, Japan

Cover: Foto ©Andreas Hilbeck / pixelio.de

More available books at **www.hansebooks.com**

H. DE BALZAC

FATHER GORIOT

(LE PÈRE GORIOT)

AND

M. GOBSECK

TRANSLATED BY

ELLEN MARRIAGE

WITH A PREFACE BY

GEORGE SAINTSBURY

PHILADELPHIA

THE GEBBIE PUBLISHING CO., Ltd.

1898

CONTENTS.

	PAGE
PREFACE	ix
FATHER GORIOT	1
M. GOBSECK	305

LIST OF ILLUSTRATIONS.

THERE WAS A SPLENDID CARRIAGE WAITING—— AND *she* GOT INTO IT . . . . *Frontispiece*

                                                                               PAGE

THE HORSE TOOK FRIGHT AT THE UMBRELLA 59

"AM I TO YOUR TASTE?" 151

VAUTRIN CAME IN IN HIGH SPIRITS 183

CLOTHES AND PAPERS AND RAGS LAY TOSSED ABOUT IN CONFUSION 363

PREFACE.

"FATHER GORIOT" perhaps deserves to be ranked as that one of Balzac's novels which has united the greatest number of suffrages, and which exhibits his peculiar merits, not indeed without any of his faults, but with the merits in eminent, and the faults not in glaring, degree. It was written (the preface is dated 1834) at the time when his genius was at its very height, when it had completely burst the strange shell which had so long enveloped and cramped it, when the scheme of the "Comédie Humaine" was not quite finally settled (it never was that), but elaborated to a very considerable extent, when the author had already acquired most of the knowledge of the actual world which he possessed, and when his physical powers were as yet unimpaired by his enormous labor and his reckless disregard of "burning the candle at both ends." Although it exhibits, like nearly all his work, the complication of interest and scheme which was almost a necessity to him, that complication is kept within reasonable bounds, and managed with wonderful address. The history of Goriot and his daughters, the fortunes of Eugène de Rastignac, and the mysterious personality and operations of Vautrin, not only all receive due and unperplexed development, but work upon each other with that correspondence and interdependence which form the rarest gift of the novelist, and which, when present, too commonly have attached to them the curse of over-minuteness and complexity. No piece of Balzac's Dutch painting is worked out with such marvelous minuteness as the Maison Vauquer, and hardly any book of his has more lifelike studies of character.

It would, however, not be difficult to find books with an almost, if not quite, equal accumulation of attractions, which have somehow failed to make the mark that has been made by "Father Goriot." And the practiced critic of novels knows perfectly well why this is. It is almost invariably, and perhaps quite invariably, because there is no sufficiently central interest, or because that interest is not of the broadly human kind. Had Goriot had no daughters, he would undoubtedly have been a happier man (or a less happy, for it is possible to take it both ways); but the history of his decadence and death never could have been such a good novel. It is because this history of the daughters—not exactly unnatural, not wholly without excuse, but as surely murderesses of their father as Goneril and Regan—at once unites and overshadows the whole, because of its intensity, its simple and suasive appeal, that "Father Goriot" holds the place it does hold. That it owes something in point of suggestion to "Lear" does not in the least impair its claims. The circumstances and treatment have that entire difference which, when genius is indebted to genius, pays all the score there is at once. And, besides, "Lear" has offered its motive for three hundred years to thousands and millions of people who have been writing plays and novels, and yet there is only one "Father Goriot."

It is, however, a fair subject of debate for those who like critical argument of the nicer kind, whether Balzac has or has not made a mistake in representing the ex-dealer in floury compounds as a sort of idiot outside his trade abilities and his love for his daughters. That in doing so he was guided by a sense of poetical justice and consistency—the same sense which made Shakespeare dwell on the ungovernable temper and the undignified haste to get rid of the cares of sovereignty that bring on and justify the woes of Lear—is undeniable. But it would perhaps not have been unnatural, and it would have been even more tragic, if the *ci-devant* manufacturer had been represented as more intellectually capable, and as ruining himself in spite of his better judgment. On this point, however, both sides may be held with equal ease and cogency, and I do not decide either way. Of the force and pathos of the actual representation, no two opinions are possible. There is hardly a touch of the one fault which can be urged against Balzac very often with some, and sometimes with very great, justice—the fault of exaggeration and phantasmagoric excess. Here at least the possibilities of actual life, as translatable into literature, are not one whit exceeded; and the artist has his full reward for being true to art.

Almost equally free from the abnormal and the gigantic is the portraiture of Rastignac. Even those who demur to the description of Balzac as an impeccable chronicler of society must admit the extraordinary felicity of the pictures of the young man's introduction to the drawing-rooms of Mesdames de Restaud and de Beauséant. Neither Fielding nor Thackeray—that is to say, no one else in the world of letters—could have drawn with more absolute vividness and more absolute veracity a young man, not a *parvenu* in point of birth, not devoid of native cleverness and "star," but hampered by the consciousness of poverty and by utter ignorance of the actual ways and current social fashions of the great world when he is first thrown, to sink or swim, into this great world itself. We may pass from the certain to the dubious, or at least the debatable, when we pass from Rastignac's first appearance to his later experiences. Here comes in what has been said in the general introduction as to the somewhat fantastic and imaginary, the conventional and artificial character of Balzac's world. But it must be remembered that for centuries the whole structure of Parisian society has been to a very great extent fantastic and imaginary, conventional and artificial. Men and women have always played parts there as they have played them nowhere else. And it must be confessed that some of the parts here, if planned to the stage, are played to the life—that of Madame de Beauséant especially.

It is Vautrin on whom Balzac's decriers, if they are so hardy as to attack this most unattackable book of his at all, must chiefly fasten. It was long ago noticed—indeed, sober eyes both in France and elsewhere noticed it at the time— that the criminal, more or less virtuous, more or less terrible, more or less superhuman, exercised a kind of sorcery over minds in France from the greatest to the least at this particular time, and even later. Not merely Balzac, but Victor Hugo and George Sand, succumbed to his fascinations; and after these three names it is quite unnecessary to mention any others. And Balzac's proneness to the enormous and gigantesque made the fascination peculiarly dangerous in his case. Undoubtedly the Vautrin who talks to Rastignac in the arbor is neither quite a real man nor quite the same man who is somewhat ignominiously caught by the treachery of his boarding-house fellows; undoubtedly we feel that with him we have left Shakespeare a long way behind, and are getting rather into the society of Bouchardy or Eugène Sue. But the genius is here likewise, and, as usual, it saves everything.

How it extends to the minutest and even the least savory details of Madame Vauquer's establishment, how it irradiates the meannesses and the sordidnesses of the inhabitants thereof, those who have read know, and those who are about to read this new presentation in English will find. Let it only be repeated, that if the rarest and strangest charms which Balzac can produce are elsewhere, nowhere else is his charm presented in a more pervading and satisfactory manner.

In "M. Gobseck" we find the hero quite interesting, the story of Derville and Fanny escapes mawkishness, and all the scenes in which the Restauds and Maxime de Trailles figure are admirably done and well worth reading. It is not necessary to take into consideration the important part which the Dutch Jew's grand-daughter or grandniece, Esther, afterwards plays in the "Comédie." He is good in himself, and a famous addition to Balzac's gallery of misers, the most interesting, if not the most authentic, ever arranged on that curious subject.

"M. Gobseck" was a "Scène de la vie Privée" from the first use of that title in 1830. Its own title, however, "Les Dangers de l'Inconduit," and "Papa Gobseck" varied a little, and it once made an excursion to the "Scènes de la vie Parisienne," but returned.

"Father Goriot" originally appeared as a book in 1835, published by Werdet and Spahmann, in two volumes. It had, however, appeared serially in the *Revue de Paris* during the previous winter. The first and some subsequent editions had seven chapter-divisions, six of them headed. These, according to Balzac's usual practice, were swept away when the book became, in 1843, part of the "Scènes de la vie Parisienne" and the "Comèdie" itself. The transferrence to the "Vie Privée," which is accomplished in the "Edition Définitive," was only executed in accordance with notes found after Balzac's death, and is far from happy, the book being essentially Parisian.

G. S.

FATHER GORIOT.

To the great and illustrious Geoffroy Saint-Hilaire, a token of admiration for his works and genius.

DE BALZAC.

MME. VAUQUER (*née* de Conflans) is an elderly person, who for the past forty years has kept a lodging-house in the Rue Neuve-Sainte-Geneviève, in the district that lies between the Latin Quarter and the Faubourg-Saint-Marcel. Her house (known in the neighborhood as the *Maison Vauquer*) receives men and women, old and young, and no word has ever been breathed against her respectable establishment; but, at the same time, it must be said that as a matter of fact no young woman has been under her roof for thirty years, and that if a young man stays there for any length of time it is a sure sign that his allowance must be of the slenderest. In 1819, however, the time when this drama opens, there was an almost penniless young girl among Mme. Vauquer's boarders.

That word drama has been somewhat discredited of late; it has been overworked and twisted to strange uses in these days of dolorous literature; but it must do service again here, not because this story is dramatic in the restricted sense of the word, but because some tears may perhaps be shed *intra et extra muros* before it is over.

Will any one without the walls of Paris understand it? It is open to doubt. The only audience who could appreciate the results of close observation, the careful reproduction of minute detail and local color, are dwellers between the heights of Montrouge and Montmartre, in a vale of crumbling stucco watered by streams of black mud, a vale of sorrows which are real and of joys too often hollow; but this audience is so accustomed to terrible sensations, that only some unimaginable and well-nigh impossible woe could produce any lasting impression there. Now and again there are tragedies so awful and so grand by reason of the complication of virtues and vices that bring them about, that egoism and selfishness are forced to pause and are moved to pity; but the impression that they receive is like a luscious fruit, soon consumed. Civilization, like the car of Juggernaut, is scarcely stayed perceptibly in its progress by a heart less easy to break than the others that lie in its course; this also is broken, and civilization continues on her course triumphant. And you, too, will do the like; you who with this book in your white hand will sink back among the cushions of your armchair, and say to yourself, "Perhaps this may amuse me." You will read the story of Father Goriot's secret woes, and, dining thereafter with an unspoiled appetite, will lay the blame of your insensibility upon the writer, and accuse him of exaggeration, of writing romances. Ah! once for all, this drama is neither a fiction nor a romance! *All is true*—so true, that every one can discern the elements of the tragedy in his own house, perhaps in his own heart.

The lodging-house is Mme. Vauquer's own property. It is still standing at the lower end of the Rue Neuve-Sainte-Geneviève, just where the road slopes so sharply down to the Rue de l'Arbalète, that wheeled traffic seldom passes that way, because it is so stony and steep. This position is sufficient to account for the silence prevalent in the streets shut in between the dome of the Panthéon and the dome of the Val-de-Grâce, two conspicuous public buildings which give a yellowish tone to the landscape and darken the whole district that lies beneath the shadow of their leaden-hued cupolas.

In that district the pavements are clean and dry, there is neither mud nor water in the gutters, grass grows in the chinks of the walls. The most heedless passer-by feels the depressing influences of a place where the sound of wheels creates a sensation; there is a grim look about the houses, a suggestion of a jail about those high garden walls. A Parisian straying into a suburb apparently composed of lodging-houses and public institutions would see poverty and dulness, old age lying down to die, and joyous youth condemned to drudgery. It is the ugliest quarter of Paris, and, it may be added, the least known. But, before all things, the Rue Neuve-Sainte-Geneviève is like a bronze frame for a picture for which the mind cannot be too well prepared by the contemplation of sad hues and sober images. Even so, step by step the daylight decreases, and the cicerone's droning voice grows hollower as the traveler descends into the catacombs. The comparison holds good! Who shall say which is more ghastly, the sight of the bleached skulls or of dried-up human hearts?

The front of the lodging-house is at right-angles to the road, and looks out upon a little garden, so that you see the side of the house in section, as it were, from the Rue Neuve-Sainte-Geneviève. Beneath the wall of the house-front there lies a channel, a fathom wide, paved with cobble-stones, and beside it runs a graveled walk bordered by geraniums and oleanders and pomegranates set in great blue and white glazed earthenware pots. Access into the graveled walk is afforded by a door, above which the words MAISON VAUQUER may be read, and beneath, in rather smaller letters, "*Lodgings for both sexes, etc.*"

During the day a glimpse into the garden is easily obtained through a wicket to which a bell is attached. On the opposite wall, at the farther end of the graveled walk, a green marble arch was painted once upon a time by a local artist, and in this semblance of a shrine a statue representing Cupid is installed; a Parisian Cupid, so blistered and disfigured that he looks like a candidate for one of the adjacent hospitals, and might suggest an allegory to lovers of symbolism. The half-obliterated inscription on the pedestal beneath determines the date of this work of art, for it bears witness to the widespread enthusiasm felt for Voltaire on his return to Paris in 1777—

"Whoe'er thou art, thy master see;
He is, or was, or ought to be."

At night the wicket gate is replaced by a solid door. The little garden is no wider than the front of the house; it is shut in between the wall of the street and the partition wall of the neighboring house. A mantle of ivy conceals the bricks and attracts the eyes of passers-by to an effect which is picturesque in Paris, for each of the walls is covered with trellised vines that yield a scanty, dusty crop of fruit, and furnish besides a subject of conversation for Mme. Vauquer and her lodgers; every year the widow trembles for her vintage.

A straight path beneath the walls on either side of the garden leads to a clump of lime trees at the farther end of it; *line* trees, as Mme. Vauquer persists in calling them, in spite of the fact that she was a de Conflans, and regardless of repeated corrections from her lodgers.

The central space between the walks is filled with artichokes and rows of pyramid fruit-trees, and surrounded by a border of lettuce, potherbs, and parsley. Under the lime trees there are a few green-painted garden seats and a wooden table, and hither, during the dog-days, such of the lodgers as are rich enough to indulge in a cup of coffee come to take their pleasure, though it is hot enough to roast eggs even in the shade.

The house itself is three stories high, without counting the attics under the roof. It is built of rough stone, and covered with the yellowish stucco that gives a mean appearance to almost every house in Paris. There are five windows in each story in the front of the house; all the blinds visible through the small square panes are drawn up awry, so that the lines are all at cross-purposes. At the side of the house there are but two windows on each floor, and the lowest of all are adorned with a heavy iron grating.

Behind the house a yard extends for some twenty feet, a space inhabited by a happy family of pigs, poultry, and rabbits; the wood-shed is situated on the farther side, and on the wall between the wood-shed and the kitchen window hangs the meat-safe, just above the place where the sink discharges its greasy streams. The cook sweeps all the refuse out through a little door into the Rue Neuve-Sainte-Geneviève, and frequently cleanses the yard with copious supplies of water, under pain of pestilence.

The house might have been built on purpose for its present uses. Access is given by a French window to the first room on the ground floor, a sitting-room which looks out upon the street through the two barred windows already mentioned. Another door opens out of it into the dining-room, which is separated from the kitchen by the wall of the staircase, the steps being constructed partly of wood, partly of tiles, which are colored and beeswaxed. Nothing can be more depressing than the sight of that sitting-room. The furniture is covered with horsehair woven in alternate dull and glossy stripes. There is a round table in the middle, with a purplish-red marble top, on which there stands, by way of ornament, the inevitable white china tea-service, covered with a half-effaced gilt network. The floor is sufficiently uneven, the wainscot rises to elbow height, and the rest of the wall space is decorated with a varnished paper, on which the principal scenes from *Télémaque* are depicted, the various classical personages being colored. The subject between the two windows is the banquet given by Calypso to the son of Ulysses, displayed thereon for the admiration of the boarders, and has furnished jokes these forty years to the young men who show themselves superior to their position by making fun of the dinners to which poverty condemns them. The hearth is always so clean and neat that it is evident that a fire is only kindled there on great occasions; the stone chimney-piece is adorned by a couple of vases filled with faded artificial flowers imprisoned under glass shades, on either side of a bluish-marble clock in the very worst taste.

The first room exhales an odor for which there is no name in the language, and which should be called the *odeur de pension*. The damp atmosphere sends a chill through you as you breathe it; it has a stuffy, musty, and rancid quality; it permeates your clothing; after-dinner scents seem to be mingled in it with smells from the kitchen and scullery and the reek of a hospital. It might be possible to describe it if some one should discover a process by which to distil from the atmosphere all the nauseating elements with which it is charged by the catarrhal exhalations of every individual lodger, young or old. Yet, in spite of these stale horrors, the sitting-room is as charming and as delicately perfumed as a boudoir, when compared with the adjoining dining-room.

The paneled walls of that apartment were once painted some color, now a matter of conjecture, for the surface is incrusted with accumulated layers of grimy deposit, which cover it with fantastic outlines. A collection of dim-ribbed glass decanters, metal discs with a satin sheen on them, and piles of blue-edged earthenware plates of Touraine ware cover the sticky surfaces of the sideboards that line the room. In a corner stands a box containing a set of numbered pigeon-holes, in which the lodgers' table napkins, more or less soiled and stained with wine, are kept. Here you see that indestructible furniture never met with elsewhere, which finds its way into lodging-houses much as the wrecks of our civilization drift into hospitals for incurables. You expect in such places as these to find the weather-house whence a Capuchin issues on wet days; you look to find the execrable engravings which spoil your appetite, framed every one in a black varnished frame, with a gilt beading round it; you know the sort of tortoise-shell clock-case, inlaid with brass; the green stove, the Argand lamps, covered with oil and dust, have met your eyes before. The oilcloth which covers the long table is so greasy that a waggish outsider will write his name on the surface, using his thumb-nail as a style. The chairs are broken-down invalids; the wretched little hempen mats slip away from under your feet without slipping away for good; and, finally, the foot-warmers are miserable wrecks, hingeless, charred, broken away about the holes. It would be impossible to give an idea of the old, rotten, shaky, cranky, worm-eaten, halt, maimed, one-eyed, rickety, and ramshackle condition of the furniture without an exhaustive description, which would delay the progress of the story to an extent that impatient people would not pardon. The red tiles of the floor are full of depressions brought about by scouring and periodical renewings of color. In short, there is no illusory grace left to the poverty that reigns here; it is dire, parsimonious, concentrated, threadbare poverty; as yet it has not sunk into the mire, it is only splashed by it, and, though not in rags as yet, its clothing is ready to drop to pieces.

This apartment is in all its glory at seven o'clock in the morning, when Mme. Vauquer's cat appears, announcing the near approach of his mistress, and jumps upon the sideboards to sniff at the milk in the bowls, each protected by a plate, while he purrs his morning greeting to the world. A moment later the widow shows her face; she is tricked out in a net cap attached to a false front set on awry, and shuffles into the room in her slipshod fashion. She is an oldish woman, with a bloated countenance, and a nose like a parrot's beak set in the middle of it; her fat little hands (she is as sleek as a church rat) and her shapeless, slouching figure are in keeping with the room that reeks of misfortune, where hope is reduced to speculate for the meanest stakes. Mme. Vauquer alone can breathe that tainted air without being disheartened by it. Her face is as fresh as a frosty morning in autumn; there are wrinkles about the eyes that vary in their expression from the set smile of a ballet-dancer to the dark, suspicious scowl of a discounter of bills; in short, she is at once the embodiment and interpretation of her lodging-house, as surely as her lodging-house implies the existence of its mistress. You can no more imagine the one without the other, than you can think of a jail without a turnkey. The unwholesome corpulence of the little woman is produced by the life she leads, just as typhus fever is bred in the tainted air of a hospital. The very knitted woolen petticoat that she wears beneath a skirt made of an old gown, with the wadding protruding through the rents in the material, is a sort of epitome of the sitting-room, the dining-room, and the little garden; it discovers the cook; it foreshadows the lodgers—the picture of the house is completed by the portrait of its mistress.

Mme. Vauquer at the age of fifty is like all women who "have seen a deal of trouble." She has the glassy eyes and innocent air of a trafficker in flesh and blood, who will wax virtuously indignant to obtain a higher price for her services, but who is quite ready to betray a Georges or a Pichegru, if a Georges or a Pichegru were in hiding and still to be betrayed, or for any other expedient that may alleviate her lot. Still, "she is a good woman at bottom," said the lodgers, who believed that the widow was wholly dependent upon the money that they paid her, and sympathized when they heard her cough and groan like one of themselves.

What had M. Vauquer been? The lady was never very explicit on this head. How had she lost her money? "Through trouble," was her answer. He had treated her badly, had left her nothing but her eyes to cry over his cruelty, the house she lived in, and the privilege of pitying nobody, because, so she was wont to say, she herself had been through every possible misfortune.

Sylvie, the stout cook, hearing her mistress' shuffling footsteps, hastened to serve the lodgers' breakfast. Besides those who lived in the house, Mme. Vauquer took boarders who came for their meals; but these outsiders usually only came to dinner, for which they paid thirty francs a month.

At the time when this story begins, the lodging-house contained seven inmates. The best rooms in the house were on the first story, Mme. Vauquer herself occupying the least important, while the rest were let to a Mme. Couture, the widow of a commissary-general in the service of the Republic. With her lived Victorine Taillefer, a school-girl, to whom she filled the place of mother. These two ladies paid eighteen hundred francs a year.

The two sets of rooms on the second floor were respectively occupied by an old man named Poiret and a man of forty or thereabouts, the wearer of a black wig and dyed whiskers, who gave out that he was a retired merchant, and was addressed as M. Vautrin. Two of the four rooms on the third floor were also let—one to an elderly spinster, a Mlle. Michonneau, and the other to a retired manufacturer of vermicelli, Italian paste and starch, who allowed the others to address him as "Father Goriot." The remaining rooms were allotted to various birds of passage, to impecunious students, who, like "Father Goriot" and Mlle. Michonneau, could only muster forty-five francs a month to pay for their board and lodging. Mme. Vauquer had little desire for lodgers of this sort; they ate too much bread, and she only took them in default of better.

At that time one of the rooms was tenanted by a law student, a young man from the neighborhood of Angoulême, one of a large family who pinched and starved themselves to spare twelve hundred francs a year for him. Misfortune had accustomed Eugène de Rastignac, for that was his name, to work. He belonged to the number of young men who know as children that their parents' hopes are centred on them, and deliberately prepare themselves for a great career, subordinating their studies from the first to this end, carefully watching the indications of the course of events, calculating the probable turn that affairs will take, that they may be the first to profit by them. But for his observant curiosity, and the skill with which he managed to introduce himself into the salons of Paris, this story would not have been colored by the tones of truth which it certainly owes to him, for they are entirely due to his penetrating sagacity and desire to fathom the mysteries of an appalling condition of things which was concealed as carefully by the victim as by those who had brought it to pass.

Above the third story there was a garret where the linen was hung to dry, and a couple of attics. Christophe, the man-of-all-work, slept in one, and Sylvie, the stout cook, in the other. Besides the seven inmates thus enumerated, taking one year with another, some eight law or medical students dined in the house, as well as two or three regular comers who lived in the neighborhood. There were usually eighteen people at dinner, and there was room, if need be, for twenty at Mme. Vauquer's table; at breakfast, however, only the seven lodgers appeared. It was almost like a family party. Every one came down in dressing-gown and slippers, and the conversation usually turned on anything that had happened the evening before; comments on the dress or appearance of the dinner contingent were exchanged in friendly confidence.

These seven lodgers were Mme. Vauquer's spoiled children. Among them she distributed, with astronomical precision, the exact proportion of respect and attention due to the varying amounts they paid for their board. One single consideration influenced all these human beings thrown together by chance. The two second-floor lodgers only paid seventy-two francs a month. Such prices as these are confined to the Faubourg Saint-Marcel and the district between La Bourbe and the Salpêtrière; and, as might be expected, poverty, more or less apparent, weighed upon them all, Mme. Couture being the sole exception to the rule.

The dreary surroundings were reflected in the costumes of the inmates of the house; all were alike threadbare. The color of the men's coats was problematical; such shoes, in more fashionable quarters, are only to be seen lying in the gutter; the cuffs and collars were worn and frayed at the edges; every limp article of clothing looked like the ghost of its former self. The women's dresses were faded, old-fashioned, dyed and re-dyed; they wore gloves that were glazed with hard wear, much-mended lace, dingy ruffles, crumpled muslin fichus. So much for their clothing; but, for the most part, their frames were solid enough; their constitutions had weathered the storms of life; their cold, hard faces were worn like coins that have been withdrawn from circulation, but there were greedy teeth behind the withered lips. Dramas brought to a close or still in progress are foreshadowed by the sight of such actors as these, not the dramas that are played before the footlights and against a background of painted canvas, but dumb dramas of life frost-bound dramas that sear hearts like fire, dramas that do not end with the actors' lives.

Mlle. Michonneau, that elderly young lady, screened her weak eyes from the daylight by a soiled green silk shade with a rim of brass, an object fit to scare away the Angel of Pity himself. Her shawl, with its scanty, draggled fringe, might have covered a skeleton, so meagre and angular was the form beneath it. Yet she must have been pretty and shapely once. What corrosive had destroyed the feminine outlines? Was it trouble, or vice, or greed? Had she loved too well? Had she been a second-hand clothes dealer, a frequenter of the back-stairs of great houses, or had she been merely a courtesan? Was she expiating the flaunting triumphs of a youth overcrowded with pleasures by an old age in which she was shunned by every passer-by? Her vacant gaze sent a chill through you; her shriveled face seemed like a menace. Her voice was like the shrill, thin note of the grasshopper sounding from the thicket when winter is at hand. She said that she had nursed an old gentleman, ill of catarrh of the bladder, and left to die by his children, who thought that he had nothing left. His bequest to her, a life annuity of a thousand francs, was periodically disputed by his heirs, who mingled slander with their persecutions. In spite of the ravages of conflicting passions, her face retained some traces of its former fairness and fineness of tissue, some vestiges of the physical charms of her youth still survived.

M. Poiret was a sort of automaton. He might be seen any day sailing like a gray shadow along the walks of the Jardin des Plantes, on his head a shabby cap, a cane with an old yellow ivory handle in the tips of his thin fingers; the outspread skirts of his threadbare overcoat failed to conceal his meagre figure; his breeches hung loosely on his shrunken limbs; the thin, blue-stockinged legs trembled like those of a drunken man; there was a notable breach of continuity between the dingy white waistcoat and crumpled shirt frills and the cravat twisted about a throat like a turkey gobler's; altogether, his appearance set people wondering whether this outlandish ghost belonged to the audacious race of the sons of Japhet who flutter about on the Boulevard Italien. What kind of toil could have so shriveled him? What devouring passions had darkened that bulbous countenance, which would have seemed outrageous as a caricature? What had he been? Well, perhaps he had been part of the machinery of justice, a clerk in the office to which the executioner sends in his accounts—so much for providing black veils for parricides, so much for sawdust, so much for pulleys and cord for the knife. Or he might have been a receiver at the door of a public slaughter-house, or a sub-inspector of nuisances. Indeed, the man appeared to have been one of the beasts of burden in our great social mill; one of those Parisian ratons whom their Bertrands do not even know by sight; a pivot in the obscure machinery that disposes of misery and things unclean; one of those men, in short, at sight of whom we are prompted to remark that, "After all, we cannot do without them."

Stately Paris ignores the existence of these faces bleached by moral or physical suffering; but, then, Paris is in truth an ocean that no line can fathom. You may survey its surface and describe it; but no matter what pains you take with your investigations and recognizances, no matter how numerous and painstaking the toilers in this sea, there will always be lonely and unexplored regions in its depths, caverns unknown, flowers and pearls and monsters of the deep overlooked or forgotten by the divers of literature. The Maison Vauquer is one of these curious monstrosities.

Two, however, of Mme. Vauquer's boarders formed a striking contrast to the rest. There was a sickly pallor, such as is often seen in anæmic girls, in Mlle. Victorine Taillefer's face; and her unvarying expression of sadness, like her embarrassed manner and pinched look, was in keeping with the general wretchedness of the establishment in the Rue Neuve-Sainte-Geneviève, which forms a background to this picture; but her face was young, there was youthfulness in her voice and elasticity in her movements. This young unfortunate was not unlike a shrub, newly planted in an uncongenial soil, where its leaves have already begun to wither. The outlines of her figure, revealed by her dress of the simplest and cheapest materials, were also youthful. There was the same kind of charm about her too slender form, her faintly colored face and light-brown hair, that modern poets find in mediæval statuettes; and a sweet expression, a look of Christian resignation in the dark-gray eyes. She was pretty by force of contrast; if she had been happy, she would have been charming. Happiness is the poetry of woman, as the toilet is her tinsel. If the delightful excitement of a ball had made the pale face glow with color; if the delights of a luxurious life had brought the color to the wan cheeks that were slightly hollowed already; if love had put light into the sad eyes, then Victorine might have ranked among the fairest; but she lacked the two things which create woman a second time—pretty dresses and love-letters.

A book might have been made of her story. Her father

was persuaded that he had sufficient reason for declining to acknowledge her, and allowed her a bare six hundred francs a year; he had further taken measures to disinherit his daughter, and had converted all his real estate into personalty, that he might leave it undivided to his son. Victorine's mother had died broken-hearted in Mme. Couture's house; and the latter, who was a near relation, had taken charge of the little orphan. Unluckily, the widow of the commissary-general to the armies of the Republic had nothing in the world but her jointure and her widow's pension, and some day she might be obliged to leave the helpless, inexperienced girl to the mercy of the world. The good soul, therefore, took Victorine to mass every Sunday, and to confession once a fortnight, thinking that, in any case, she would bring up her ward to be devout. She was right; religion offered a solution of the problem of the young girl's future. The poor child loved the father who refused to acknowledge her. Once every year she tried to see him to deliver her mother's message of forgiveness, but every year hitherto she had knocked at that door in vain; her father was inexorable. Her brother, her only means of communication, had not come to see her for four years, and had sent her no assistance; yet she prayed to God to unseal her father's eyes and to soften her brother's heart, and no accusations mingled with her prayers. Mme. Couture and Mme. Vauquer exhausted the vocabulary of abuse, and failed to find words that did justice to the banker's iniquitous conduct; but while they heaped execrations on the millionaire, Victorine's words were as gentle as the moan of the wounded dove, and affection found expression even in the cry drawn from her by pain.

Eugène de Rastignac was a thoroughly southern type; he had a fair complexion, blue eyes, black hair. In his figure, manner, and his whole bearing it was easy to see that he either came of a noble family, or that, from his earliest childhood, he had been gently bred. If he was careful of his wardrobe, only taking last year's clothes into daily wear, still upon occasion he could issue forth as a young man of fashion. Ordinarily he wore a shabby coat and waistcoat, the limp black cravat, untidily knotted, that students affect, trousers that matched the rest of his costume, and boots that had been re-soled.

Vautrin (the man of forty with the dyed whiskers) marked a transition stage between these two young people and the others. He was the kind of man that calls forth the remark: "He looks a jovial sort!" He had broad shoulders, a well-developed chest, muscular arms, and strong square-fisted hands; the joints of his fingers were covered with tufts of fiery red hair. His face was furrowed by premature wrinkles; there was a certain hardness about it in spite of his bland and insinuating manner. His bass voice was by no means unpleasant, and was in keeping with his boisterous laughter. He was always obliging, always in good spirits; if anything went wrong with one of the locks, he would soon unscrew it, take it to pieces, file it, oil and clean and set it in order, and put it back in its place again: "I am an old hand at it," he used to say. Not only so, he knew all about ships, the sea, France, foreign countries, men, business, law, great houses and prisons—there was nothing that he did not know. If any one complained rather more than usual, he would offer his services at once. He had several times loaned money to Mme. Vauquer, or to the boarders; but, somehow, those whom he obliged felt that they would sooner face death than fail to repay him; a certain resolute look, sometimes seen on his face, inspired fear of him, for all his appearance of easy good-nature. In the way he spat there was an imperturbable coolness which seemed to indicate that this was a man who would not stop at a crime to extricate himself from a false position. His eyes, like those of a pitiless judge, seemed to go to the very bottom of all questions, to read all natures, all feelings, and thoughts. His habit of life was very regular; he usually went out after breakfast, returning in time for dinner, and disappeared for the rest of the evening, letting himself in about midnight with a latch-key, a privilege that Mme. Vauquer accorded to no other boarder. But then he was on very good terms with the widow; he used to call her "mamma," and put his arm round her waist, a piece of flattery perhaps not appreciated to the full! The worthy woman might imagine this to be an easy feat; but, as a matter of fact, no arm but Vautrin's was long enough to encircle her.

It was a characteristic trait of his generosity to pay fifteen francs a month for the cup of coffee with a dash of brandy in it, which he took after dinner. Less superficial observers than young men engulfed by the whirlpool of Parisian life, or old men, who took no interest in anything that did not directly concern them, would not have stopped short at the vaguely unsatisfactory impression that Vautrin made upon them. He knew or guessed the concerns of every one about him; but none of them had been able to penetrate his thoughts, or to discover his occupation. He had deliberately made his apparent good-nature, his unfailing readiness to oblige, and his high spirits into a barrier between himself and the rest of them, but not seldom he gave glimpses of appalling depths of character. He seemed to delight in scourging the upper class of society with the lash of his tongue, to take pleasure in convicting it of inconsistency, in mocking at law and order with some grim jest worthy of Juvenal, as if some grudge against the social system rankled in him, as if there were some mystery carefully hidden away in his life.

Mlle. Taillefer felt attracted, perhaps unconsciously by the strength of the one man, and the good looks of the other; her stolen glances and secret thoughts were divided between them; but neither of them seemed to take any notice of her, although some day a chance might alter her position and she would be a wealthy heiress. For that matter, there was not a soul in the house who took any trouble to investigate the various chronicles of misfortunes, real or imaginary, related by the rest. Each one regarded the others with indifference, tempered by suspicion; it was the natural result of their relative positions. Practical assistance not one of them could give, this they all knew, and they had long since exhausted their stock of condolence over previous discussions of their grievances. They were in something the same position as an elderly couple who have nothing left to say to each other. The routine of existence kept them in contact, but they were parts of a mechanism which wanted oil. There was not one of them but would have passed a blind man begging in the street, not one that felt moved to pity by a tale of misfortune, not one that did not see in death the solution of the all-absorbing problem of misery which left them cold to the most terrible anguish in others.

The happiest of these hapless beings was certainly Mme. Vauquer, who reigned supreme over this hospital supported by voluntary contributions. For her the little garden, which silence, and cold, and rain and drought combined to make as dreary as an Asian *steppe*, was a pleasant shaded nook; the gaunt yellow house, the musty odors of a back shop had charms for her, and for her alone. Those cells belonged to her. She fed those convicts condemned to penal servitude for life, and her authority was recognized among them. Where else in Paris would they have found wholesome food in sufficient quantity at the prices she charged them, and rooms which they were at liberty to make, if not exactly elegant or comfortable, at any rate, clean and healthy? If she had committed some flagrant act of injustice, the victim would have borne it in silence.

Such a gathering contained, as might have been expected, the elements out of which a complete society might be constructed. And, as in a school, as in the world itself, there was among the eighteen men and women who met round the dinner table a poor creature, despised by all the others,

2

condemned to be the butt of all their jokes. At the beginning of Eugène de Rastignac's second twelvemonth, this figure suddenly started out into bold relief against the background of human forms and faces among which the law student was yet to live for another two years to come. This laughing-stock was the retired vermicelli-merchant, Father Goriot, upon whose face a painter, like the historian, would have concentrated all the light in his picture.

How had it come about that the boarders regarded him with a half-malignant contempt? Why did they subject the oldest among their number to a kind of persecution, in which there was mingled some pity, but no respect for his misfortunes? Had he brought it upon himself by some eccentricity or absurdity, which is less easily forgiven or forgotten than more serious defects? The question strikes at the root of many a social injustice. Perhaps it is only human nature to inflict suffering on anything that will endure suffering, whether by reason of its genuine humility, or indifference, or sheer helplessness. Do we not, one and all, like to feel our strength even at the expense of some one or of something? The poorest sample of humanity, the street arab, will pull the bell-handle at every street-door in bitter weather, and scramble up to write his name on the unsullied marble of a monument.

In the year 1813, at the age of sixty-nine or thereabouts, "Father Goriot" had sold his business and retired—to Mme. Vauquer's boarding-house. When he first came there he had taken the rooms now occupied by Mme. Couture; he had paid twelve hundred francs a year like a man to whom five louis more or less was a mere trifle. For him Mme. Vauquer had made various improvements in the three rooms destined for his use, in consideration of a certain sum paid in advance, so it was said, for the miserable furniture, that is to say, for some yellow cotton curtains, a few chairs of stained wood covered with Utrecht velvet, several wretchedly colored prints in frames, and wall papers that a little suburban tavern would have disdained. Possibly it was the careless generosity with which Father Goriot allowed himself to be overreached at this period of his life (they called him Monsieur Goriot very respectfully then) that gave Mme. Vauquer the meanest opinion of his business abilities; she looked on him as an imbecile where money was concerned.

Goriot had brought with him a considerable wardrobe, the gorgeous outfit of a retired tradesman who denies himself nothing. Mme. Vauquer's astonished eyes beheld no less than eighteen cambric-fronted shirts, the splendor of their fineness being enhanced by a pair of pins each bearing a large diamond, and connected by a short chain, an ornament which adorned the vermicelli-maker's shirt-front. He usually wore a coat of cornflower blue; his rotund and portly person was still further set off by a clean white waistcoat, and a gold chain and seals which dangled over that broad expanse. When his hostess accused him of being "a bit of a beau," he smiled with the vanity of a citizen whose foible is gratified. His cupboards (*ormoires*, as he called them in the popular dialect) were filled with a quantity of plate that he brought with him. The widow's eyes gleamed as she obligingly helped him to unpack the soup ladles, tablespoons, forks, cruet-stands, tureens, dishes, and breakfast services—all of silver—which were duly arranged upon the shelves, beside a few more or less handsome pieces of plate, all weighing no inconsiderable number of ounces; he could not bring himself to part with these gifts that reminded him of past domestic festivals.

"This was my wife's present to me on the first anniversary of our wedding-day," he said to Mme. Vauquer, as he put away a little silver posset dish, with two turtle-doves billing on the cover. "Poor dear! she spent on it all the money she had saved before we married. Do you know, I would sooner scratch the earth with my nails for a living, madame, than part with that. But I shall be able to take my coffee out of it every morning for the rest of my days, thank the Lord!

I am not to be pitied. There's not much fear of my starving for some time to come."

Finally, Mme. Vauquer's magpie's eye had discovered and read certain entries in the list of shareholders in the funds, and, after a rough calculation, was disposed to credit Goriot (worthy man) with something like ten thousand francs a year. From that day forward Mme. Vauquer (*née* de Conflans), who, as a matter of fact, had seen forty-eight summers, though she would only own to thirty-nine of them—Mme. Vauquer had her own ideas. Though Goriot's eyes seemed to have shrunk in their sockets, though they were weak and watery, owing to some glandular affection which compelled him to wipe them continually, she considered him to be a very gentlemanly and pleasant-looking man. Moreover, the widow saw favorable indications of character in the well-developed calves of his legs and in his square-shaped nose, indications still further borne out by the worthy man's full-moon countenance and look of stupid good-nature. This, in all probability, was a strongly-built animal, whose brains mostly consisted in a capacity for affection. His hair, worn in *ailes de pigeon*, and duly powdered every morning by the barber from the École Polytechnique, described five points on his low forehead, and made an elegantly setting to his face. Though his manners were somewhat boorish, he was always as neat as a new pin, and he took his snuff in a lordly way, like a man who knows that his snuff-box is always likely to be filled with maccaboy; so that when Mme. Vauquer lay down to rest on the day of M. Goriot's installation, her heart, like a larded partridge, sweltered before the fire of a burning desire to shake off the shroud of Vauquer and rise again as Goriot. She would marry again, sell her boarding-house, give her hand to this fine flower of citizenship, become a lady of consequence in the Quarter, and ask for subscriptions for charitable purposes; she would make little Sunday excursions to Choisy, Soisy, Gentilly; she would have a box at the theatre when she liked, instead of waiting for the author's tickets that one of her boarders sometimes gave her, in July; the whole Eldorado of a little Parisian household rose up before Mme. Vauquer in her dreams. Nobody knew that she herself possessed forty thousand francs, accumulated *sou* by *sou*, that was her secret; surely as far as money was concerned she was a very tolerable match. "And in other respects, I am quite his equal," she said to herself, turning as if to assure herself of the charms of a form that the portly Sylvie found moulded in down feathers every morning.

For three months from that day Mme. Veuve Vauquer availed herself of the services of M. Goriot's coiffeur, and went to some expense over her toilet, expense justifiable on the ground that she owed it to herself and her establishment to pay some attention to appearances when such highly respectable persons honored her house with their presence. She expended no small amount of ingenuity in a sort of weeding process of her lodgers, announcing her intention of receiving henceforward none but people who were in every way select. If a stranger presented himself, she let him know that M. Goriot, one of the best-known and most highly respected merchants in Paris, had singled out her boarding-house for a residence. She drew up a prospectus headed MAISON VAUQUER, in which it was asserted that hers was "*one of the oldest and most highly recommended boarding-houses in the Latin Quarter.*" "From the windows of the house," thus ran the prospectus, "there is a charming view of the Vallée des Gobelins (so there is— from the third floor), and a *beautiful* garden, *extending* down to *an avenue of lindens* at the farther end." Mention was made of the bracing air of the place and its quiet situation.

It was this prospectus that attracted Mme. la Comtesse de l'Ambermesnil, a widow of six and thirty, who was awaiting the final settlement of her husband's affairs, and of another matter regarding a pension due to her as the wife of a general who had died "on the field of battle." On this Mme. Vauquer saw to her table, lighted a fire daily in the sitting-room for nearly six months, and kept the promise of her prospectus, even going to some expense to do so. And the Countess, on her side, addressed Mme. Vauquer as "my dear," and promised her two more boarders, the Baronne de Vaumerland and the widow of a colonel, the late Comte de Picquoisie, who were about to leave a boarding-house in the Marais, where the terms were higher than at the Maison Vauquer. Both these ladies, moreover, would be very well to do when the people at the War Office had come to an end of their formalities. "But government departments are always so dilatory," the lady added.

After dinner the two widows went together up to Mme. Vauquer's room, and had a snug little chat over some cordial and various delicacies reserved for the mistress of the house. Mme. Vauquer's ideas as to Goriot were cordially approved by Mme. de l'Ambermesnil; it was a capital notion, which for that matter she had guessed from the very first; in her opinion the vermicelli-maker was an excellent man.

"Ah! my dear lady, such a well-preserved man of his age, as sound as my eyesight—a man who might make a woman happy!" said the widow.

The good-natured Countess turned to the subject of Mme. Vauquer's dress, which was not in harmony with her projects. "You must put yourself on a war footing," said she.

After much serious consideration the two widows went shopping together—they purchased a hat adorned with ostrich feathers and a cap at the Palais Royal, and the Countess took her friend to the Magasin de la Petite Jeannette, where they chose a dress and a scarf. Thus equipped for the campaign, the widow looked exactly like the prize animal hung out for a sign above an *à la mode* beef-shop; but she herself was so much pleased with the improvement, as she considered it, in her appearance, that she felt that she lay under some obligation to the Countess; and, though by no means open-handed, she begged that lady to accept a hat that cost twenty francs. The fact was that she needed the Countess' services on the delicate mission of sounding Goriot; the Countess must sing her praises in his ears. Mme. de Ambermesnil lent herself very good-naturedly to this manœuvre, began her operations, and succeeded in obtaining a private interview; but the overtures that she made, with a view to securing him for herself, were received with embarrassment, not to say a repulse. She left him, revolted by his coarseness.

"My angel," said she to her dear friend, "you will make nothing of that man yonder. He is absurdly suspicious, and he is a mean curmudgeon, an idiot, a fool; you would never be happy with him."

After what had passed between M. Goriot and Mme. de l'Ambermesnil, the Countess would no longer live under the same roof. She left the next day, forgot to pay for six months' board, and left behind her her wardrobe, cast-off clothing to the value of five francs. Eagerly and persistently as Mme. Vauquer sought her quondam lodger, the Comtesse de l'Ambermesnil was never heard of again in Paris. The widow often talked of this deplorable business, and regretted her own too confiding disposition. As a matter of fact, she was as suspicious as a cat; but she was like many other people, who cannot trust their own kin and put themselves at the mercy of the next chance comer—an odd but common phenomenon, whose causes may readily be traced to the depths of the human heart.

Perhaps there are people who know that they have nothing more to look for from those with whom they live; they have shown the emptiness of their hearts to their housemates, and in their secret selves they are conscious that they are severely judged, and that they deserve to be judged severely; but still they feel an unconquerable craving for praises that they do not hear, or they are consumed by a desire to appear to possess, in the eyes of a new audience, the qualities which they have not, hoping to win the admiration or affection of strangers at the risk of forfeiting it again some day. Or, once more, there are other mercenary natures who never do a kindness to a friend or a relation simply because these have a claim upon them, while a service done to a stranger brings its reward to self-love. Such natures feel but little affection for those who are nearest to them; they keep their kindness for remoter circles of acquaintance, and show most to those who dwell on its utmost limits. Mme. Vauquer belonged to both these essentially mean, false, and execrable classes.

"If I had been here at the time," Vautrin would say at the end of the story, "I would have shown her up, and that misfortune would not have befallen you. I know that kind of phiz!"

Like all narrow natures, Mme. Vauquer was wont to confine her attention to events, and did not go very deeply into the causes that brought them about; she likewise preferred to throw the blame of her own mistakes on other people, so she chose to consider that the honest vermicelli-maker was responsible for her misfortune. It had opened her eyes, so she said, with regard to him. As soon as she saw that her blandishments were in vain, and that her outlay on her toilet was money thrown away, she was not slow to discover the reason of his indifference. It became plain to her at once that there was *some other attraction*, to use her own expression. In short, it was evident that the hope she had so fondly cherished was a baseless delusion, and that she would "never make anything out of that man yonder," in the Countess' forcible phrase. The Countess seemed to have been a judge of character. Mme. Vauquer's aversion was naturally more energetic than her friendship, for her hatred was not in proportion to her love, but to her disappointed expectations. The human heart may find here and there a resting-place short of the highest height of affection, but we seldom stop in the steep, downward slope of hatred. Still, M. Goriot was a lodger, and the widow's wounded self-love could not vent itself in an explosion of wrath; like a monk harassed by the prior of his convent, she was forced to stifle her sighs of disappointment, and to gulp down her cravings for revenge. Little minds find gratification for their feelings, benevolent or otherwise, by a constant exercise of petty ingenuity. The widow employed her woman's malice to devise a system of covert persecution. She began by a course of retrenchment—various luxuries which had found their way to the table appeared there no more.

"No more gherkins, no more anchovies; they have made a fool of me!" she said to Sylvie one morning, and they returned to the old bill of fare.

The thrifty frugality necessary to those who mean to make their way in the world had become an inveterate habit of life with M. Goriot. Soup, boiled beef, and a dish of vegetables had been, and always would be, the dinner he liked best, so Mme. Vauquer found it very difficult to annoy a boarder whose tastes were so simple. He was proof against her malice, and in desperation she spoke to him and of him slightingly before the other lodgers, who began to amuse themselves greatly at his expense, and so deeply graitfied her desire for revenge.

Towards the end of the first year the widow's suspicions had reached such a pitch that she began to wonder how it was that a retired merchant with a secure income of seven or eight thousand livres, the owner of such magnificent plate and jewelry handsome enough for a kept mistress, should be living in her house. Why should he devote so small a proportion of his money to his expenses? Until the first year was nearly at an end, Goriot had dined out once or twice every week, but these occasions came less frequently, and at last he was scarcely absent from the dinner table twice a month. It was hardly to be expected that Mme. Vauquer should regard the increased regularity of her boarder's habits with complacency, when those little excursions of his had been so much to her interest. She attributed the change not so much to a gradual diminution of fortune as to a spiteful wish to annoy his hostess. It is one of the most detestable habits of a liliputian mind to credit other people with its own malignant pettiness.

Unluckily, towards the end of the second year, M. Goriot's conduct gave some color to the idle talk about him. He asked Mme. Vauquer to give him a room on the second floor, and to make a corresponding reduction in her charges. Apparently, such strict economy was called for, that he did without a fire all through the winter. Mme. Vauquer asked to be paid in advance, an arrangement to which M. Goriot consented, and thenceforward she spoke of him as "Father Goriot."

What had brought about this decline and fall? Conjecture was keen, but investigation was difficult. Father Goriot was not communicative; in the sham Countess' phrase, he was "a curmudgeon." Empty-headed people who babble about their own affairs because they have nothing else to occupy them, naturally conclude that if people say nothing of their doings it is because their doings will not bear being talked about; so the highly respectable merchant became a scoundrel, and the late beau was an old rogue. Opinion fluctuated. Sometimes, according to Vautrin, who came about this time to live in the Maison Vauquer, Father Goriot was a man who went on 'Change and *dabbled* (to use the sufficiently expressive language of the Stock Exchange) in stocks and shares after he had ruined himself by heavy speculation. Sometimes it was held that he was one of those petty gamblers who nightly play for small stakes until they win a few francs. A theory that he was a detective in the employ of the Home Office found favor at one time, but Vautrin urged that "Goriot was not sharp enough for one of that sort." There were yet other solutions; Father Goriot was a skinflint, a shark of a money-lender, a man who lived by selling lottery tickets. He was by turns all the most mysterious brood of vice and shame and misery; yet, however vile his life might be, the feeling of repulsion which he aroused in others was not so strong that he must be banished from their society—he paid his way. Besides, Goriot had his uses, every one vented his spleen or sharpened his wit on him; he was pelted with jokes and belabored with hard words. The general consensus of opinion was in favor of a theory which seemed the most likely; this was Mme. Vauquer's view. According to her, the man so well preserved at his time of life, as sound as her eyesight, with whom a woman might be very happy, was a libertine who had strange tastes. These are the facts upon which Mme. Vauquer's slanders were based.

Early one morning, some few months after the departure of the unlucky Countess who had managed to live for six months at the widow's expense, Mme. Vauquer (not yet dressed) heard the rustle of a silk dress and a young woman's light footstep on the stair; some one was going to Goriot's room. He seemed to expect the visit, for his door stood ajar. The portly Sylvie presently came up to tell her mistress that a girl too pretty to be honest, "dressed like a goddess," and not a speck of mud on her laced cashmere boots, had glided in from the street like a snake, had found the kitchen, and asked for M. Goriot's room. Mme. Vauquer and the cook, listening, overheard several words affectionately spoken during the visit, which lasted for some time. When M. Goriot went downstairs with the lady, the stout Sylvie forthwith took her basket and followed the lover-like couple, under pretext of going to do her marketing.

"M. Goriot must be awfully rich, all the same, madame," she reported on her return, "to keep her in such style. Just imagine it! There was a splendid carriage waiting at the corner of the Place de l'Estrapade, and *she* got into it."

While they were at dinner that evening, Mme. Vauquer

went to the window and drew the curtain, as the sun was shining into Goriot's eyes.

"You are beloved of fair ladies, M. Goriot—the sun seeks you out," she said, alluding to his visitor. "*Peste!* you have good taste; she was very pretty."

"That was my daughter," he said, with a kind of pride in his voice, and the rest chose to consider this as the fatuity of an old man who wishes to save appearances.

A month after this visit M. Goriot received another. The same daughter who had come to see him that morning came again after dinner, this time in evening dress. The boarders, in deep discussion in the dining-room, caught a glimpe of a lovely, fair-haired woman, slender, graceful, and much too distinguished-looking to be a daughter of Father Goriot.

"Two of them!" cried the portly Sylvie, who did not recognize the lady of the first visit.

A few days later, and another young lady—a tall, well-moulded brunette, with dark hair and bright eyes—came to ask for M. Goriot.

"Three of them!" said Sylvie.

Then the second daughter, who had first come in the morning to see her father, came shortly afterwards in the evening. She wore a ball dress, and came in a carriage.

"Four of them!" commented Mme. Vauquer and her plump handmaid. Sylvie saw not a trace of resemblance between this great lady and the girl in her simple morning dress who had entered her kitchen on the occasion of her first visit.

At that time Goriot was paying twelve hundred francs a year to his landlady, and Mme. Vauquer saw nothing out of the common in the fact that a rich man had four or five mistresses; nay, she thought it very knowing of him to pass them off as his daughters. She was not at all inclined to draw a hard-and-fast line, or to take umbrage at his sending for them to the Maison Vauquer; yet, inasmuch as these visits explained her boarder's indifference to her, she went so far (at the end of the second year) as to speak of him as an "ugly old wretch." When at length her boarder declined to nine hundred francs a year, she asked him very insolently what he took her house to be, after meeting one of these ladies on the stairs. Father Goriot answered that the lady was his eldest daughter.

"So you have two or three dozen daughters, have you?" said Mme. Vanquer sharply.

"I have only two," her boarder answered meekly, like a ruined man who is broken in to all the cruel usage of misfortune.

Towards the end of the third year Father Goriot reduced his expenses still further; he went up to the third story, and now paid forty-five francs a month. He did without snuff, told his hairdresser that he no longer required his services, and gave up wearing powder. When Goriot appeared for the first time in this condition, an exclamation of astonishment broke from his hostess at the color of his hair—a dingy olive gray. He had grown sadder day by day under the influence of some hidden trouble; among all the faces round the table, his was the most woe-begone. There was no longer any doubt. Goriot was an elderly libertine, whose eyes had only been preserved by the skill of the physician from the malign influence of the remedies necessitated by the state of his health. The disgusting color of his hair was a result of his excesses, and of the drugs which he had taken that he might continue his career. The poor old man's mental and physical condition afforded some ground for the absurd rubbish talked about him. When his outfit was worn out, he replaced the fine linen by calico at fourteen *sous* the ell. His diamonds, his old snuff-box, watch-chain and trinkets, disappeared one by one. He had left off wearing the cornflower blue coat, and was sumptuously arrayed, summer as winter, in a coarse chestnut-brown coat, a plush waistcoat, and doeskin breeches. He grew thinner and thinner; his legs were shrunken, his cheeks, once so puffed out by contented bourgeois prosperity, were covered with wrinkles, and the outlines of the jawbones were distinctly visible; there were deep furrows in his forehead. In the fourth year of his residence in the Rue Neuve-Sainte-Geneviève he was no longer like his former self. The hale vermicelli manufacturer, sixty-two years of age, who had looked scarce forty, the stout, comfortable, prosperous tradesman, with an almost bucolic air, and such a brisk demeanor that it did you good to look at him; the man with something boyish in his smile, had suddenly sunk into his dotage, and had become a feeble, vacillating septuagenarian.

The keen, bright blue eyes had grown dull, and faded to a steel-gray color; the red inflamed rims looked as though they had shed tears of blood. He excited feelings of repulsion in some, and of pity in others. The young medical students who came to the house noticed the drooping of his lower lip and the conformation of the facial angle; and, after teasing him for some time to no purpose, they declared that crétinism was setting in.

One evening after dinner Mme. Vauquer said half-banteringly to him, "So those daughters of yours don't come to see you any more, eh?" meaning to imply her doubts as to his paternity; but Father Goriot shrank as if his hostess had touched him with a sword-point.

"They come sometimes," he said in a tremulous voice.

"Aha! you still see them sometimes?" cried the students. "Bravo, Father Goriot!"

The old man scarcely seemed to hear the witticisms at his expense that followed on the words; he had relapsed into the dreamy state of mind that these superficial observers took for senile torpor, due to his lack of intelligence. If they had only known, they might have been deeply interested by the problem of his condition; but few problems were more obscure. It was easy, of course, to find out whether Goriot had really been a vermicelli manufacturer; the amount of his fortune was readily discoverable; but the old people, who were most inquisitive as to his concerns, never went beyond the limits of the Quarter, and lived in the lodging-house much as oysters cling to a rock. As for the rest, the current of life in Paris daily awaited them, and swept them away with it; so soon as they left the Rue Neuve-Sainte-Geneviève, they forgot the existence of the old man, their butt at dinner. For those narrow souls, or for careless youth, the misery in Father Goriot's withered face and its dull apathy were quite incompatible with wealth or any sort of intelligence. As for the creatures whom he called his daughters, all Mme. Vauquer's boarders were of her opinion. With the faculty for severe logic sedulously cultivated by elderly women during long evenings of gossip till they can always find an hypothesis to fit all circumstances, she was wont to reason thus—

"If Father Goriot had daughters of his own as rich as those ladies who came here seemed to be, he would not be lodging in my house, on the third floor, at forty-five francs a month; and he would not go about dressed like a poor man."

No objection could be raised to these inferences. So by the end of the month of November, 1819, at the time when the curtain rises on this drama, every one in the house had come to have a very decided opinion as to the poor old man. He had never had either wife or daughter; excesses had reduced him to this sluggish condition; he was a sort of human mollusc who should be classed among the capu*lidæ*, so said one of the dinner contingent, an employé at the Muséum, who had a pretty wit of his own. Poiret was an eagle, a gentleman, compared with Goriot. Poiret would join the talk, argue, answer when he was spoken to; as a matter of fact, his talk, arguments, and responses contributed nothing to the conversation, for Poiret had a habit of repeating what the others said in different words; still, he did join in the talk; he was alive, and seemed capable of feeling; while Father Goriot (to quote the Muséum official again) was invariably at zero—Réaumur.

Eugène de Rastignac had just returned to Paris in a state of mind not unknown to young men who are conscious of unusual powers, and to those whose faculties are so stimulated by a difficult position, that for the time being they rise above the ordinary level.

Rastignac's first year of study for the preliminary examinations in law had left him free to see the sights of Paris and to enjoy some of its amusements. A student has not much time on his hands if he sets himself to learn the repertory of every theatre, and to study the ins and outs of the labyrinth of Paris. To know its customs; to learn the language, and become familiar with the amusements of the capital, he must explore its recesses, good and bad, follow the studies that please him best, and form some idea of the treasures contained in galleries and museums.

At this stage of his career a student grows eager and excited about all sorts of follies that seem to him to be of immense importance. He has his hero, his great man, a professor at the Collége de France, paid to talk down to the level of his audience. He adjusts his cravat, and strikes various attitudes for the benefit of the women in the first galleries at the Opéra-Comique. As he passes through all these successive initiations, and breaks out of his sheath, the horizons of life widen around him, and at length he grasps the plan of society with the different human strata of which it is composed.

If he begins by admiring the procession of carriages on sunny afternoons in the Champs-Élysées, he soon reaches the further stage of envying their owners. Unconsciously, Eugène had served his apprenticeship before he went back to Angoulême for the long vacation after taking his degrees as bachelor of arts and bachelor of law. The illusions of childhood had vanished, so also had the ideas he brought with him from the provinces; he had returned thither with an intelligence developed, with loftier ambitions, and saw things as they were at home in the old manor house. His father and mother, his two brothers and two sisters, with an aged aunt, whose whole fortune consisted in annuities, lived on the little estate of Rastignac. The whole property brought in about three thousand francs; and though the amount varied with the season (as must always be the case in a vine-growing district), they were obliged to spare an unvarying twelve hundred francs out of their income for him. He saw how constantly the poverty, which they had generously hidden from him, weighed upon them; he could not help comparing the sisters, who had seemed so beautiful to his boyish eyes, with women in Paris, who had realized the beauty of his dreams. The uncertain future of the whole family depended upon him. It did not escape his eyes that not a crumb was wasted in the house, nor that the wine they drank was made from the second pressing; a multitude of small things, which it is useless to speak of in detail here, made him burn to distinguish himself, and his ambition to succeed increased tenfold.

He meant, like all great souls, that his success should be owing entirely to his merits; but his was pre-eminently a southern temperament, the execution of his plans was sure to be marred by the vertigo that seizes on youth when youth sees itself alone in a wide sea, uncertain how to spend its energies, whither to steer its course, how to adapt its sails to the winds. At first he determined to fling himself heart and soul into his work, but he was diverted from this purpose by the need of society and connections; then he saw how great an influence women exert in social life, and suddenly made up his mind to go out into this world to seek a protectress there. Surely a clever and high-spirited young man, whose wit and courage were set off to advantage by a graceful figure, and the vigorous kind of beauty that readily strikes a woman's imagination, need not despair of finding a protectress. These ideas occurred to him in his country walks with his sisters, whom he had once joined so gaily. The girls thought him very much changed.

His aunt, Mme. de Marcillac, had been presented at court, and had moved among the highest heights of that lofty region. Suddenly the young man's ambition discerned in those recollections of hers, which had been like nursery fairy tales to her nephews and nieces, the elements of a social success at least as important as the success which he had achieved at the École de droit. He began to ask his aunt about those relations; some of the old ties might still hold good. After much shaking of the branches of the family tree, the old lady came to the conclusion that of all persons who could be useful to her nephew among the selfish genius of rich relations, the Vicomtesse de Beauséant was the least likely to refuse. To this lady, therefore, she wrote in the old-fashioned style, recommending Eugène to her; pointing out to her nephew that if he succeeded in pleasing Mme. de Beauséant, the Vicomtesse would introduce him to other relations. A few days after his return to Paris, therefore, Rastignac sent his aunt's letter to Mme. de Beauséant. The Vicomtesse replied by an invitation to a ball for the following evening. This was the position of affairs at the Maison Vauquer at the end of November, 1819.

A few days later, after Mme. de Beauséant's ball, Eugène came in at two o'clock in the morning. The persevering student meant to make up for the lost time by working until daylight. It was the first time that he had attempted to spend the night in this way in that silent quarter. The spell of a factitious energy was upon him; he had beheld the pomp and splendor of the world. He had not dined at the Maison Vauquer; the boarders probably would think that he would walk home at daybreak from the dance, as he had done sometimes on former occasions, after a fête at the Prado, or a ball at the Odéon, splashing his silk stockings thereby, and ruining his pumps.

It so happened that Christophe took a look into the street before drawing the bolts of the door; and Rastignac, coming in at that moment, could go up to his room without making any noise, followed by Christophe, who made a great deal. Eugène exchanged his dress suit for a shabby overcoat and slippers, kindled a fire with some blocks of patent fuel, and prepared for his night's work in such a way that the faint sounds he made were drowned by Christophe's heavy tramp on the stairs.

Eugène sat absorbed in thought for a few moments before plunging into his law books. He had just become aware of the fact that the Vicomtesse de Beauséant was one of the queens of fashion, that her house was thought to be the pleasantest in the Faubourg Saint-Germain. And not only so, she was, by right of her fortune, and the name she bore, one of the most conspicuous figures in that aristocratic world. Thanks to his aunt, thanks to Mme. de Marcillac's letter of introduction, the poor student had been kindly received in that house before he knew the extent of the favor thus shown to him. It was almost like a patent of nobility to be admitted to those gilded salons; he had appeared in the most exclusive circle in Paris, and now all doors were open for him. Eugène had been dazzled at first by the brilliant assembly, and had scarcely exchanged a few words with the Vicomtesse; he had been content to single out a goddess from among this throng of Parisian divinities, one of those women who are sure to attract a young man's fancy.

The Comtesse Anastasie de Restaud was tall and gracefully made; she had one of the prettiest figures in Paris. Imagine a pair of great dark eyes, a magnificently moulded hand, a shapely foot. There was a fiery energy in her movements; the Marquis de Ronquerolles had called her a "thoroughbred," but this fineness of nervous organization had brought no accompanying defect; the outlines of her form were full and rounded, without any tendency to stoutness. "A thoroughbred," "a pure pedigree," these figures of speech have replaced the "heavenly angel" and Ossianic nomenclature; the old mythology of love is extinct, doomed to perish by modern dandyism. But for Rastignac, Mme. Anastasie de Restaud was the woman for whom he had sighed. He had contrived to write his name twice upon the list of partners upon her fan, and had snatched a few words with her during the first quadrille.

"Where shall I meet you again, madame?" he asked abruptly, and the tones of his voice were full of the vehement energy that women like so well.

"Oh, everywhere!" said she, "in the Bois, at the Bouffons, in my own house."

With the impetuosity of his adventurous southern temper, he did all he could to cultivate an acquaintance with this lovely Countess, making the best of his opportunities in the quadrille and during a waltz that she gave him. When he had told her that he was a cousin of Mme. de Beauséant, the Countess, whom he took for a great lady, asked him to call at her house, and, after her parting smile, Rastignac felt convinced that he must make this visit. He was so lucky as to light upon some one who did not laugh at his ignorance, a fatal defect among the gilded and insolent youth of that period; the coterie of Maulincourts, Maximes de Trailles, de Marsays, Ronquerolles, Ajuda-Pintos, and Vandenesses, who shone there in all the glory of coxcombry among the best-dressed women of fashion in Paris—Lady Brandon, the Duchesse de Langeais, the Comtesse de Kergarouët, Mme. de Sérizy, the Duchesse de Carigliano, the Comtesse Ferraud, Mme. de Lanty, the Marquise d'Aiglemont, Mme. Firmiani, the Marquise de Listomère and the Marquise d'Espard, the Duchesse de Maufrigneuse and the Grandlieus. Luckily, therefore, for him, the novice happened upon the Marquis de Montriveau, the lover of the Duchesse de Langeais, a general as simple as a child; from him Rastignac learned that the Comtesse lived in the Rue du Helder.

Ah, what it is to be young, eager to see the world, greedily on the watch for any chance that brings you nearer the woman of your dreams, and behold two houses open their doors to you! To set foot in the Vicomtesse de Beauséant's house in the Faubourg Saint-Germain; to fall on your knees before a Comtesse de Restaud in the Chaussée d'Antin; to look at one glance across a vista of Paris drawing-rooms, conscious that, possessing sufficient good looks, you may hope to find aid and protection there in a feminine heart! To feel ambitious enough to spurn the tight-rope on which you must walk with the steady head of an acrobat for whom a fall is impossible, and to find in a charming woman the best of all balancing poles.

He sat there with his thoughts for a while, law on the one hand and poverty on the other, beholding a radiant vision of a woman rise above the dull, smoldering fire. Who would not have paused and questioned the future as Eugène was doing? who would not have pictured it full of success? His wandering thoughts took wings; he was transported out of the present into that blissful future; he was sitting by Mme. de Restaud's side, when a sort of sigh, like the grunt of an overburdened St. Joseph, broke the silence of the night. It vibrated through the student, who took the sound for a death-groan. He opened his door noiselessly, went out upon the landing, and saw a thin streak of light under Father Goriot's door. Eugène feared that his neighbor had been taken ill; he went over and looked through the key-hole; the old man was busily engaged in an occupation so singular and so suspicious that Rastignac thought he was only doing a piece of necessary service to society to watch the self-styled vermicelli-maker's nocturnal industries.

The table was upturned, and Goriot had doubtless in some

way secured a silver plate and cup to the bar before knotting a thick rope round them; he was pulling at this rope with such enormous force that they were being crushed and twisted out of shape; to all appearance he meant to convert the richly wrought metal into ingots.

"*Peste!* what a man!" said Rastignac, as he watched Goriot's muscular arms; there was not a sound in the room while the old man, with the aid of the rope, was kneading the silver like dough. "Was he, then, indeed, a thief, or a receiver of stolen goods, who affected imbecility and decrepitude, and lived like a beggar that he might carry on his pursuits the more securely?" Eugène stood for a moment revolving these questions in his mind, then he looked again through the keyhole as before.

Father Goriot had unwound his coil of rope; he had covered the table with a blanket, and was now employed in rolling the flattened mass of silver into a bar, an operation which he performed with marvelous dexterity.

"Why, he must be as strong as Augustus, King of Poland!" said Eugène to himself when the bar was nearly finished.

Father Goriot looked sadly at his handiwork, tears fell from his eyes, he blew out the dip which had served him for a light while he manipulated the silver, and Eugène heard him sigh as he lay down again.

"He is mad," thought the student.

"*Poor child!*" Father Goriot said aloud. Rastignac, hearing those words, concluded to keep silence; he would not hastily condemn his neighbor. He was just in the doorway of his room when a strange sound from the staircase below reached his ears; it might have been made by two men coming up in list slippers. Eugène listened; two men there certainly were, he could hear their breathing. Yet there had been no sound of opening the street-door, no footsteps in the passage. Suddenly, too, he saw a faint gleam of light on the second story; it came from M. Vautrin's room.

"There are a good many mysteries here for a lodging-house!" he said to himself.

He went part of the way downstairs and listened again. The rattle of gold reached his ears. In another moment the light was put out, and again he distinctly heard the breathing of two men, but no sound of a door being opened or shut. The two men went downstairs, the faint sounds growing fainter as they went.

"Who is there?" cried Mme. Vauquer out of her bedroom window, she having heard slight sounds of the departing footsteps and the closing of the outer door.

"I, Mme. Vauquer," answered Vautrin's deep bass voice. "I am coming in."

"That is odd! Christophe drew the bolts," said Eugène, going back to his room. "You have to sit up at night, it seems, if you really mean to know all that is going on about you in Paris."

These incidents turned his thoughts from his ambitious dreams; he betook himself to his work, but his thoughts wandered back to Father Goriot's suspicious occupation; Mme. de Restaud's face swam again and again before his eyes like a vision of a brilliant future, and at last he lay down and slept with clenched fists. When a young man makes up his mind that he will work all night, the chances are that seven times out of ten he will sleep till morning. Such vigils do not begin before we are turned twenty.

The next morning Paris was wrapped in one of the dense fogs that throw the most punctual people out in their calculations as to the time; even the most business-like folk fail to keep their appointments in such weather, and ordinary mortals wake up at noon and fancy it is eight o'clock. On this morning it was half-past nine, and Mme. Vauquer still lay abed. Christophe was late, Sylvie was late, but the two sat comfortably taking their coffee as usual. It was Sylvie's custom to take the cream off the milk destined for the boarders' breakfast for her own, and to boil the remainder for some time, so that madame should not discover this illegal exaction.

"Sylvie," said Christophe, as he dipped a piece of toast into the coffee, "M. Vautrin, who is not such a bad sort, all the same, had two people come to see him again last night. If madame says anything, mind you say nothing about it."

"Has he given you something?"

"He gave me a five-franc piece this month, which is as good as saying, 'Hold your tongue.'"

"Except him and Mme. Couture, who don't look twice at every penny, there's no one in the house that doesn't try to get back with the left hand all that they give with the right at New Year," said Sylvie.

"And, after all," said Christophe, "what do they give you? A miserable five-franc piece. There is Father Goriot, who has cleaned his shoes himself these two years past. There is that old beggar Poiret, who goes without blacking altogether; he would sooner drink it than put it on his boots. Then there is that whipper-snapper of a student, who gives me a couple of francs. Two francs will not pay for my brushes, and he sells his old clothes, and gets more for them than they are worth. Oh! they're a shabby lot!"

"Pooh!" said Sylvie, sipping her coffee, "our places are the best in the Quarter, that I know. But about that great big chap Vautrin, Christophe; has any one told you anything about him?"

"Yes. I met a gentleman in the street a few days ago; he said to me, 'There's a gentleman at your place, isn't there? a tall man that dyes his whiskers?' I told him, 'No, sir; they aren't dyed. A gay fellow like him hasn't the time to do it.' And when I told M. Vautrin about it afterwards, he said, 'Quite right, my boy. That is the way to answer them. There is nothing more unpleasant than to have your little weaknesses known; it might spoil many a match.'"

"Well, and for my part," said Sylvie, "a man tried to

humbug me at the market wanting to know if I had seen him put on his shirt. Such bosh! There," she cried, interrupting herself, "that's a quarter to ten striking at the Val-de-Grâce, and not a soul stirring!"

"Pooh! they are all gone out. Mme. Couture and the girl went out at eight o'clock to take the wafer at Saint-Étienne. Father Goriot started off somewhere with a parcel, and the student won't be back from his lecture till ten o'clock. I saw them go while I was sweeping the stairs; Father Goriot knocked up against me, and his parcel was as hard as iron. What is the old fellow up to I wonder? He is as good as a plaything for the rest of them; they can never let him alone; but he is a good man, all the same, and worth more than all of them put together. He doesn't give you much himself, but he sometimes sends you with a message to ladies who fork out famous tips; they are dressed grandly, too."

"His daughters, as he calls them, eh? There are a dozen of them."

"I have never been to more than two—the two who came here."

"There is madame moving overhead; I shall have to go, or she will raise a fine racket. Just keep an eye on the milk, Christophe! don't let the cat get at it."

Sylvie went up to her mistress' room.

"Sylvie! How is this? It's nearly ten o'clock, and you let me sleep on like a dormouse! Such a thing has never happened before."

"It is the fog; it is that thick, you could cut it with a knife."

"But how about breakfast?"

"Bah! the boarders are possessed, I'm sure. They all cleared out before there was a wink of daylight."

"Do speak properly, Sylvie," Mme. Vauquer retorted; "say a blink of daylight."

"Ah, well, madame, whichever you please. Anyhow, you

can have breakfast at ten o'clock. La Michonnette and Poireau have neither of them stirred. There are only those two upstairs, and they are sleeping like the logs they are."

"But, Sylvie, you put their names together as if——"

"As if what?" said Sylvie, bursting into a guffaw. "The two of them make a pair."

"It is a strange thing, isn't it, Sylvie, how M. Vautrin got in last night after Christophe had bolted the door?"

"Not at all, madame. Christophe heard M. Vautrin, and went down and undid the door for him. And here are you imagining that——"

"Give me my bodice, and be quick and get breakfast ready. Dish up the rest of the mutton with the potatoes, and you can put the stewed pears on the table, those at five a penny."

A few moments later Mme. Vauquer came down, just in time to see the cat knock down a plate that covered a bowl of milk, and begin to lap in all haste.

"Mistigris!" she cried.

The cat fled, but promptly returned to rub against her ankles.

"Oh! yes, you can wheedle, you old hypocrite!" she said. "Sylvie! Sylvie!"

"Yes, madame; what is it?"

"Just see what the cat has done!"

"It is all that stupid Christophe's fault. I told him to stop and lay the table. What has become of him? Don't you worry, madame; Father Goriot shall have it. I will fill it up with water, and he won't know the difference; he never notices anything, not even what he eats."

"I wonder where the old heathen can have gone?" said Mme. Vauquer, setting the plates round the table.

"Who knows? He is up to all sorts of tricks."

"I have overslept myself," said Mme. Vauquer.

"But madame looks as fresh as a rose, all the same."

The door-bell rang at that moment, and Vautrin came through the sitting-room, singing loudly—

> "'Tis the same old story everywhere,
> A roving heart and a roving glance——"

"Oh! Mamma Vauquer! good-morning!" he cried at the sight of his hostess, and he put his arm gaily round her waist.

"There! have done——"

"'Impertinence!' Say it!" he answered. "Come, say it! Now isn't that what you really mean? Stop a bit, I will help you to set the table. Ah! I am a nice man, am I not?

> "'For the locks of brown and the golden hair
> A sighing lover.'

"Oh! I have just seen something so funny——

> "'——led by chance.'"

"What?" asked the widow.

"Father Goriot in the goldsmith's shop in the Rue Dauphine at half-past eight this morning. They buy old spoons and forks and gold lace there, and Goriot sold a piece of silver plate for a good round sum. It had been twisted out of shape very neatly for a man that's not used to the trade."

"Really? You don't say so?"

"Yes. One of my friends is expatriating himself; I had been to see him off on board the Royal Mail steamer, and was coming back here. I waited after that to see what Father Goriot would do; it is a comical affair. He came back to this quarter of the world, to the Rue des Grès, and went into a money-lender's house; everybody knows him, Gobseck, a stuck-up rascal, that would make dominoes out of his father's bones; a Turk, a heathen, an old Jew, a Greek; it would be a difficult matter to rob *him*, for he puts all his coin into the bank."

"Then what was Father Goriot doing there?"

"Doing?" said Vautrin. "Nothing; he was bent on his own undoing. He is a simpleton, stupid enough to ruin himself by running after——"

"There he is!" said Sylvie.

"Christophe," cried Father Goriot's voice, "come upstairs with me."

Christophe went up, and shortly afterwards came down again.

"Where are you going?" Mme. Vauquer asked of her servant.

"Out on an errand for M. Goriot."

"What may that be?" said Vautrin, pouncing on a letter in Christophe's hand. "*Mme. la Comtesse Anastasie de Restaud*," he read. "Where are you going with it?" he added, as he gave the letter back to Christophe.

"To the Rue du Helder. I have orders to give this into her hands myself."

"What is there inside it?" said Vautrin, holding the letter up to the light. "A bank-note? No." He peered into the envelope. "A receipted account!" he cried. "My word! 'tis a gallant old dotard. Off with you, old chap," he said, bringing down a hand on Christophe's head, and spinning the man round like a thimble; "you will have a famous tip."

By this time the table was set. Sylvie was boiling the milk; Mme. Vauquer was lighting a fire in the stove with some assistance from Vautrin, who kept on humming to himself—

"*The same old story everywhere,*
A roving heart and a roving glance."

When everything was ready, Mme. Couture and Mlle. Taillefer came in.

"Where have you been this morning, fair lady?" said Mme. Vauquer, turning to Mme. Couture.

"We have just been to say our prayers at Saint-Étienne du Mont. To-day is the day when we must go to see M. Taillefer. Poor little thing! She is trembling like a leaf," Mme. Couture went on, as she seated herself before the fire and held the steaming soles of her boots to the blaze.

"Warm yourself, Victorine," said Mme. Vauquer.

"It is quite right and proper, mademoiselle, to pray to heaven to soften your father's heart," said Vautrin, as he drew a chair nearer to the orphan girl; "but that is not enough. What you want is a friend who will give the monster a piece of his mind; a barbarian that has three millions (so they say), and will not give you a dowry; and a pretty girl needs a dowry nowadays."

"Poor child!" said Mme. Vauquer. "Never mind, my pet, your wretch of a father is going just the way to bring trouble upon himself."

Victorine's eyes filled with tears at the words, and the widow checked herself at a sign from Mme. Couture.

"If we could only see him!" said the commissary-general's widow; "if I could speak to him myself and give him his wife's last letter! I have never dared to run the risk of sending it by post; he knew my handwriting——"

"'Oh woman, persecuted and injured innocent!'" exclaimed Vautrin, breaking in upon her. "So that is how you are, is it? In a few days' time I will look into your affairs, and it will be all right, you shall see."

"Oh! sir," said Victorine, with a tearful but eager glance at Vautrin, who showed no sign of being touched by it, "if you know of any way of communicating with my father, please be sure and tell him that his affection and my mother's honor are more to me than all the money in the world. If you can induce him to relent a little towards me, I will pray to God for you. You may be sure of my gratitude——"

"*The same old story everywhere,*" sang Vautrin, with a satirical intonation. At this juncture, Goriot, Mlle. Michonneau, and Poiret came downstairs together; possibly the scent of the gravy which Sylvie was making to serve with the mutton had announced breakfast. The seven people thus assembled bade each other good-morning, and took their places at the table; the clock struck ten, and the student's footsteps were heard outside.

"Ah! here you are, M. Eugène," said Sylvie; "every one is breakfasting at home to-day."

The student exchanged greetings with the lodgers, and sat down beside Goriot.

"I have just met with a queer adventure," he said, as he helped himself abundantly to the mutton, and cut a slice of bread, which Madame Vauquer's sharp and watchful eyes gauged as usual.

"An adventure?" queried Poiret.

"Well, and what is there to astonish you in that, old boy?" Vautrin asked of Poiret. "M. Eugène is cut out for that kind of thing."

Mlle. Taillefer stole a timid glance at the young student.

"Tell us about your adventure," said Mme. Vauquer.

"Yesterday evening I went to a ball given by a cousin of mine, the Vicomtesse de Beauséant. She has a magnificent house; the rooms were hung with silk—in short, it was a splendid affair, and I was as happy as a king——"

"Fisher," put in Vautrin, interrupting.

"What do you mean, sir?" said Eugène sharply.

"I said 'fisher,' because kingfishers see a good deal more fun than kings."

"Quite true; I would much rather be the little careless bird than a king," said Poiret the ditto-ist, "because——"

"In fact"—the law student cut him short—"I danced with one of the handsomest women in the room, a charming countess, the most exquisite creature I have ever seen. There was peach blossom in her hair, and she had the loveliest bouquet of flowers—real flowers, that scented the air—— but there! it is no use trying to describe a woman glowing with the dance. You ought to have seen her! Well, and this morning I met this divine countess about nine o'clock, on foot in the Rue des Grès. Oh! how my heart beat! I began to think——"

"That she was coming here," said Vautrin, with a keen look at the student. "I expect that she was going to call on old Gobseck, a money-lender. If ever you explore a Parisian woman's heart, you will find the money-lender first, and the lover afterwards. Your countess is called Anastasie de Restaud, and she lives in the Rue de Helder."

The student stared hard at Vautrin. Father Goriot raised his head at the words, and gave the two speakers a glance so full of intelligence and uneasiness that the lodgers beheld him with astonishment.

"Then Christophe was too late, and she must have gone to him!" cried Goriot, with anguish in his voice.

"It is just as I guessed," said Vautrin, leaning over to whisper in Mme. Vauquer's ear.

Goriot went on with his breakfast, but seemed unconscious of what he was doing. He had never looked more stupid nor more taken up with his own thoughts than he did at that moment.

"Who the devil could have told you her name, M. Vautrin?" asked Eugène.

"Aha! there you are!" answered Vautrin. Old Father Goriot there knew it quite well! and why should not I know it too?"

"M. Goriot?" the student cried.

"What is it?" said the old man. "So she was very beautiful, was she, yesterday night?"

"Who?"

"Mme. de Restaud."

"Look at the old wretch," said Mme. Vauquer, speaking to Vautrin; "how his eyes light up!"

"Then does he really keep her?" said Mlle. Michonneau, in a whisper to the student.

"Oh! yes, she was tremendously pretty," Eugène answered. Father Goriot watched him with eager eyes. "If Mme. de Beauséant had not been there, my divine countess would have been the queen of the ball; none of the younger men had eyes for any one else. I was the twelfth on her list, and she danced every quadrille. The other women were furious. She must have enjoyed herself, if ever creature did! It is a true saying that there is no more beautiful sight than a frigate in full sail, a galloping horse, or a woman dancing."

"So the wheel turns," said Vautrin; "yesterday night at a duchess' ball, this morning in a money-lender's office, on the lowest rung of the ladder—just like a Parisienne! If their husbands cannot afford to pay for their frantic extravagance, they will sell themselves. Or if they cannot do that, they will tear out their mothers' hearts to find something to pay for their splendor. They will turn the world upside down. Just a Parisienne through and through!"

Father Goriot's face, which had shone at the student's words like the sun on a bright day, clouded over all at once at this cruel speech of Vautrin's.

"Well," said Mme. Vauquer, "but where is your adventure? Did you speak to her? Did you ask her if she wanted to study law?"

"She did not see me," said Eugène. "But only think of meeting one of the prettiest women in Paris in the Rue des Grès at nine o'clock! She could not have reached home after the ball till two o'clock this morning. Wasn't it queer? There is no place like Paris for these sort of adventures."

"Pshaw! much funnier things than *that* happen here!" exclaimed Vautrin.

Mlle. Taillefer had scarcely heeded the talk, she was so absorbed by the thought of the new attempt that she was about to make. Mme. Couture made a sign that it was time to go upstairs and dress; the two ladies went out, and Father Goriot followed their example.

"Well, did you see?" said Mme. Vauquer, addressing Vautrin and the rest of the circle. "He is ruining himself for those women, that is plain."

"Nothing will ever make me believe that that beautiful Comtesse de Restaud is anything to Father Goriot," cried the student.

"Well, and if you don't," broke in Vautrin, "we are not set on convincing you. You are too young to know Paris thoroughly yet; later on you will find out that there are what we call men with a passion——"

Mlle. Michonneau gave Vautrin a quick glance at these words. They seemed to be like the sound of a trumpet to a trooper's horse. "Aha!" said Vautrin, stopping in his speech to give her a searching glance, "so we have had our little experiences, have we?"

The old maid lowered her eyes like a nun who sees a statue.

"Well," he went on, "when folk of that kind get a notion into their heads, they cannot drop it. They must drink the water from some particular spring—it is stagnant as often as not; but they will sell their wives and families, they will sell their own souls to the devil to get it. For some this spring is play, or the stock exchange, or music, or a collection of pictures or insects; for others it is some woman who can give them the dainties they like. You might offer these last all the women on earth—they would turn up their noses; they will have the only one who can gratify their passion. It often happens that the woman does not care for them at all, and treats them cruelly; they buy their morsels of satisfaction very dear; but no matter, the fools are never tired of it; they will take their last blanket to the pawnbroker to give their last five-franc piece to her. Father Goriot here is one of that sort. He is discreet, so the Countess exploits him—just the way of the gay world. The poor old fellow thinks of her and of nothing else. In all other respects you see he is a stupid animal; but get him on that subject, and his eyes sparkle like diamonds. That secret is not difficult to guess. He took some plate himself this morning to the melting-pot, and I saw him at Daddy Gobseck's in the Rue des Grès. And now, mark what follows—he came back here, and gave a letter for the Comtesse de Restaud to that noodle of a Christophe, who showed us the address; there was a receipted bill inside it. It is clear that it was an urgent matter if the Countess also went herself to the old money-lender. Father Goriot has financed her handsomely. There is no need to tack a tale together; the thing is self-evident. So that shows you, sir student, that all the time your countess was smiling, dancing, flirting, swaying her peach-flower crowned head, with her gown gathered into her hand, her slippers were pinching her, as they say; she was thinking of her protested bills, or her lover's protested bills."

"You have made me wild to know the truth," cried Eugène de Rastignac; "I will go to call on Mme. de Restaud to-morrow."

"Yes," echoed Poiret; "you must go and call on Mme. de Restaud."

"And perhaps you will find Father Goriot there, who will take payment for the assistance he politely rendered."

Eugène looked disgusted. "Why, then, this Paris of yours is a slough."

"And an uncommonly queer slough, too," replied Vautrin. "The mud splashes you as you drive through it in your carriage—you are a respectable person; you go afoot and are splashed—you are a scoundrel. You are so unlucky as to walk off with something or other belonging to somebody else, and they exhibit you as a curiosity in the Place du Palais-de-Justice; you steal a million, and you are pointed out in every salon as a model of virtue. And you pay thirty millions for the police and the courts of justice, for the maintenance of law and order! A pretty state of things it is!"

"What," cried Mme. Vauquer, "has Father Goriot really melted down his silver posset-dish?"

"There were two turtle-doves on the lid, were there not?" asked Eugène.

"Yes, that there were."

"Then, was he fond of it!" said Eugène. "He cried while he was breaking up the cup and plate. I happened to see him by accident."

"It was dear to him as his own life," answered the widow.

"There! you see how infatuated the old fellow is," cried Vautrin. "The woman yonder can coax the soul out of him."

The student went up to his room. Vautrin went out, and a few minutes later Mme. Couture and Victorine drove away in a cab which Sylvie had called for them. Poiret gave his arm to Mlle. Michonneau, and they went together to spend the two sunniest hours of the day in the Jardin des Plantes.

"Well, those two are as good as married," was the portly Sylvie's comment. "They are going out together to-day for the first time. They are such a couple of dry sticks that if they happen to strike against each other they will draw sparks like flint and steel."

"Keep clear of Mlle. Michonneau's shawl, then," said Mme. Vauquer, laughing; "it would flare up like tinder."

At four o'clock that evening, when Goriot came in, he saw, by the light of two smoky lamps, that Victorine's eyes were red. Mme. Vauquer was listening to the history of the visit made that morning to M. Taillefer; it had been made in vain. Taillefer was tired of the annual application made by his daughter and her elderly friend; he gave them a personal interview in order to arrive at an understanding with them.

"My dear lady," said Mme. Couture, addressing Mme. Vauquer, "just imagine it; he did not even ask Victorine to sit down, she was standing the whole time. He said to me quite coolly, without putting himself in a passion, that we might spare ourselves the trouble of going there; that the young lady (he would not call her his daughter) was injuring her cause by importuning him (*importuning!* once a year, the wretch!); that as Victorine's mother had nothing when he married her, Victorine ought not to expect anything from him; in fact, he said the most cruel things, that made the poor child burst out crying. The little thing threw herself at her father's feet and spoke up bravely; she said that she only persevered in her visits for her mother's sake; that she would obey him without a murmur, but that she begged him to read her poor dead mother's farewell letter. She took it up and gave it to him, saying the most beautiful things in the world, most beautifully expressed; I do not know where she learned them; God must have put them into her head, for the poor child was inspired to speak so nicely that it made me cry like a fool to hear her talk. And what do you think the monster was doing all the time? Cutting his nails! He took the letter that poor Mme. Taillefer had soaked with tears, and flung it on to the chimney-piece. 'That is all right,' he said. He held out his hands to raise his daughter, but she covered them with kisses, and he drew them away again. Scandalous, isn't it? And his great booby of a son came in and took no notice of his sister."

"Very singular conduct, indeed!" exclaimed Mme. Vauquer.

"What inhuman wretches they must be!" said Father Goriot.

"And then they both went out of the room," Mme. Couture went on, without heeding the worthy vermicelli-maker's exclamation; "father and son bowed to me, and asked me to excuse them on account of urgent business! That is the history of our call. Well, he has seen his daughter at any rate.

How he can refuse to acknowledge her I cannot think, for they are as like as two peas."

The boarders dropped in one after another, interchanging greetings and the empty jokes that certain classes of Parisians regard as humorous and witty. Dulness is their prevailing ingredient, and the whole point consists in mispronouncing a word or in a gesture This kind of argot is always changing. The essence of the jest consists in some catchword suggested by a political event, an incident in the police courts, a street song, or a bit of burlesque at some theatre, and forgotten in a month. Anything and everything serves to keep up a game of battle-dore and shuttlecock with words and ideas. The diorama, a recent invention, which carried an optical illusion, a degree farther than panoramas, had given rise to a mania among art students for ending every word with *rama*. The Maison Vauquer had caught the infection from a young artist among the boarders.

"Well, Monsieur-r-r Poiret," said the employé from the Muséum, "how is your health-orama?" Then, without waiting for an answer, he turned to Mme. Couture and Victorine with a " Ladies, you seem melancholy."

"Is dinner ready?" cried Horace Bianchon, a medical student, and a friend of Rastignac's; "my stomach is sinking *usque ad talones.*"

"There is an uncommon *frozerama* outside!" said Vautrin. "Make room there, Father Goriot! Confound it! your foot covers the whole front of the stove. Let somebody else have a show."

"Illustrious M. Vautrin," put in Bianchon, "why do you say *frozerama?* It is incorrect; it should be *frozenrama.*"

"No, it shouldn't," said the official from the Muséum; "*frozerama* is right by the same rule that you say ' My feet are *froze.*' "

"Ah! ah!"

"Here is his excellency the Marquis de Rastignac, Doctor

of the Law of Contraries," cried Bianchon, seizing Eugène by the throat, and almost throttling him.

"Hallo there! hallo!"

Mlle. Michonneau came noiselessly in, bowed to the rest of the party, and took her place beside the three women without saying a word.

"That old bat always makes me shudder," said Bianchon in a low voice, indicating Mlle. Michonneau to Vautrin. "I have studied Gall's system, and I am sure she has the bump of Judas."

"Then you have seen a case before?" said Vautrin.

"Who has not?" answered Bianchon. "Upon my word, that ghastly old maid looks just like one of the long worms that will gnaw a beam through, give them time enough."

"That is the way, young man," returned he of the forty years and the dyed whiskers—

> *"The rose has lived the life of a rose—*
> *A morning's space."*

"Aha! here is a magnificent *soupe-au-rama*," cried Poiret as Christophe came in bearing the soup with cautious heed.

"I beg your pardon, sir," said Mme. Vauquer; "it is *soupe aux choux*."

All the young men roared with laughter.

"Had you there, Poiret!"

"Poir-r-r-rette! she had you there!"

"Score two points to Mamma Vauquer," said Vautrin.

"Did any one notice the fog this morning?" asked the official.

"It was a frantic fog," said Bianchon, "a fog unparalleled, doleful, melancholy, sea-green, asthmatical—a Goriot of a fog!"

"A Goriorama," said the art student, "because you couldn't see a thing in it."

"Hey! Milord Gâôriotte, they air talking about yoo-o-ou."

Father Goriot, seated at the lower end of the table, close to the door through which the servant entered, raised his face; he had smelt at a scrap of bread that lay under his table napkin, an old trick acquired in his commercial capacity, that still showed itself at times.

"Well," Mme. Vauquer cried in sharp tones, that rang above the rattle of spoons and plates and the sound of other voices, "and is there anything the matter with the bread?"

"Nothing whatever, madame," he answered; "on the contrary, it is made of the best quality of corn; flour from Etampes."

"How could you tell?" asked Eugène.

"By the color, by the flavor."

"You knew the flavor by the smell, I suppose," said Mme. Vauquer. "You have grown so economical, you will find out how to live on the smell of cooking at last."

"Take out a patent for it then," cried the Muséum official; "you would make a handsome fortune."

"Never mind him," said the artist; "he does that sort of thing to delude us into thinking that he was a vermicelli-maker."

"Your nose is a corn-sampler, it appears?" inquired the official.

"Corn *what?*" asked Bianchon.

"Corn-el."

"Corn-et."

"Corn-elian."

"Corn-ice."

"Corn-ucopia."

"Corn-crake."

"Corn-cockle."

"Corn-orama."

The eight responses came like a rolling fire from every part of the room, and the laughter that followed was the more uproarious because poor Father Goriot stared at the other with a puzzled look, like a foreigner trying to catch the meaning of words in a language that he does not understand.

"Corn?——" he said, turning to Vautrin, his next neighbor.

"Corn on your foot, old man!" said Vautrin, and he drove Father Goriot's cap down over his eyes by a blow on the crown.

The poor old man thus suddenly attacked was for a moment too bewildered to do anything. Christophe carried off his plate, thinking that he had finished his soup, so that when Goriot had pushed back his cap from his eyes his spoon encountered the table. Every one burst out laughing. "You are a disagreeable joker, sir," said the old man, "and if you take any further liberties with me——"

"Well, what then, old boy?" Vautrin interrupted.

"Well, then, you shall pay dearly for it some day——"

"Down below, eh?" said the artist, "in the little dark corner where they put naughty boys."

"Well, mademoiselle," Vautrin said, turning to Victorine, "you are eating nothing. So papa was refractory, was he?"

"A monster!" said Mme. Couture.

"Mademoiselle might make application for aliment pending her suit; she is not eating anything. Eh! eh! just see how Father Goriot is staring at Mlle. Victorine."

The old man had forgotten his dinner, he was so absorbed in gazing at the poor girl; the sorrow in her face was unmistakable—the slighted love of a child whose father would not recognize her.

"We are mistaken about Father Goriot, my dear boy," said Eugène in a low voice. "He is not an idiot, nor wanting in energy. Try your Gall system on him, and let me know what you think. I saw him crush a silver dish last night as if it had been made of wax; there seems to be something extraordinary going on in his mind just now, to judge by his face. His life is so mysterious that it must be worth studying. Oh, you may laugh, Bianchon; I am not joking."

"The man is a subject, is he?" said Bianchon; "all right! I will dissect him if he will give me a chance."

"No; feel his bumps."

"Hm!—his stupidity might perhaps be contagious."

The next day Rastignac dressed himself very elegantly, and about three o'clock in the afternoon went to call on Mme. de Restaud. On the way thither he indulged in the wild intoxicating dreams which fill a young head so full of delicious excitement. Young men at his age take no account of obstacles nor of dangers; they see success in every direction; imagination has free play, and turns their lives into a romance; they are saddened or discouraged by the collapse of one of the wild visionary schemes that have no existence save in their heated fancy. If youth were not ignorant and timid, civilization would be impossible.

Eugène took unheard-of pains to keep himself in a spotless condition, but on his way through the streets he began to think about Mme. de Restaud and what he should say to her. He equipped himself with wit, rehearsed repartees in the course of an imaginary conversation, and prepared certain neat speeches à la Talleyrand, conjuring up a series of small events which should prepare the way for the declaration on which he had based his future; and during these musings the law student was bespattered with mud, and by the time he reached the Palais Royal he was obliged to have his boots blacked and his trousers brushed.

"If I were rich," he said, as he changed the five-franc piece he had brought with him in case anything might happen, "I would take a cab, then I could think at my ease."

At last he reached the Rue de Helder, and asked for the Comtesse de Restaud. He bore the contemptuous glances of the servants, who had seen him cross the court on foot, with the cold fury of a man who knows that he will succeed some day. He understood the meaning of their glances at once, for he had felt his inferiority as soon as he entered the court, where a smart cab was waiting. All the delights of life in Paris seemed to be implied by this visible and manifest sign of luxury and extravagance. A fine horse, in magnificent harness, was pawing the ground, and all at once the law student felt out of humor with himself. Every compartment in his brain which he had thought to find so full of wit was bolted fast; he grew positively stupid. He sent up his name to the Countess, and waited in the ante-chamber, standing on one foot before a window that looked out upon the court; mechanically he leaned his elbow against the sash, and stared before him. The time seemed long; he would have left the house but for the southern tenacity of purpose which works miracles when it is single-minded.

"Madame is in her boudoir, and cannot see any one at present, sir," said the servant. "She gave me no answer; but if you will go into the dining-room, there is some one already there."

Rastignac was impressed with a sense of the formidable power of the lackey who can accuse or condemn his masters by a word; he coolly opened the door by which the man had just entered the ante-chamber, meaning, no doubt, to show these insolent flunkeys that he was familiar with the house; but he found that he had thoughtlessly precipitated himself into a small room full of dressers, where lamps were standing, and hot-water pipes, on which towels were being dried; a dark passage and a back staircase lay beyond it. Stifled laughter from the ante-chamber added to his confusion.

"This way to the drawing-room, sir," said the servant, with the exaggerated respect which seemed to be one more jest at his expense.

Eugène turned so quickly that he stumbled against a bath,

THE HORSE TOOK FRIGHT AT THE UMBRELLA.

By good luck, he managed to keep his hat on his head, and saved it from immersion in the water; but just as he turned, a door opened at the farther end of the dark passage, dimly lighted by a small lamp. Rastignac heard voices and the sound of a kiss; one of the speakers was Mme. de Restaud, the other was Father Goriot. Eugène followed the servant through the dining-room into the drawing-room; he went to a window that looked out into the courtyard, and stood there for a while. He meant to know whether this Goriot was really the Goriot that he knew. His heart beat unwontedly fast; he remembered Vautrin's hideous insinuations. A well-dressed young man suddenly emerged from the room almost as Eugène entered it, saying impatiently to the servant who stood at the door: "I am going, Maurice. Tell Madame la Comtesse that I waited more than half an hour for her."

Whereupon this insolent being, who, doubtless, had a right to be insolent, sang an Italian trill, and went towards the window where Eugène was standing, moved thereto quite as much by a desire to see the student's face as by a wish to look out into the courtyard.

"But M. le Comte had better wait a moment longer; madame is disengaged," said Maurice, as he returned to the ante-chamber.

Just at that moment Father Goriot appeared close to the gate; he had emerged from a door at the foot of the back staircase. The worthy soul was preparing to open his umbrella regardless of the fact that the great gate had opened to admit a tilbury, in which a young man with a ribbon at his button-hole was seated. Father Goriot had scarcely time to start back and save himself. The horse took fright at the umbrella, swerved, and dashed forward towards the flight of steps. The young man looked round in annoyance, saw Father Goriot, and greeted him as he went out with constrained courtesy, such as people usually show to a money-lender so long as they require his services, or the sort of respect they feel it necessary to show for some one whose reputation has been blown upon, so that they blush to acknowledge his acquaintance. Father Goriot gave him a little friendly nod and a good-natured smile. All this happened with lightning speed. Eugène was so deeply interested that he forgot that he was not alone till he suddenly heard the Countess' voice.

"Oh! Maxime, were you going away?" she said reproachfully, with a shade of pique in her manner. The Countess had not seen the incident nor the entrance of the tilbury. Rastignac turned abruptly and saw her standing before him, coquettishly dressed in a loose white cashmere gown with knots of rose-colored ribbon here and there; her hair was carelessly coiled about her head, as is the wont of Parisian women in the morning; there was a soft fragrance about her—doubtless she was fresh from a bath—her graceful form seemed more flexible, her beauty more luxuriant. Her eyes glistened. A young man can see everything at a glance; he feels the radiant influence of woman as a plant discerns and absorbs its nutriment from the air; he did not need to touch her hands to feel their cool freshness. He saw faint rose tints through the cashmere of the dressing-gown; it had fallen slightly open, giving glimpses of a bare throat, on which the student's eyes rested. The Countess had no need of the adventitious aid of corsets; her girdle defined the outlines of her slender waist; her throat was a challenge to love; her feet, thrust into slippers, were daintily small. As Maxime took her hand and kissed it, Eugène became aware of Maxime's existence, and the Countess saw Eugène.

"Oh! is that you M. de Rastignac? I am very glad to see you," she said, but there was something in her manner that a shrewd observer would have taken as a hint to depart.

Maxime, as the Countess Anastasie had called the young man with the haughty insolence of bearing, looked from Eugène to the lady, and from the lady to Eugène; it was sufficiently evident that he wished to be rid of the latter.

An exact and faithful rendering of the glance might be given in the words: "Look here, my dear; I hope you intend to send this little whipper-snapper about his business."

The Countess consulted the young man's face with an intent submissiveness that betrays all the secrets of a woman's heart, and Rastignac all at once began to hate him violently. To begin with, the sight of the fair carefully arranged curls on the other's comely head had convinced him that his own crop was hideous; Maxime's boots, moreover, were elegant and spotless, while his own, in spite of all his care, bore some traces of his recent walk; and, finally, Maxime's overcoat fitted the outline of his figure gracefully, he looked like a pretty woman, while Eugène was wearing a black coat at half-past two. The quick-witted child of the Charente felt the disadvantage at which he was placed beside this tall, slender dandy, with the clear gaze and the pale face, one of those men who would ruin orphan children without scruple. Mme. de Restaud fled into the next room without waiting for Eugène to speak; shaking out the skirts of her dressing-gown in her flight, so that she looked like a white butterfly, and Maxime hurried after her. Eugène, in a fury, followed Maxime and the Countess, and the three stood once more face to face by the hearth in the large drawing-room. The law student felt quite sure that the odious Maxime found him in the way, and even at the risk of displeasing Mme. de Restaud, he meant to annoy the dandy. It had struck him all at once that he had seen the young man before at Mme. de Beauséant's ball; he guessed the relation between Maxime and Mme. de Restaud; and with the youthful audacity that commits prodigious blunders or achieves signal success, he said to himself, "This is my rival; I mean to cut him out."

Rash resolve! He did not know that M. le Comte Maxime de Trailles would wait till he was insulted, so as to fire first and kill his man. Eugène was a sportsman and a good shot, but he had not yet hit the bull's eye twenty times out of twenty-two. The young Count dropped into a low chair by the hearth, took up the tongs, and made up the fire so violently and so sulkily, that Anastasie's fair face suddenly clouded over. She turned to Eugène with a cool, questioning glance that asked plainly, "Why do you not go?" a glance which well-bred people regard as a cue to make their exit.

Eugène assumed an amiable expression.

"Madame," he began, "I hastened to call upon you——"

He stopped short. The door opened, and the owner of the tilbury suddenly appeared. He had left his hat outside, and did not greet the Countess; he looked meditatively at Rastignac, and held out his hand to Maxime with a cordial "Good-morning," that astonished Eugène not a little. The young provincial did not understand the amenities of a triple alliance.

"M. de Restaud," said the Countess, introducing her husband to the law student.

Eugène bowed profoundly.

"This gentleman," she continued, presenting Eugène to her husband, "is M. de Rastignac; he is related to Mme. la Vicomtesse de Beauséant through the Marcillacs; I had the pleasure of meeting him at her last ball."

Related to Mme. la Vicomtesse de Beauséant through the Marcillacs! These words, on which the Countess threw ever so slight an emphasis, by reason of the pride that the mistress of the house takes in showing that she only receives people of distinction as visitors in her house, produced a magical effect. The Count's stiff manner relaxed at once as he returned the student's bow.

"Delighted to have an opportunity of making your acquaintance," he said.

Maxime de Trailles himself gave Eugène an uneasy glance, and suddenly dropped his insolent manner. The mighty name had all the power of a fairy's wand; those closed compartments in the southern brain flew open again; Rastignac's carefully drilled faculties returned. It was as if a sudden light had pierced the obscurity of this upper world of Paris, and he began to see, though everything was indistinct as yet. Mme. Vauquer's lodging-house and Father Goriot were very far remote from his thoughts.

"I thought that the Marcillacs were extinct," the Comte de Restaud said, addressing Eugène.

"Yes, they are extinct," answered the law student. "My great uncle, the Chevalier de Rastignac, married the heiress of the Marcillac family. They had only one daughter, who married the Maréchal de Clarimbault, Mme. de Beauséant's grandfather on the mother's side. We are the younger branch of the family, and the younger branch is all the poorer because my great-uncle, the vice-admiral, lost all that he had in the King's service. The government during the Revolution refused to admit our claims when the Compagnie des Indes was liquidated."

"Was not your great-uncle in command of the *Vengeur* before 1789?"

"Yes."

"Then he would be acquainted with my grandfather, who commanded the *Warwick*."

Maxime looked at Mme. de Restaud and shrugged his shoulders, as much as to say, "If he is going to discuss nautical matters with that fellow, it is all over with us." Anastasie understood the glance that M. de Trailles gave her. With a woman's admirable tact and shrdewness, she began to smile and said:

"Come with me, Maxime; I have something to say to you. We will leave you two gentlemen to sail in company on board the *Warwick* and the *Vengeur*."

She rose to her feet and signed to Maxime to follow her, mirth and mischief in her whole attitude, and the two went in the direction of the boudoir. The *morganatic* couple (to use a convenient German expression which has no exact equivalent) had reached the door, when the Count interrupted himself in his talk with Eugène.

"Anastasie!" he cried pettishly, "just stay a moment, dear; you know very well that——"

"I am coming back in a minute," she interrupted; "I have a commission for Maxime to execute, and I want to tell him about it."

She came back almost immediately. She had noticed the inflection in her husband's voice, and knew that it would not be safe to retire to the boudoir: like all women who are compelled to study their husband's characters in order to have their own way, and whose business it is to know exactly how far they can go without endangering a good understanding, she was very careful to avoid petty collisions in domestic life. It was Eugène who had brought about this untoward incident; so the Countess looked at Maxime and indicated the law student with an air of exasperation. M. de Trailles addressed the Count, the Countess, and Eugène with the pointed remark, "You are busy, I do not want to interrupt you; good-day," and he went.

"Just wait a moment, Maxime!" the Count called after him.

"Come and dine with us," said the Countess, leaving Eugène and her husband together once more. She followed Maxime into the little drawing-room, where they sat together sufficiently long to feel sure that Rastignac had taken his leave.

The law student heard their laughter, and their voices, and the pauses in their talk; he grew malicious, exerted his conversational powers for M. de Restaud, flattered him, and drew him into discussions, to the end that he might see the Countess again and discover the nature of her relations with Father Goriot. This countess, with a husband and a lover, for Maxime clearly was her lover, was a mystery. What was the secret tie that bound her to the old tradesman? This mystery he meant to penetrate, hoping by its means to gain a sovereign ascendancy over this fair typical Parisian.

"Anastasie!" the Count called again to his wife.

"Poor Maxime!" she said, addressing the young man. "Come, we must resign ourselves. This evening——"

"I hope, Nasie," he said in her ear, "that you will give orders not to admit that youngster, whose eyes light up like live coals when he looks at you. He will make you a declaration, and compromise you, and then you will compel me to kill him."

"Are you mad, Maxime?" she said. "A young lad of a student is, on the contrary, a capital lightning-conductor; is not that so? Of course, I mean to make Restaud furiously jealous of him."

Maxime burst out laughing, and went out, followed by the Countess, who stood at the window to watch him into his carriage; he shook his whip, and made his horse prance. She only returned when the great gate had been closed after him.

"What do you think, dear?" cried the Count, her husband, "this gentleman's family estate is not far from Verteuil, on the Charente; his great-uncle and my grandfather were acquainted."

"Delighted to find that we have acquaintances in common," said the Countess, with a preoccupied manner.

"More than you think," said Eugène, in a low voice.

"What do you mean?" she asked quickly.

"Why, only just now," said the student, "I saw a gentleman go out at the gate, Father Goriot, my next-door neighbor in the house where I am lodging."

At the sound of this name, and the prefix that embellished it, the Count, who was stirring the fire, let the tongs fall as though they had burned his fingers, and rose to his feet.

"Sir," he cried, "you might have called him 'Monsieur Goriot!'"

The Countess turned pale at first at the sight of her husband's vexation, then she reddened; clearly she was embarrassed, her answer was made in a tone that she tried to make natural, and with an air of assumed carelessness—

"You could not know any one who is dearer to us both——"

She broke off, glanced at the piano as if some fancy had crossed her mind, and asked, "Are you fond of music, M. de Rastignac?"

"Exceedingly," answered Eugène, flushing, and disconcerted by a dim suspicion that he had somehow been guilty of a clumsy piece of folly.

"Do you sing?" she cried, going to the piano, and, sitting down before it, she swept her fingers over the keyboard from end to end. R-r-r-r-ah!

"No, madame."

The Comte de Restaud walked to and fro.

"That is a pity; you are without one great means of success. *Ca-ro, ca-a-ro, ca-a-a-ro, non du-bi-ta-re,*" sang the Countess.

Eugène had a second time waved a magic wand when he uttered Goriot's name, but the effect seemed to be entirely opposite to that produced by the formula "related to Mme. de Beauséant." His position was not unlike that of some visitor permitted as a favor to inspect a private collection of curiosities, when by inadvertence he comes into collision with a glass case full of sculptured figures, and three or four heads, imperfectly secured, fall at the shock. He wished the earth would open and swallow him. Mme. de Restaud's expression was reserved and chilly, her eyes had grown indifferent, and sedulously avoided meeting those of the unlucky student of law.

"Madame," he said, "you wish to talk with M. de Restaud; permit me to wish you good-day——"

The Countess interrupted him by a gesture, saying hastily,

"Whenever you come to see us, both M. de Restaud and I shall be delighted to see you."

Eugène made a profound bow and took his leave, followed by M. de Restaud, who insisted, in spite of his remonstrances, on accompanying him into the hall.

"Neither your mistress nor I are at home to that gentleman when he calls," the Count said to Maurice, his servant, when the door had closed after Eugène.

As Eugène set foot on the steps, he saw that it was raining.

"Come," said he to himself, "somewhow I have just made a mess of it, I do not know how. And now I am going to spoil my hat and coat into the bargain. I ought to stop in my corner, grind away at law, and never look to be anything but a boorish country magistrate. How can I go into society, when to manage properly you want a lot of cabs, varnished boots, gold watch-chains, and all sorts of things; you have to wear white doeskin gloves that cost six francs in the morning, and primrose kid gloves every evening? A fig for that old humbug of a Goriot!"

When he reached the street-door, the driver of a hackney coach, who had probably just deposited a wedding party at their door, and asked nothing better than a chance of making a little money for himself without his employer's knowledge, saw that Eugène had no umbrella, remarked his black coat, white waistcoat, yellow gloves, and varnished boots, and stopped and looked at him inquiringly. Eugène, in the blind desperation that drives a young man to plunge deeper and deeper into an abyss, as if he might hope to find a fortunate issue in its lowest depths, nodded in reply to the driver's signal, and stepped into the cab; a few stray petals of orange blossom and scraps of wire bore witness to its recent occupation by a wedding party.

"Where am I to drive, sir?" demanded the man, who, by this time, had taken off his white gloves.

"Confound it!" Eugène said to himself, "I am in for

it now, and at least I will not spend cab-hire for nothing! Drive to the Hôtel Beauséant," he said aloud.

"Which?" asked the man, a portentous word that reduced Eugène to confusion. This young man of fashion, *species incerta*, did not know that there were two Hôtels Beauséant; he was not aware how rich he was in relations who did not care about him.

"The Vicomte de Beauséant, Rue——"

"De Grenelle," interrupted the driver, with a jerk of his head. "You see, there are the hôtels of the Marquis and Comte de Beauséant in the Rue Saint-Dominique," he added, drawing up the step.

"I know all about that," said Eugène, severely. "Everybody is laughing at me to-day, it seems!" he said to himself, as he deposited his hat on the opposite seat. "This escapade will cost me a king's ransom, but, at any rate, I shall call on my so-called cousin in a thoroughly aristocratic fashion. Goriot has cost me ten francs already, the old scoundrel! My word! I will tell Mme. de Beauséant about my adventure; perhaps it may amuse her. Doubtless she will know the secret of the criminal relation between that handsome woman and the old rat without a tail. It would be better to find favor in my cousin's eyes than to come in contact with that shameless woman, who seems to me to have very expensive tastes. Surely the beautiful Vicomtesse's personal interest would turn the scale for me, when the mere mention of her name produces such an effect. Let us look higher. If you set yourself to carry the heights of heaven, you must face God."

The innumerable thoughts that surged through his brain might be summed up in these phrases. He grew calmer, and recovered something of his assurance as he watched the falling rain. He told himself that though he was about to squander two of the precious five-franc pieces that remained to him, the money was well laid out in preserving his coat, boots, and hat; and his cabman's cry of "Gate, if you please," almost put him in spirits. A Swiss, in scarlet and gold, appeared, the great door groaned on its hinges, and Rastignac, with sweet satisfaction, beheld his equipage pass under the archway and stop before the flight of steps beneath the awning. The driver, in a blue-and-red greatcoat, dismounted and let down the step. As Eugène stepped out of the cab, he heard smothered laughter from the peristyle. Three or four lackeys were making merry over the festal appearance of the vehicle. In another moment the law student was enlightened as to the cause of their hilarity; he felt the full force of the contrast between his equipage and one of the smartest broughams in Paris; a coachman, with powdered hair, seemed to find it difficult to hold a pair of spirited horses, who stood chafing the bit. In Mme. de Restaud's courtyard, in the Chaussée d'Antin, he had seen the neat turnout of a young man of six-and-twenty; in the Faubourg Saint-Germain he found the luxurious equipage of a man of rank; thirty thousand francs would not have purchased it.

"Who can be here?" said Eugène to himself. He began to understand, though somewhat tardily, that he must not expect to find many women in Paris who were not already appropriated, and that the capture of one of these queens would be likely to cost something more than bloodshed. "Confound it all! I expect my cousin also has her Maxime."

He went up the steps, feeling that he was a blighted being. The glass door was opened for him; the servants were as solemn as jackasses under the currycomb. So far, Eugène had only been in the ballroom on the ground floor of the Hôtel Beauséant; the fête had followed so closely on the invitation that he had not had time to call on his cousin, and had therefore never seen Mme. de Beauséant's apartments; he was about to behold for the first time a great lady among the wonderful and elegant surroundings that reveal her character and reflect her daily life. He was the more curious, because Mme. de Restaud's drawing-room had provided him with a standard of comparison.

At half-past four the Vicomtesse de Beauséant was visible. Five minutes earlier she would not have received her cousin, but Eugène knew nothing of the recognized routine of various houses in Paris. He was conducted up the wide, white-painted, crimson-carpeted staircase, between the gilded balusters and masses of flowering plants, to Mme. de Beauséant's apartments. He did not know the rumor current about Mme. de Beauséant, one of the biographies told, with variations, in whispers, every evening in the salons of Paris.

For three years past her name had been spoken of in connection with that of one of the most wealthy and distinguished Portuguese nobles, the Marquis d'Ajuda-Pinto. It was one of those innocent *liaisons* which possess so much charm for the two thus attached to each other that they find the presence of a third person intolerable. The Vicomte de Beauséant, therefore, had himself set an example to the rest of the world by respecting, with as good a grace as might be, this morganatic union. Any one who came to call on the Vicomtesse in the early days of this friendship was sure to find the Marquis d'Ajuda-Pinto there. As, under the circumstances, Mme. de Beauséant could not very well shut her door against these visitors, she gave them such a cold reception, and showed so much interest in the study of the ceiling, that no one could fail to understand how much he bored her; and when it became known in Paris that Mme. de Beauséant was bored by callers between two and four o'clock, she was left in perfect solitude during that interval. She went to the Bouffons or to the Opéra with M. de Beauséant and M. d'Ajuda-Pinto; and M. de Beauséant, like a well-bred man of the world, always left his wife and the Portuguese as soon as he had installed them. But M. d'Ajuda-Pinto must marry, and a Mlle. de Rochefide was the young lady. In the whole fashionable world there was but one person who as yet knew nothing of the arrangement, and that was Mme. de Beauséant. Some of her friends had hinted at the possibility, and she had laughed at them, believing that envy had prompted those ladies to try to make mischief. And now, though the banns were about to be published, and although the handsome Portuguese had come that day to break the news to the Vicomtesse, he had not found courage as yet to say one word about his treachery. How was it? Nothing is doubtless more difficult than the notification of an *ultimatum* of this kind. There are men who feel more at their ease when they stand up before another man who threatens their lives with sword or pistol than in the presence of a woman who, after two hours of lamentations and reproaches, falls into a dead swoon and requires salts. At this moment, therefore, M. d'Ajuda-Pinto was on thorns, and anxious to take his leave. He told himself that in some way or other the news would reach Mme. de Beauséant; he would write, it would be much better to do it by letter, and not to utter the words that should stab her to the heart.

So when the servant announced M. Eugène de Rastignac, the Marquis d'Ajuda-Pinto trembled with joy. To be sure, a loving woman shows even more ingenuity in inventing doubts of her lover than in varying the monotony of his happiness; and when she is about to be forsaken, she instinctively interprets every gesture as rapidly as Virgil's courser detected the presence of his companion by snuffing the breeze. It was impossible, therefore, that Mme. de Beauséant should not detect that involuntary thrill of satisfaction; slight though it was, it was appalling in its artlessness.

Eugène had yet to learn that no one in Paris should present himself in any house without first making himself acquainted with the whole history of its owner, and of its owner's wife and family, so that he may avoid making any of the terrible blunders which in Poland draw forth the picturesque exclamation, "Harness five bullocks to your cart!" probably because you will need them all to pull you out of the quagmire into which a false step has plunged you. If, down to the present day, our language has no name for these conversational disasters, it is probably because they are believed to be impossible, the publicity given in Paris to every scandal is so prodigious. After the awkward incident at Mme. de Restaud's, no one but Eugène could have reappeared in his character of bullock-driver in Mme. de Beauséant's drawing-room. But if Mme. de Restaud and M. de Trailles had found him horribly in the way, M. d'Ajuda-Pinto hailed his coming with relief.

"Good-bye," said the Portuguese, hurrying to the door, as Eugène made his entrance into a dainty little pink-and-gray drawing-room, where luxury seemed nothing more than good taste.

"Until this evening," said Mme. de Beauséant, turning her head to give the Marquis a glance. "We are going to the Bouffons, are we not?"

"I cannot go," he said, with his fingers on the door-handle.

Mme. de Beauséant rose and beckoned to him to return. She did not pay the slightest attention to Eugène, who stood there dazzled by the sparkling marvels around him; he began to think that this was some story out of the "Arabian Nights" made real, and did not know where to hide himself, when the woman before him seemed to be unconscious of his existence. The Vicomtesse had raised the forefinger of her right hand, and gracefully signed to the Marquis to seat himself beside her. The Marquis felt the imperious sway of passion in her gesture; he came back towards her. Eugène watched him, not without a feeling of envy.

"That is the owner of the brougham!" he said to himself. "But is it necessary to have a pair of spirited horses, servants in livery, and torrents of gold to draw a glance from a woman here in Paris?"

The demon of luxury gnawed at his heart, greed burned in his veins, his throat was parched with the thirst of gold.

He had a hundred and thirty francs every quarter. His father, mother, brothers, sisters, and aunt did not spend two hundred francs a month among them. This swift comparison between his present condition and the aims he had in view helped to benumb his faculties.

"Why not?" the Vicomtesse was saying, as she smiled at the Portuguese. "Why can you not come to the Italiens?"

"Affairs! I am to dine with the English ambassador."

"Throw him over."

When a man once enters on a course of deception, he is compelled to add lie to lie. M. d'Ajuda therefore said, smiling, "Do you lay your commands on me?"

"Yes, certainly."

"That was what I wanted to have you say to me," he answered, dissembling his feelings in a glance which would have reassured any other woman.

He took the Vicomtesse's hand, kissed it, and went.

Eugène ran his fingers through his hair, and constrained himself to bow. He thought that now Mme. de Beauséant would give him her attention; but suddenly she sprang forward, rushed to a window in the gallery, and watched M. d'Ajuda step into his carriage; she listened to the order that he gave, and heard the Swiss repeat it to the coachman—

"To M. de Rochefide's house."

Those words, and the way in which M. d'Ajuda flung himself back in the carriage, were like a lightning flash and a thunderbolt for her; she walked back again with a deadly fear gnawing at her heart. The most terrible catastrophes only happen among the heights. The Vicomtesse went to her own room, sat down at a table, and took up a sheet of dainty note-paper.

"When, instead of dining with the English ambassador," she wrote, "you go to the Rochefides, you owe me an explanation, which I am waiting to hear."

She retraced several of the letters, for her hand was trembling so that they were indistinct; then she signed the note with an initial C. for " Claire de Bourgogne," and rang the bell.

"Jacques," she said to the servant, who appeared immediately, "take this note to M. de Rochefide's house at half-past seven, and ask for the Marquis d'Ajuda. If M. d'Ajuda is there, leave the note without waiting for an answer; if he is not there, bring the note back to me."

"Madame la Vicomtesse, there is a visitor in the drawing-room."

"Ah! yes, of course," she said, opening the door.

Eugène was beginning to feel very uncomfortable, but at last the Vicomtesse appeared; she spoke to him, and the tremulous tones of her voice vibrated through his heart.

"Pardon me, monsieur," she said; "I had a letter to write. Now I am quite at liberty."

She scarcely knew what she was saying, for even as she spoke she thought, "Ah! he means to marry Mlle. de Rochefide! But is he still free? This evening the marriage shall be broken off, or else—— But before to-morrow I shall know."

"Cousin——" the student replied.

"Eh?" said the Countess, with an insolent glance that sent a cold shudder through Eugène; he understood what that "Eh?" meant; he had learned a great deal in three hours, and his wits were on the alert. He reddened—

"Madame——" he began; he hesitated a moment, and then went on. "Pardon me; I am in such need of protection that the merest scrap of relationship could do me no harm."

Mme. de Beauséant smiled, but there was sadness in her smile; even now she felt forebodings of the coming pain, the air she breathed was heavy with the storm that was about to burst.

"If you knew how my family are situated," he went on, "you would love to play the part of a beneficent fairy godmother who graciously clears the obstacles from the path of her protégé."

"Well, cousin," she said laughing, "and how can I be of service to you?"

"But do I know even that? I am distantly related to you, and this obscure and remote relationship is even now a perfect godsend to me. You have confused my ideas; I cannot remember the things that I meant to say to you. I know no one else here in Paris—— Ah! if I could only ask you to counsel me, ask you to look upon me as a poor child who would fain cling to the hem of your dress, who would lay down his life for you."

"Would you kill a man for me?"

"Two," said Eugène.

"You, child! Yes, you are a child," she said, keeping back the tears that came to her eyes; "you would love sincerely."

"Oh!" he cried, flinging up his head.

The audacity of the student's answer interested the Vicomtesse in him. The southern brain was beginning to scheme for the first time. Between Mme. de Restaud's blue boudoir and Mme. de Beauséant's rose-colored drawing-room he had made a three years' advance in a kind of law which is not a recognized study in Paris, although it is a sort of higher jurisprudence, and, when well understood, is a high-road to success of every kind.

"Ah! this is what I meant to say!" said Eugène. "I met Mme. de Restaud at your ball, and this morning I went to see her."

"You must have been very much in the way," said Mme. de Beauséant, smiling as she spoke.

"Yes, indeed. I am a novice, and my blunders will set every one against me, if you do not give me your counsel. I believe that in Paris it is very difficult to meet with a young, beautiful, and wealthy woman of fashion who would be willing to teach me, what you women can explain so well—life. I shall find a M. de Trailles everywhere. So I have come to you to ask you to give me a key to a puzzle, to entreat you to tell me what sort of blunder I made this morning. I mentioned an old man——"

"Madame la Duchesse de Langeais!" Jacques cut the student short; Eugène gave expression to his intense annoyance by a gesture.

"If you mean to succeed," said the Vicomtesse in a low voice, "in the first place you must not be so demonstrative."

"Ah! good-morning, dear," she continued, and, rising and crossing the room, she grasped the Duchess' hand as affectionately as if they had been sisters; the Duchess responded in the prettiest and most gracious way.

"Two intimate friends!" said Rastignac to himself. "Henceforward I shall have two protectresses; those two women are great friends, no doubt, and this new-comer will doubtless interest herself in her friend's cousin."

"To what happy inspiration do I owe this piece of good fortune, dear Antoinette?" asked Mme. de Beauséant.

"Well, I saw M. d'Ajuda-Pinto at M. de Rochefide's door, so I thought that if I came I should find you alone."

Mme. de Beauséant's mouth did not tighten, her color did not rise, her expression did not alter, or rather, her brow seemed to clear as the Duchess uttered those deadly words.

"If I had known that you were engaged——" the speaker added, glancing at Eugène.

"This gentleman is M. Eugène de Rastignac, one of my cousins," said the Vicomtesse. "Have you any news of General de Montriveau?" she continued. "Sérizy told me yesterday that he never goes anywhere now; has he been to see you to-day?"

It was believed that the Duchess was desperately in love

with M. de Montriveau, and that he was a faithless lover; she felt the question in her very heart, and her face flushed as she answered.

"He was at the Élysée yesterday."

"In attendance?"

"Claire," returned the Duchess, and hatred overflowed in the glances she threw at Mme. de Beauséant; "of course you know that M. d'Ajuda-Pinto is going to marry Mlle. de Rochefide; the banns will be published to-morrow."

This thrust was too cruel; the Vicomtesse's face grew white, but she answered, laughing, "One of those rumors that fools amuse themselves with. What should induce M. d'Ajuda to take one of the noblest names in Portugal to the Rochefides? The Rochefides were only ennobled yesterday."

"But Bertha will have two hundred thousand livres a year, they say."

"M. d'Ajuda is too wealthy to marry for money."

"But, my dear, Mlle. de Rochefide is a charming girl."

"Indeed?"

"And, as a matter of fact, he is dining with them to-day; the thing is settled. It is very surprising to me that you should know so little about it."

Mme. de Beauséant turned to Rastignac. "What was the blunder that you made, monsieur?" she asked. "The poor boy is only just launched into the world, Antoinette, so that he understands nothing of all this that we are speaking of. Be merciful to him, and let us finish our talk to-morrow. Everything will be announced to-morrow, you know, and your kind informal communication can be accompanied by official confirmation."

The Duchess gave Eugène one of those insolent glances that measure a man from head to foot and leave him crushed and annihilated.

"Madame, I have unwittingly plunged a dagger into Mme. de Restaud's heart; unwittingly—therein lies my offense," said the student of law, whose keen brain had served him sufficiently well, for he had detected the biting epigrams that lurked beneath this friendly talk. "You continue to receive, possibly you fear, those who know the amount of pain that they deliberately inflict; but a clumsy blunderer who has no idea how deeply he wounds is looked upon as a fool who does not know how to make use of his opportunities, and every one despises him."

Mme. de Beauséant gave the student a glance, one of those glances in which a great soul can mingle dignity and gratitude. It was like balm to the law student, who was still smarting under the Duchess' insolent scrutiny; she had looked at him as an auctioneer might look at some article to appraise its value.

"Imagine, too, that I had just made some progress with the Comte de Restaud; for I should tell you, madame," he went on, turning to the Duchess with a mixture of humility and malice in his manner, "that as yet I am only a poor devil of a student, very much alone in the world, and very poor——"

"You should not tell us that, M. de Rastignac. We women never care about anything that no one else will take."

"Bah!" said Eugène. "I am only two-and-twenty, and I must make up my mind to the drawbacks of my time of life. Besides, I am confessing my sins, and it would be impossible to kneel in a more charming confessional; you commit your sins in one drawing-room, and receive absolution for them in another."

The Duchess' expression grew colder; she did not like the flippant tone of these remarks, and showed that she considered them to be in bad taste by turning to the Vicomtesse with—
"This gentleman has only just come——"

Mme. de Beauséant began to laugh outright at her cousin and at the Duchess both.

"He has only just come to Paris, dear, and is in search of some one who will give him lessons in good taste."

"Mme. la Duchesse," said Eugène, "is it not natural to wish to be initiated into the mysteries which charm us?" ("Come, now," he said to himself, "my language is superfinely elegant, I'm sure.")

"But Mme. de Restaud is herself, I believe, M. de Trailles' pupil," said the Duchess.

"Of that I had no idea, madame," answered the law student, "so I rashly came between them. In fact, I got on very well with the lady's husband, and his wife tolerated me for a time until I took it into my head to tell them that I knew some one of whom I had just caught a glimpse as he went out by a back staircase, a man who had given the Countess a kiss at the end of a passage."

"Who was it?" both women asked together.

"An old man who lives at the rate of two louis a month in the Faubourg Saint-Marceau, where I, a poor student, lodge likewise. He is a truly unfortunate creature, everybody laughs at him—we call him Father Goriot."

"Why, child that you are," cried the Vicomtesse, "Mme. de Restaud was a Mlle. Goriot!"

"The daughter of a vermicelli manufacturer," the Duchess added; "and when the little creature went to court, the daughter of a pastry-cook was presented on the same day. Do you remember, Claire? The King began to laugh, and made some joke in Latin about flour. People—what was it?—people——"

"*Ejusdem farinæ*," said Eugène.

"Yes, that was it," said the Duchess.

"Oh! is that her father?" the law student continued, aghast.

"Yes, certainly; the old man had two daughters; he dotes on them, so to speak, though they will scarcely acknowledge him."

"Didn't the second daughter marry a banker with a German name?" the Vicomtesse asked, turning to Mme. de

Langeais, "a Baron de Nucingen? And her name is Delphine, is it not? Isn't she a fair-haired woman who has a side-box at the Opéra? She comes sometimes to the Bouffons, and laughs loudly to attract attention."

The Duchess smiled and said—

"I wonder at you, dear. Why do you take so much interest in people of that kind? One must have been as madly in love as Restaud was, to be infatuated with Mlle. Anastasie and her flour-sacks. Oh! he will not find her a good bargain! She is in M. de Trailles' hands, and he will ruin her."

"And they do not acknowledge their father!" Eugène repeated.

"Oh! well, yes, their father, the father, a father," replied the Vicomtesse, "a kind father who gave them each five or six hundred thousand francs, it is said, to secure their happiness by marrying them well; while he only kept eight or ten thousand livres a year for himself, thinking that his daughters would always be his daughters, thinking that in them he would live his life twice over again, that in their houses he should find two homes, where he would be loved and looked up to, and made much of. And in two years' time both his sons-in-law had turned him out of their houses as if he were one of the lowest outcasts."

Tears came into Eugène's eyes. He was still under the spell of youthful beliefs, he had but just left home, pure and sacred feelings had been stirred within him, and this was his first day on the battlefield of civilization in Paris. Genuine feeling is so infectious that for a moment the three looked at each other in silence.

"*Eh, mon Dieu!*" said Mme. de Langeais; "yes, it seems very horrible, and yet we see such things every day. Is there not a reason for it? Tell me, dear, have you ever really thought what a son-in-law is? A son-in-law is the man for whom we bring up, you and I, a dear little one, bound to us very closely in innumerable ways; for seventeen years she will be the joy of her family, its 'white soul,' as Lamartine says, and suddenly she will become its scourge. When *he* comes and takes her from us, his love from the very beginning is like an axe laid to the root of all the old affection in our darling's heart, and all the ties that bound her to her family are severed. But yesterday our little daughter thought of no one but her mother and father, as we had no thought that was not for her; by to-morrow she will have become a hostile stranger. The tragedy is always going on under our eyes. On the one hand you see a father who has sacrificed himself to his son, and his daughter-in-law shows him the last degree of insolence. On the other hand, it is the son-in-law who turns his wife's mother out of the house. I sometimes hear it said that there is nothing dramatic about society in these days; but the Drama of the Son-in-law is appalling, to say nothing of our marriages, which have come to be very poor farces. I can explain how it all came about in the old vermicelli-maker's case. I think I recollect that Foriot—"

"Goriot, madame."

"Yes, that Moriot was once president of his section during the Revolution. He was in the secret of the famous scarcity of grain, and laid the foundation of his fortune in those days by selling flour for ten times its cost. He had as much flour as he wanted. My grandmother's steward sold him immense quantities. No doubt Noriot shared the plunder with the Committee of Public Salvation, as that sort of person always did. I recollect the steward telling my grandmother that she might live at Grandvilliers in complete security, because her corn was as good as a certificate of civism. Well, then, this Loriot, who sold corn to those butchers, has never had but one passion, they say—he idolizes his daughters. He settled one of them under Restaud's roof, and grafted the other into the Nucingen family tree, the Baron de Nucingen being a rich banker who had turned Royalist. You can quite understand that so long as Bonaparte was Emperor, the two sons-in-law could manage to put up with old Ninety-three; but after the restoration of the Bourbons, M. de Restaud felt bored by the old man's society, and the banker was still more tired of it. His daughters were still fond of him; they wanted 'to keep the goat and the cabbage,' so they used to see the Joriot whenever there was no one there, under pretense of affection. 'Come to-day, papa, we shall have you all to ourselves, and that will be much nicer!' and all that sort of thing. As for me, dear, I believe that love has second sight: poor Ninety-three, his heart must have bled! He saw that his daughters were ashamed of him, that if they loved their husbands his visits must make mischief. So he immolated himself. He made the sacrifice because he was a father; he went into voluntary exile. His daughters were satisfied, so he thought that he had done the best thing he could; but it was a family crime, and father and daughters were accomplices. You see this sort of thing everywhere. What could this Father Doriot have been but a splash of mud in his daughters' drawing-rooms? He would only have been in the way and bored other people, besides being bored himself. And this that happened between father and daughters may happen to the prettiest woman in Paris and the man she loves best; if her love grows tiresome, he will go; he will descend to the basest trickery to leave her. It is the same with all love and friendship. Our heart is a treasury; if you pour out all its wealth at once, you are bankrupt. We show no more mercy to the affection that reveals its utmost extent than we do to another kind of prodigal who has not a penny left. Their father had given them all he had. For twenty years he had given his whole heart to them; then, one day, he gave them all his fortune too. The lemon was squeezed; the girls left the rest in the gutter."

"The world is very base," said the Vicomtesse, plucking at the threads of her shawl. See did not raise her eyes as she spoke; the words that Mme. de Langeais had meant for her in the course of the story had cut her to the quick.

"Base? Oh, no," answered the Duchess; "the world goes its own way, that is all. If I speak in this way, it is only to show that I am not duped by it. I think as you do," she said, pressing the Vicomtesse's hand. "The world is a slough; let us try to live on the heights above it."

She rose to her feet and kissed Mme. de Beauséant on the forehead as she said: "You look very charming to-day, dear. I have never seen such a lovely color in your cheeks before."

Then she went out, with a slight inclination of the head to the cousin.

"Father Goriot is sublime!" said Eugène to himself, as he remembered how he had watched his neighbor work the silver vessel into a shapeless mass that night.

Mme. de Beauséant did not hear him; she was absorbed in her own thoughts. For several minutes the silence remained unbroken till the law student became almost paralyzed with embarrassment, and was equally afraid to go or stay or speak a word.

"The world is basely ungrateful and ill-natured," said the Vicomtesse at last. "No sooner does a trouble befall you than a friend is ready to bring the tidings and to probe your heart with the point of a dagger while calling on you to admire the handle. Epigrams and sarcasms already! Ah! I will defend myself!"

She raised her head like the great lady that she was, and lightnings flashed from her proud eyes.

"Ah!" she said, as she saw Eugène, "are you there?"

"Still," he said piteously.

"Well, then, M. de Rastignac, deal with the world as it deserves. You are determined to succeed? I will help you. You shall sound the depths of corruption in woman; you shall measure the extent of man's pitiful vanity. Deeply as I am versed in such learning, there were pages in the book of life that I had not read. Now I know all. The more cold-blooded your calculations, the farther you will go. Strike ruthlessly; you will be feared. Men and women for you must be nothing more than post-horses; take a fresh relay, and leave the last to drop by the roadside; in this way you will reach the goal of your ambition. You will be nothing here, you see, unless a woman interests herself in you; and she must be young and wealthy, and a woman of the world. Yet, if you have a heart, lock it carefully away like a treasure; do not let any one suspect it, or you will be lost; you would cease to be the executioner, you would take the victim's place. And if ever you should love, never let your secret escape you! Trust no one until you are very sure of the heart to which you open your heart. Learn to mistrust every one; take every precaution for the sake of the love which does not exist as yet. Listen, Miguel"—the name slipped from her so naturally that she did not notice her mistake—"there is something still more appalling than the ingratitude of daughters who have cast off their old father and wish that he were dead, and that is a rivalry between the two sisters. Restaud comes of a good family; his wife has been received into their circle; she has been presented at court; and her sister, her wealthy sister, Mme. Delphine de Nucingen, the wife of a great capitalist, is consumed with envy, and ready to die of spleen. There is a gulf set between the sisters—indeed, they are sisters no longer—the two women who refuse to acknowledge their father do not acknowledge each other. So Mme. de Nucingen would lap all the mud that lies between the Rue Saint-Lazare and the Rue de Grenelle to gain admittance to my salon. She fancied that she should gain her end through de Marsay; she has made herself de Marsay's slave, and she bores him. De Marsay cares very little about her. If you will introduce her to me, you will be her darling, her Benjamin; she will idolize you. If, after that, you can love her, do so; if not, make her useful. I will ask her to come once or twice to one of my great crushes, but I will never receive her here in the morning. I will bow to her when I see her, and that will be quite sufficient. You have shut the Comtesse de Restaud's door against you by mentioning Father Goriot's name. Yes, my good friend, you may call at her house twenty times, and every time out of the twenty you will find that she is not at home. The servants have their orders, and will not admit you. Very well, then, now let Father Goriot gain the right of entry into her sister's house for you. The beautiful Mme. de Nucingen will give the signal for a battle. As soon as she singles you out, other women will begin to lose their heads about you, and her enemies and rivals and intimate friends will all try to take you from her. There are women who will fall in love with a man because another woman has chosen him; like the city madames, poor things, who copy our millinery, and hope thereby to acquire our manners. You will have a success, and in Paris success is everything; it is the key of power. If the women credit you with wit and talent, the men will follow suit so long as you do not undeceive them yourself. There will be nothing you may not aspire to; you will go everywhere, and you will find out what the world is—an assemblage of fools and knaves. But you must be neither the one nor the other. I am giving you my name like Ariadne's clue of thread to take with you into this labyrinth; make no unworthy use of it," she said, with a queenly glance and curve of her throat; "give it back to me unsullied. And now, go; leave me. We women also have our battles to fight."

"And if you should ever need some one who would gladly set a match to a train for you——"

"Well?" she asked.

He tapped his heart, smiled in answer to his cousin's smile, and went.

It was five o'clock, and Eugène was hungry; he was afraid lest he should not be in time for dinner, a misgiving which made him feel that it was pleasant to be borne so quickly across Paris. This sensation of physical comfort left his mind free to grapple with the thoughts that assailed him. A mortification usually sends a young man of his age into a furious rage; he shakes his fists at society, and vows vengeance when his belief in himself is shaken. Just then Rastignac was overwhelmed by the words, "You have shut the Countess' door against you."

"I shall call!" he said to himself, "and if Mme. de Beauséant is right, if I never find her at home—I—— well, Mme. de Restaud shall meet me in every salon in Paris. I will learn to fence, and have some pistol practice, and kill that Maxime of hers!"

"And money?" cried an inward monitor. "How about money, where is that to come from?" And all at once the wealth displayed in the Comtesse de Restaud's drawing-room rose before his eyes. That was the luxury which Goriot's daughter had loved too well; the gilding, the ostentatious splendor, the unintelligent luxury of the parvenu, the riotous extravagance of a courtesan. Then the attractive vision suddenly went under an eclipse as he remembered the stately grandeur of the Hôtel de Beauséant. As his fancy wandered among these lofty regions in the great world of Paris, innumerable dark thoughts gathered in his heart; his ideas widened, and his conscience grew more elastic. He saw the world as it is; saw how the rich lived beyond the jurisdiction of law and public opinion, and found in success the *ultima ratio mundi*.

"Vautrin is right, success is virtue!" he said to himself.

Arrived in the Rue Neuve-Sainte-Geneviève, he rushed up to his room for ten francs wherewith to satisfy the demands of the cabman, and went in to dinner. He glanced round the squalid room, saw the eighteen poverty-stricken creatures about to feed like cattle in their stalls, and the sight filled him with loathing. The transition was too sudden, and the contrast was so violent that it could not but act as a powerful stimulant; his ambition developed and grew beyond all bounds. On the one hand, he beheld a vision of social life in its most charming and refined forms, of quick-pulsed youth, of fair, impassioned faces invested with all the charm of poetry, framed in a marvelous setting of luxury or art; and, on the other hand, he saw a sombre picture, the miry verge beyond these faces, in which passion was extinct and nothing was left of the drama but the cords and pulleys and bare mechanism. Mme. de Beauséant's counsels, the words uttered in anger by the forsaken lady, her petulant offer, came to his mind, and poverty was a ready expositor. Rastignac determined to open two parallel trenches, so as to insure success; he would be a learned doctor of law and a man of fashion. Clearly he was still a child! Those two lines are asymptotes, and will never meet.

"You are very dull, my lord marquis," said Vautrin, with one of the shrewd glances that seem to read the innermost secrets of another mind.

"I am not in the humor to stand jokes from people who call me 'my lord marquis,'" answered Eugène. "A marquis here in Paris, if he is not the veriest sham, ought to have a hundred thousand livres a year at least; and a lodger in the Maison Vauquer is not exactly fortune's favorite."

Vautrin's glance at Rastignac was half-paternal, half-contemptuous. "Puppy!" it seemed to say; "I should make one mouthful of him!" Then he answered—

"Your are in a bad humor; perhaps your visit to the beautiful Comtesse de Restaud was not a success."

"She has shut her door against me because I told her that her father dined at our table," cried Rastignac.

Glances were exchanged all round the room; Father Goriot looked down.

"You have sent some snuff into my eye," he said to his

neighbor, turning a little aside to rub his hand over his face.

"Any one who molests Father Goriot will have henceforward to reckon with me," said Eugène, looking at the old man's neighbor; "he is worth all the rest of us put together—I am not speaking of the ladies," he added, turning in the direction of Mlle. Taillefer.

Eugène's remarks produced a sensation, and his tone silenced the dinner table. Vautrin alone spoke. "If you are going to champion Father Goriot, and set up for his responsible editor into the bargain, you had need be a crack-shot and know how to handle the foils," he said, banteringly.

"So I intend," said Eugène.

"Then are you taking the field to-day?"

"Perhaps," Rastignac answered. "But I owe no account of myself to any one, especially as I do not try to find out what other people do of a night."

Vautrin looked askance at Rastignac.

"If you do not mean to be deceived by the puppets, my boy, you must go behind and see the whole show, and not peep through holes in the curtain. That is enough," he added, seeing that Eugène was about to fly into a passion. "We can have a little talk whenever you like."

There was a general feeling of gloom and constraint. Father Goriot was so deeply dejected by the student's remark that he did not notice the change in the disposition of his fellow-lodgers, nor know that he had met with a champion capable of putting an end to the persecution.

"Then, M. Goriot sitting there is the father of a countess," said Mme. Vauquer in a low voice.

"And of a baroness," answered Rastignac.

"That is about all he is capable of," said Bianchon to Rastignac; "I have taken a look at his head; there is only one bump—the bump of paternity; he must be an *eternal father*."

Eugène was too intent on his thoughts to laugh at Bianchon's joke. He determined to profit by Mme. de Beauséant's counsels, and was asking himself how he could obtain the necessary money. He grew grave. The wide savannahs of the world stretched before his eyes; all things lay before him, nothing was his. Dinner came to an end, the others went, and he was left in the dining-room.

"So you have seen my daughter?" Goriot spoke tremulously, and the sound of his voice broke in upon Eugène's dreams. The young man took the elder's hand, and looked at him with something like kindness in his eyes.

"You are a good and noble man," he said. "We will have some talk about your daughters by and by."

He rose without waiting for Goriot's answer, and went to his room. There he wrote the following letter to his mother:

"MY DEAR MOTHER:—Can you nourish your child from your breast again? I am in a position to make a rapid fortune, but I want twelve hundred francs—I must have them at all costs. Say nothing about this to my father; perhaps he might make objections, and unless I have the money, I may be led to put an end to myself, and so escape the clutches of despair. I will tell you everything when I see you. I will not begin to try to describe my present situation; it would take volumes to put the whole story clearly and fully. I have not been gambling, my kind mother, I owe no one a penny; but if you would preserve the life that you gave me, you must send me the sum I mention. As a matter of fact, I go to see the Vicomtesse de Beauséant; she is using her influence for me; I am obliged to go into society, and I have not a penny to lay out on clean gloves. I can manage to exist on bread and water, or go without food, if need be, but I cannot do without the tools with which they cultivate the vineyards in this country. I must resolutely make up my mind at once to make my way, or stick in the mire for the rest of my days. I know that all your hopes are set on me, and I want to realize them quickly. Sell some of your old jewelry, my kind mother; I will give you other jewels very soon. I know enough of our affairs at home to know all that such a sacrifice means, and you must not think that I would lightly ask you to make it; I should be a monster if I could. You must think of my entreaty as a cry forced from me by imperative necessity. Our whole future lies in the subsidy with which I must begin my first campaign, for life in Paris is one continual battle. If you cannot otherwise procure the whole of the money, and are forced to sell our aunt's lace, tell her that I will send her some still handsomer," and so forth.

He wrote to ask each of his sisters for their savings—would they despoil themselves for him, and keep the sacrifice a secret from the family? To his request he knew that they would not fail to respond gladly, and he added to it an appeal to their delicacy by touching the chord of honor that vibrates so loudly in young and highly strung natures.

Yet when he had written the letters, he could not help feeling misgivings in spite of his youthful ambition; his heart beat fast, and he trembled. He knew the spotless nobleness of the lives buried away in the lonely manor house; he knew what trouble and what joy his request would cause his sisters, and how happy they would be as they talked at the bottom of the orchard of that dear brother of theirs in Paris. Visions rose before his eyes; a sudden strong light revealed his sisters secretly counting over their little store, devising some girlish stratagem by which the money could be sent to him *incognito*, essaying, for the first time in their lives, a piece of deceit that reached the sublime in its unselfishness.

"A sister's heart is a diamond for purity, a deep sea of tenderness!" he said to himself. He felt ashamed of those letters.

What power there must be in the petitions put up by such

hearts; how pure the fervor that bears their souls to heaven in prayer! What exquisite joy they would find in self-sacrifice! What a pang for his mother's heart if she could not send him all that he asked for! And this noble affection, these sacrifices made at such terrible cost, were to serve as the ladder by which he meant to climb to Delphine de Nucingen. A few tears, like the last grains of incense flung upon the sacred altar fire of the hearth, fell from his eyes. He walked up and down, and despair mingled with his emotion. Father Goriot saw him through the half-open door.

"What is the matter, sir?" he asked from the threshold.

"Ah! my good neighbor, I am as much a son and brother as you are a father. You do well to fear for the Comtesse Anastasie; there is one M. Maxime de Trailles, who will be her ruin."

Father Goriot withdrew, stammering some words, but Eugène failed to catch their meaning.

The next morning Rastignac went out to post his letters. Up to the last moment he wavered and doubted, but he ended by flinging them into the box. "I shall succeed!" he said to himself. So says the gambler; so says the great captain; but the three words that have been the salvation of some few have been the ruin of many more.

A few days after this Eugène called at Mme. de Restaud's house; she was not at home. Three times he tried the experiment, and three times he found her doors closed against him, though he was careful to choose an hour when M. de Trailles was not there. The Vicomtesse was right.

The student studied no longer. He put in an appearance at lectures simply to answer to his name, and, after thus attesting his presence, departed forthwith. He had been through a reasoning process familiar to most students. He had seen the advisability of deferring his studies to the last moment before going up for his examinations; he made up his mind to cram his second and third year's work into the third year, when he meant to begin to work in earnest and to complete his studies in law with one great effort. In the meantime he had fifteen months in which to navigate the ocean of Paris, to spread the nets and set the lines that should bring him a protectress and a fortune. Twice during that week he saw Mme. de Beauséant; he did not go to her house until he had seen the Marquis d'Ajuda drive away.

Victory for yet a few more days was with the great lady, the most poetic figure in the Faubourg Saint-Germain; and the marriage of the Marquis d'Ajuda-Pinto with Mlle. de Rochefide was postponed. The dread of losing her happiness filled those days with a fever of joy unknown before, but the end was only so much the nearer. The Marquis d'Ajuda and the Rochefides agreed that this quarrel and reconciliation was a very fortunate thing; Mme. de Beauséant (so they hoped) would gradually become reconciled to the idea of the marriage, and in the end would be brought to sacrifice d'Ajuda's morning visits to the exigencies of a man's career, exigencies which she must have foreseen. In spite of the most solemn promises, daily renewed, M. d'Ajuda was playing a part, and the Vicomtesse was eager to be deceived. "Instead of taking the leap heroically from the window, she is falling headlong down the staircase," said her most intimate friend, the Duchesse de Langeais. Yet this after-glow of happiness lasted long enough for the Vicomtesse to be of service to her young cousin. She had a half-superstitious affection for him. Eugène had shown her sympathy and devotion at a crisis when a woman sees no pity, no real comfort in any eyes; when if a man is ready with soothing flatteries, it is because he has an interested motive.

Rastignac made up his mind that he must learn the whole of Goriot's previous history; he would come to his bearings before attempting to board the Maison de Nucingen. The results of his inquiries may be given briefly as follows:

In the days before the Revolution, Jean-Joachim Goriot

was simply a workman in the employ of a vermicelli-maker. He was a skillful, thrifty workman, sufficiently enterprising to buy his master's business when the latter fell a chance victim to the disturbances of 1789. Goriot established himself in the Rue de la Jussienne, close to the Corn Exchange. His plain good sense led him to accept the position of president of the section, so as to secure for his business the protection of those in power at that dangerous epoch. This prudent step had led to success; the foundations of his fortune were laid in the time of the scarcity (real or artificial), when the price of grain of all kinds rose enormously in Paris. People used to fight for bread at the bakers' doors; while other persons went to the grocers' shops and bought Italian paste foods without brawling over it. It was during this year that Goriot made the money, which, at a later time, was to give him all the advantage of the great capitalist over the small buyer; he had, moreover, the usual luck of average ability; his mediocrity was the salvation of him. He excited no one's envy; it was not even suspected that he was rich till the peril of being rich was over, and all his intelligence was concentrated, not on political, but on commercial speculations. Goriot was an authority second to none on all questions relating to corn, flour, and "middlings;" and the production, storage, and quality of grain. He could estimate the yield of the harvest, and foresee market prices; he bought his cereals in Sicily, and imported Russian wheat. Any one who had heard him hold forth on the regulations that control the importation and exportation of grain, who had seen his grasp of the subject, his clear insight into the principles involved, his appreciation of weak points in the way that the system worked, would have thought that here was the stuff of which a minister is made. Patient, active, and persevering, energetic and prompt in action, he surveyed his business horizon with an eagle's eye. Nothing there took him by surprise; he foresaw all things, knew all that was happening, and kept his own counsel; he was a diplomatist in his quick comprehension of a situation; and in the routine of business he was as patient and plodding as a soldier on the march. But beyond this business horizon he could not see. He used to spend his hours of leisure on the threshold of his shop, leaning against the framework of the door. Take him from his dark little counting-house, and he became once more the rough, slow-witted workman, a man who cannot understand a piece of reasoning, who is indifferent to all intellectual pleasures, and falls asleep at the play, a Parisian Dolibom in short, against whose stupidity other minds are powerless.

Natures of this kind are nearly all alike; in almost all of them you will find some hidden depth of sublime affection. Two all-absorbing affections filled the vermicelli-maker's heart to the exclusion of every other feeling; into them he seemed to put all the forces of his nature, as he put the whole power of his brain into the corn trade. He had regarded his wife, the only daughter of a rich farmer of La Brie, with a devout admiration; his love for her had been boundless. Goriot had felt the charm of a lovely and sensitive nature, which, in its delicate strength, was the very opposite of his own. Is there any instinct more deeply implanted in the heart of man than the pride of protection, a protection which is constantly exerted for a fragile and defenseless creature? Join love thereto, the warmth of gratitude that all generous souls feel for the source of their pleasures, and you have the explanation of many strange incongruities in human nature.

After seven years of unclouded happiness, Goriot lost his wife. It was very unfortunate for him. She was beginning to gain an ascendancy over him in other ways; possibly she might have brought that barren soil under cultivation, she might have widened his ideas and given other directions to his thoughts. But when she was dead, the instinct of fatherhood developed in him till it almost became a mania. All the affection balked by death seemed to turn to his daughters, and he found full satisfaction for his heart in loving them. More or less brilliant proposals were made to him from time to time; wealthy merchants or farmers with daughters vied with each other in offering inducements to him to marry again; but he determined to remain a widower. His father-in-law, the only man for whom he felt a decided friendship, gave out that Goriot had made a vow to be faithful to his wife's memory. The frequenters of the Corn Exchange, who could not comprehend this sublime piece of folly, joked about it among themselves, and found a ridiculous nickname for him. One of them ventured (after a glass over a bargain) to call him by it, and a blow from the vermicelli-maker's fist sent him headlong into a gutter in the Rue Oblin. He could think of nothing else when his children were concerned; his love for them made him fidgety and anxious; and this was so well known, that one day a competitor, who wished to get rid of him to secure the field to himself, told Goriot that Delphine had just been knocked down by a cab. The vermicelli-maker turned ghastly pale, left the Exchange at once, and did not return for several days afterwards; he was ill in consequence of the shock and the subsequent relief on discovering that it was a false alarm. This time, however, the offender did not escape with a bruised shoulder; at a critical moment in the man's affairs, Goriot drove him into bankruptcy, and forced him to disappear from the Corn Exchange.

As might have been expected, the two girls were spoiled. With an income of sixty thousand francs, Goriot scarcely spent twelve hundred on himself, and found all his happiness in satisfying the whims of the two girls. The best masters were engaged, that Anastasie and Delphine might be endowed with all the accomplishments which distinguish a good education. They had a chaperon—luckily for them, she was a woman who had sense and good taste; they learned to ride; they had a carriage for their use; they lived as the mistress of a rich old lord might live; they had only to express a wish, their father would hasten to give them their most extravagant desires, and asked nothing of them in return but a kiss. Goriot had raised the two girls to the level of the angels; and, quite naturally, he himself was left beneath them. Poor man! he loved them even for the pain that they gave him.

When the girls were old enough to be married, they were left free to choose for themselves. Each had half her father's fortune as her dowry; and when the Comte de Restaud came to woo Anastasie for her beauty, her social aspirations led her to leave her father's house for a more exalted sphere. Delphine wished for money; she married Nucingen, a banker of German extraction, who became a baron of the Holy Roman Empire. Goriot remained a vermicelli-maker as before. His daughters and his sons-in-law began to demur; they did not like to see him still engaged in trade, though his whole life was bound up with his business. For five years he stood out against their entreaties, then he yielded, and consented to retire on the amount realized by the sale of his business and the savings of the last few years. It was this capital that Mme. Vauquer, in the early days of his residence with her, had calculated would bring in eight or ten thousand livres in a year. He had taken refuge in her lodging-house, driven there by despair when he knew that his daughters were compelled by their husbands not only to refuse to receive him as an inmate in their houses, but even to see him no more except in private.

This was all the information which Rastignac gained from a M. Muret who had purchased Goriot's business, information which confirmed the Duchesse de Langeais' suppositions, and herewith the preliminary explanation of this obscure but terrible Parisian tragedy comes to an end.

Towards the end of the first week in December Rastignac received two letters—one from his mother and one from his eldest sister. His heart beat fast, half with happiness, half with fear, at the sight of the familiar handwriting. Those two little scraps of paper contained life or death for his hopes. But while he felt a shiver of dread as he remembered their dire poverty at home, he knew their love for him so well that he could not help fearing that he was draining their very life-blood. His mother's letter ran as follows:

"MY DEAR CHILD:—I am sending you the money that you asked for. Make a good use of it. Even to save your life I could not raise so large a sum a second time without your father's knowledge, and there would be trouble about it. We should be obliged to mortgage the land. It is impossible to judge of the merits of schemes of which I am ignorant; but what sort of schemes can they be that you should fear to tell me about them! Volumes of explanation would not have been needed; we mothers can understand at a word, and that word would have spared me the anguish of uncertainty. I do not know how to hide the painful impression that your letter has made upon me, my dear son. What can you have felt when you were moved to send this chill of dread through my heart? It must have been very painful to you to write the letter that gave me so much pain as I read it. To what courses are you committed? You are going to appear to be something that you are not, and your whole life and success depends upon this? You are about to see a society into which you cannot enter without rushing into expense that you cannot afford, without losing precious time that is needed for your studies? Ah! my dear Eugène, believe your mother, crooked ways cannot lead to great ends. Patience and endurance are the two qualities most needed in your position. I am not scolding you; I do not want any tinge of bitterness to spoil our offering. I am only talking like a mother whose trust in you is as great as her foresight for you. You know the steps that you must take, and I, for my part, know your purity of heart, and how good your intentions are; so I can say to you without a doubt, 'Go forward, beloved!' If I tremble, it is because I am a mother, but my prayers and blessings will be with you at every step. Be very careful, dear boy. You must have a man's prudence, for it lies with you to shape the destinies of five others who are dear to you, and must look to you. Yes, our fortunes depend upon you, and your success is ours. We all pray to God to be with you in all that you do. Your aunt Marcillac has been most generous beyond words in this matter; she saw at once how it was, even down to your gloves. 'But I have a weakness for the eldest!' she said gaily. You must love your aunt very much, dear Eugène. I shall wait till you have succeeded before telling you all that she has done for you, or her money would burn your fingers. You, who are young, do not know what it is to part with something that is a piece of your past! But what would we not sacrifice for your sake? Your aunt says that I am to send you a kiss on the forehead from her, and that kiss is to bring you luck again and again, she says. She would have written to you herself, the dear kind-hearted woman, but she is troubled with the gout in her fingers just now. Your father is very well. The vintage of 1819 has turned out better than we expected. Good-bye, dear boy; I will say nothing about your sisters, because Laure is writing to you, and I must let her have the pleasure of giving you all the home news. Heaven send that you may succeed! Oh! yes, dear Eugène, you must succeed. I have come, through you, to a knowledge of a pain so sharp that I do not think I could endure it a second time. I have come to know what it is to be poor, and to long for money for my children's sake. There, good-bye! Do not leave us for long without news of you; and here, at the last, take a kiss from your mother."

By the time Eugène had finished the letter he was in tears. He thought of Father Goriot crushing his silver keepsake into a shapeless mass before he sold it to meet his daughter's bill of exchange.

"Your mother has broken up her jewels for you," he said to himself; "your aunt shed tears over those relics of hers before she sold them for your sake. What right have you to heap execrations on Anastasie? You have followed her example; you have selfishly sacrificed others to your own future, and she sacrifices her father to her lover; and of you two, which is the worse?"

He was ready to renounce his attempts; he could not bear to take that money. The fires of remorse burned in his heart, and gave him intolerable pain, the generous secret remorse which men seldom take into account when they sit in judgment upon their fellow-men; but perhaps the angels in heaven, beholding it, pardon the criminal whom our justice condemns. Rastignac opened his sister's letter; its simplicity and kindness revived his heart.

"Your letter came just at the right time, dear brother. Agathe and I had thought of so many different ways of spending our money, that we did not know what to buy with it; and now you have come in, and, like the servant who upset all the watches that belonged to the King of Spain, you have restored harmony; for, really and truly, we did not know which of all the things we wanted we needed most, and we were always quarreling about it, never thinking, dear Eugène, of a way of spending our money which would satisfy us completely. Agathe jumped for joy. Indeed, we have been like two mad things all day, 'to such a prodigious degree' (as aunt would say), that mother said, with her severe expression, 'Whatever can be the matter with you, mesdemoiselles?' I think if we had been scolded a little, we should have been still better pleased. A woman ought to be very glad to suffer for one she loves! I, however, in my inmost soul, was doleful and cross in the midst of all my joy. I shall make a bad wife, I am afraid, I am too fond of spending. I had bought two sashes and a nice little stiletto for piercing eyelet-holes in my stays, trifles that I really did not want, so that I have less than that slow-coach Agathe, who is so economical, and hoards her money like a magpie. She had two hundred francs! And I have only one hundred and fifty! I am nicely punished; I could throw my sash down the well; it will be painful to me to wear it now. Poor dear, I have robbed you. And Agathe was so nice about it. She said, 'Let us send the three hundred and fifty francs in our two names!' But I could not help telling you everything just as it happened.

"Do you know how we managed to keep your commandments? We took our glittering hoard, we went out for a walk, and when once fairly on the highway we ran all the way to Ruffec, where we handed over the coin, without more ado, to M. Grimbert of the Méssageries Royales. We came back again like swallows on the wing. 'Don't you think that happiness has made us lighter?' Agathe said. We said all sorts of things, which I shall not tell you, Monsieur le Parisien, because they were all about you. Oh, we love you dearly, dear brother; it was all summed up in those few words. As for keeping the secret, little masqueraders like us are capable of anything (according to our aunt), even of holding our tongues. Our mother has been on a mysterious journey to Angoulême, and the aunt went with her, not without solemn councils, from which we were shut out, and M. le Baron likewise. They are silent as to the weighty political considerations that prompted their mission, and conjectures are rife in the State of Rastignac. The Infants are embroidering a muslin robe with open-work sprigs for her majesty the Queen; the work progresses in the most profound secrecy. There are but two more breadths to finish. A decree has gone forth that no wall shall be built on the side of Verteuil, but that a hedge shall be planted instead thereof. Our subjects may sustain some disappointment of fruit and espaliers, but strangers will enjoy a fair prospect. Should the heir-presumptive lack pocket-handkerchiefs, be it known unto him that the dowager lady of Marcillac, exploring the recesses of her drawers and boxes (known respectively as Pompeii and Herculaneum), having brought to light a fair piece of cambric whereof she wotted not, the Princesses Agathe and Laure place at their brother's disposal their thread, their needles, and hands somewhat of the reddest. The two young Princes, Don Henri and Don Gabriel, retain their fatal habits of stuffing themselves with grape-jelly, of teasing their sisters, of taking their pleasure by going a-birdnesting, and of cutting switches for themselves from the osier-beds, maugre the laws of the realm. Moreover, they list not to learn aught, wherefore the Papal Nuncio (called of the commonalty, M. le Curé) threateneth them with excommunication, since that they neglect the sacred canons of grammatical construction for the construction of other canons, deadly engines made of the stems of elder.

"Farewell, dear brother, never did letter carry so many wishes for your success, so much love fully satisfied. You will have a great deal to tell us when you come home! You will tell me everything, won't you? I am the oldest. From something the aunt let fall, we think you must have had some success.

"'*Something was said of a lady, but nothing more was said——*'

"Of course not, in our family! Oh, by-the-by, Eugène, would you rather we made that piece of cambric into shirts for you instead of pocket-handkerchiefs? If you want some really nice shirts at once, we ought to lose no time in beginning upon them; and if the fashion is different now in Paris, send us one for a pattern; we want more particularly to know about the cuffs. Good-bye! good-bye! Take my kiss on the left side of your forehead, on the temple that belongs to me, and to no one else in the world. I am leaving the other side of the sheet for Agathe, who has solemnly promised not to read a word that I have written; but, all the same, I mean to sit by her while she writes, so as to be quite sure that she keeps her word. Your loving sister,

"Laure de Rastignac."

"Yes!" said Eugène to himself. "Yes! Success at all costs now! Riches could not repay such devotion as this. I wish I could give them every sort of happiness! Fifteen hundred and fifty francs," he went on after a pause. "Every shot must go to the mark! Laure is right. Trust a woman! I have only calico shirts. Where some one else's welfare is concerned, a young girl becomes as ingenious as a thief. Guileless where she herself is in question, and full of foresight for me—she is like a heavenly angel forgiving the strange incomprehensible sins of earth."

The world lay before him. His tailor had been summoned and sounded, and had finally surrendered. When Rastignac met M. de Trailles, he had seen at once how great a part the tailor plays in a young man's career; a tailor is either a deadly enemy or a staunch friend, with an invoice for a bond of friendship; between these two extremes there is, alack! no middle term. In this representative of his craft Eugène discovered a man who understood that his was a sort of paternal function for young men at their entrance into life, who regarded himself as a stepping-stone between a young man's present and future. And Rastignac in gratitude made the man's fortune by an epigram of a kind in which he excelled at a later period of his life.

"I have twice known a pair of trousers turned out by him make a match of twenty thousand livres a year!"

Fifteen hundred francs, and as many suits of clothes as he chose to order! At that moment the poor child of the south felt no more doubts of any kind. The young man went down to breakfast with the indefinable air which the consciousness of the possession of money gives to youth. No sooner are the coins slipped into a student's pocket than his wealth, in imagination at least, is piled into a fantastic column, which affords him a moral support. He begins to hold up his head as he walks; he is conscious that he has a means of bringing his power to bear on a given point; he looks you straight in the face; his gestures are quick and decided; only yesterday he was diffident and shy, any one might have pushed him aside; to-morrow he will take the walk of a prime minister. A miracle has been wrought in him. Nothing is beyond the reach of his ambition, and his ambition soars at random; he is light-hearted, generous, and enthusiastic; in short, the fledgling bird has discovered that he has wings. A poor student snatches at every chance pleasure much as a dog runs all sorts of risks to steal a bone, cracking it and sucking the marrow as he flies from pursuit; but a young man who can rattle a few runaway gold coins in his pocket can take his pleasure deliberately, can taste the whole of the sweets of secure possession; he soars far above earth; he has forgotten what the word *poverty* means; all Paris is his. Those are days when the whole world shines radiant with light, when everything glows and sparkles before the eyes of youth, days that bring joyous energy that is never brought into harness, days of debts and of painful fears that go hand-in-hand with every delight. Those who do not know the left bank of the Seine between the Rue Saint-Jacques and the Rue des Saints-Pères know nothing of life.

"Ah! if the women of Paris but knew," said Rastignac, as he devoured Mme. Vauquer's stewed pears (at five for a penny), "they would come here in search of a lover."

Just then a porter from the Méssageries Royales appeared at the door of the room; they had previously heard the bell ring as the wicket opened to admit him. The man asked for

M. Eugène de Rastignac, holding out two bags for him to take, and a form of receipt for his signature. Vautrin's keen glance cut Eugène like a lash.

"Now you will be able to pay for those fencing lessons and go to the shooting gallery," he said.

"Your ship has come in," said Mme. Vauquer, eyeing the bags.

Mlle. Michonneau did not dare to look at the money, for fear her eyes should betray her cupidity.

"You have a kind mother," said Mme. Couture.

"You have a kind mother, sir," echoed Poiret.

"Yes, mamma has been drained dry," said Vautrin, "and now you can have your fling, go into society, and fish for heiresses, and dance with countesses who have peach blossom in their hair. But take my advice, young man, and don't neglect your pistol practice."

Vautrin struck an attitude, as if he were facing an antagonist. Rastignac, meaning to give the porter a tip, felt in his pockets and found nothing. Vautrin flung down a franc-piece on the table.

"Your credit is good," he remarked, eyeing the student, and Rastignac was forced to thank him, though, since the sharp encounter of wits at dinner that day, after Eugène came in from calling on Mme. de Beauséant, he had made up his mind that Vautrin was insufferable. For a week, in fact, they had both kept silence in each other's presence, and watched each other. The student tried in vain to account to himself for this attitude.

An idea, of course, gains in force by the energy with which it is expressed; it strikes where the brain sends it, by a law as mathematically exact as the law that determines the course of a shell from a mortar. The amount of impression it makes is not to be determined so exactly. Sometimes, in an impressible nature, the idea works havoc, but there are, no less, natures so robustly protected, that this sort of projectile falls flat and harmless on skulls of triple brass, as cannon-shot against solid masonry; then there are flaccid and spongy-fibred natures into which ideas from without sink like spent bullets into the earthworks of a redoubt. Rastignac's head was something of the powder-magazine order; the least shock sufficed to bring about an explosion. He was too quick, too young, not to be readily accessible to ideas; and open to that subtle influence of thought and feeling in others which causes so many strange phenomena that make an impression upon us of which we are all unconscious at the time. Nothing escaped his mental vision; he was lynx-eyed; in him the mental powers of perception, which seem like duplicates of the senses, had the mysterious power of swift projection that astonishes us in intellects of a high order—slingers who are quick to detect the weak spot in any armor.

In the past month Eugène's good qualities and defects had rapidly developed with his character. Intercourse with the world and the endeavor to satisfy his growing desires had brought out his defects. But Rastignac came from the south side of the Loire, and had the good qualities of his countrymen. He had the impetuous courage of the south, that rushes to the attack of a difficulty, as well as the southern impatience of delay or suspense. These traits are held to be defects in the north; they made the fortune of Murat, but they likewise cut short his career. The moral would appear to be that when the dash and boldness of the south side of the Loire meets, in a southern temperament, with the guile of the north, the character is complete, and such a man will gain (and keep) the crown of Sweden.

Rastignac, therefore, could not stand the fire from Vautrin's batteries for long without discovering whether this was a friend or a foe. He felt as if this strange being was reading his inmost soul and dissecting his feelings, while Vautrin himself was so close and secretive that he seemed to have something of the profound and unmoved serenity of a sphinx, seeing and hearing all things and saying nothing. Eugène, conscious of that money in his pocket, grew rebellious.

"Be so good as to wait a moment," he said to Vautrin, as the latter rose, after slowly emptying his coffee-cup, sip by sip.

"What for?" inquired the older man, as he put on his large-brimmed hat and took up the sword-cane that he was wont to twirl like a man who will face three or four footpads without flinching.

"I will repay you in a minute," returned Eugène. He unsealed one of the bags as he spoke, counted out a hundred and forty francs, and pushed them towards Mme. Vauquer. "Short reckonings make good friends," he added, turning to the widow; "that clears our accounts till the end of the year. Can you give me change for a five-franc piece?"

"Good friends make short reckonings," echoed Poiret, with a glance at Vautrin.

"Here is your franc," said Rastignac, holding out the coin to the sphinx in the black wig.

"Any one might think that you were afraid to owe me a trifle," exclaimed the latter, with a searching glance that seemed to read the young man's inmost thoughts; there was a satirical and cynical smile on Vautrin's face such as Eugène had seen scores of times already; every time he saw it, it exasperated him almost beyond endurance.

"Well—— so I am," he answered. He held both the bags in his hand, and had risen to go up to his room.

Vautrin made as if he were going out through the sitting-room, and the student turned to go through the second door that opened into the square lobby at the foot of the staircase.

"Do you know, Monsieur le Marquis de Rastignacorama, that what you were saying just now was not exactly polite?" Vautrin remarked, as he rattled his sword-cane across the panels of the sitting-room door, and came up to the student.

Rastignac looked coolly at Vautrin, drew him to the foot

of the staircase, and shut the dining-room door. They were standing in the little square lobby between the kitchen and the dining-room; the place was lighted by an iron-barred fanlight above a door that gave access into the garden. Sylvie came out of her kitchen, and Eugène chose that moment to say—

"*Monsieur* Vautrin, I am not a marquis, and my name is not Rastignacorama."

"They will fight," said Mlle. Michonneau, in an indifferent tone.

"Fight!" echoed Poiret.

"Not they," replied Mme. Vauquer, lovingly fingering her pile of coins.

"But there they are under the lime trees," cried Mlle. Victorine, who had risen so that she might see out into the garden. "Poor young man! he was in the right, after all."

"We must go upstairs, my pet," said Mme. Couture; "it is no business of ours."

At the door, however, Mme. Couture and Victorine found their progress barred by the portly form of Sylvie the cook.

"What ever can have happened?" she said. "M. Vautrin said to M. Eugène, 'Let us have an explanation!' then he took him by the arm, and there they are, out among the artichokes."

Vautrin came in while she was speaking. "Mamma Vauquer," he said, smiling, "don't frighten yourself at all. I am only going to try my pistols under the lime trees."

"Oh! monsieur," cried Victorine, clasping her hands as she spoke, "why do you want to kill M. Eugène?"

Vautrin stepped back a pace or two, and gazed at Victorine.

"Oh! this is something fresh!" he exclaimed in a bantering tone, that brought the color into the poor girl's face. "That young fellow yonder is very nice, isn't he?" he went on. "You have given me a notion, my pretty child; I will make you both happy."

Mme. Couture laid her hand on the arm of her ward, and drew the girl away, as she said in her ear—

"Why, Victorine, I cannot imagine what has come over you this morning."

"I don't want any shots fired in my garden," said Mme. Vauquer. "You will frighten the neighborhood and bring the police up here all in a moment."

"Come, keep cool, Mamma Vauquer," answered Vautrin. "There, there; it's all right; we will go to the shooting-gallery."

He went back to Rastignac, laying his hand familiarly on the young man's arm.

"When I have given you ocular demonstrations of the fact that I can put a bullet through the ace on a card five times running at thirty-five paces," he said, "that won't take away your appetite, I suppose. You look to me to be inclined to be a trifle quarrelsome this morning, and as if you would rush on your death like a blockhead."

"Do you draw back?" asked Eugène.

"Don't try to raise my temperature," answered Vautrin; "it is not cold this morning. Let us go and sit over there," he added, pointing to the green-painted garden seats; "no one can overhear us. I want a little talk with you. You are not a bad sort of youngster, and I have no quarrel with you. I like you, take Tromp—(confound it!)—take Vautrin's word for it. What makes me like you? I will tell you by-and-by. Meantime, I can tell you that I know you as well as if I had made you myself, as I will prove to you in a minute. Put down your bags," he continued, pointing to the round table.

Rastignac deposited his money on the table, and sat down. He was consumed with curiosity, which the sudden change in the manner of the man before him had excited to the highest pitch. Here was a strange being who, a moment ago, had talked of killing him, and now posed as his protector.

"You would like to know who I really am, what I was,

and what I do now," Vautrin went on "You want to know too much, youngster. Come! come! keep cool! You will hear more astonishing things than that. I have had my misfortunes. Just hear me out first, and you shall have your turn afterwards. Here is my past in three words. Who am I? Vautrin. What do I do? Just what I please. Let us change the subject. You want to know my character. I am goodnatured to those who do me a good turn, or to those whose hearts speak to mine. These last may do anything they like with me; they may bruise my shins, and I shall not tell them to 'mind what they are about;' but, *nom d'une pipe*, the devil himself is not an uglier customer than I can be if people annoy me, or if I don't happen to take to them; and you may just as well know at once that I think no more of killing a man than of that," and he spat before him as he spoke. "Only when it is absolutely necessary to do so, I do my best to kill him properly. I am what you call an artist. I have read Benvenuto Cellini's "Memoirs," such as you see me; and, what is more, in Italian! A fine-spirited fellow he was! From him I learned to follow the example set us by Providence, who strikes us down at random, and to admire the beautiful whenever and wherever it is found. And, setting other questions aside, is it not a glorious part to play, when you pit yourself against mankind, and the luck is on your side? I have thought a good deal about the constitution of your present social dis-order. A duel is downright childish, my boy! utter nonsense and folly! When one of two living men must be gotten out of the way, none but an idiot would leave chance to decide which it is to be; and in a duel it is a toss-up—heads or tails—and there you are! Now I, for instance, can hit the ace in the middle of a card five times running, send one bullet after another through the same hole, and at thirty-five paces, moreover! With that little accomplishment you might think yourself certain of killing your man, mightn't you? Well, I have fired at twenty paces and missed, and the rogue who had never handled a pistol in his life—look here!"—(he unbuttoned his waistcoat and exposed his chest, covered, like a bear's back, with a shaggy fell; the student gave a startled shudder)—"he was a raw lad, but he made his mark on me," the extraordinary man went on, drawing Rastignac's fingers over a deep scar on his breast. "But that happened when I myself was a mere boy; I was one-and-twenty then (your age), and I had some beliefs left—in a woman's love, and in a pack of rubbish that you will be over head and ears in directly. You and I were to have fought just now, weren't we? You might have killed me. Suppose that I were put under the earth, where would you be? You would have to clear out of this, go to Switzerland, draw on papa's purse—and he has none too much in it as it is. I mean to open your eyes to your real position, that is what I am going to do; but I shall do it from the point of view of a man who, after studying the world very closely, sees that there are but two alternatives—stupid obedience or revolt. I obey nobody; is that clear? Now, do you know how much you will want at the pace you are going? A million; and promptly, too, or that little head of ours will be swaying to and fro in the drag-nets at Saint-Cloud, while we are gone to find out whether or no there is a Supreme Being. I will put you in the way of that million."

He stopped for a moment and looked at Eugène.

"Aha! you do not look so sourly at Papa Vautrin now! At the mention of the million you look like a young girl when somebody has said, 'I will come for you this evening!' and she betakes herself to her toilet as a cat licks its whiskers over a saucer of milk. All right. Come, now, let us go into the question, young man; all between ourselves, you know. We have a papa and a mamma down yonder, a great-aunt, two sisters (aged eighteen and seventeen), two young brothers (one fifteen and the other ten), that is about the roll-call of the crew. The aunt brings up the two sisters; the curé comes and teaches the boys Latin. Boiled chestnuts are oftener on the table than white bread. Papa makes a suit of clothes last a long while; if mamma has a different dress winter and summer, it is about as much as she has; the sisters manage as best they can. I know all about it; I have lived in the south.

"That is how things are at home. They send you twelve hundred francs a year, and the whole property only brings in three thousand francs all told. We have a cook and a manservant; papa is a baron, and we must keep up appearances. Then we have our ambitions; we are connected with the Beauséants, and we go afoot through the streets; we want to be rich, and we have not a penny; we eat Mme. Vauquer's messes, and we like grand dinners in the Faubourg Saint-Germain; we sleep on a truckle-bed, and dream of a mansion! I do not blame you for wanting these things. It is not given to every one to have ambition, my little trump. What sort of men do the women run after? Men of ambition. Men of ambition have stronger frames, their blood is richer in iron, their hearts are warmer than those of ordinary men. Women feel that when their power is greatest they look their best, and that those are their happiest hours; they like power in men, and prefer the strongest even if it is a power that may be their own destruction. I am going to make an inventory of your desires in order to put the question at issue before you. Here it is—

"We are as hungry as a wolf, and those newly-cut teeth of ours are sharp; what are we to do to keep the pot boiling? In the first place, we have the Code to browse upon; it is not amusing, and we are none the wiser for it, but that cannot be helped. So far so good. We mean to make an advocate of ourselves with a prospect of one day being made president of a court of assize, when we shall send poor devils, our betters, to the galleys with a T. F.* on their shoulders, so that the rich may be convinced that they can sleep in peace.

* *Travaux forcés.*

There is no fun in that; and you are a long while coming to it; for, to begin with, there are two years of nauseous drudgery in Paris, we see all the lollipops that we long for out of our reach. It is tiresome to want things and never to have them. If you were a pallid creature of the mollusc order, you would have nothing to fear, but it is different when you have the hot blood of a lion and are ready to get into a score of scrapes every day of your life. This is the ghastliest form of torture known in this inferno of God's making, and you will give in to it. Or suppose that you are a good boy, drink nothing stronger than milk, and bemoan your hard lot; you, with your generous nature, will endure hardships that would drive a dog mad, and make a start, after long waiting, as deputy to some rascal or other in a hole of a place where the government will fling you a thousand francs a year like the scraps that are thrown to the butcher's dog. Bark at thieves, plead the cause of the rich, send men of heart to the guillotine, that is your work! Many thanks! If you have no influence, you may rot in your provincial tribunal. At thirty you will be a justice with twelve hundred francs a year (if you have not flung off the gown for good before then). By the time you are forty you may look to marry a miller's daughter, an heiress with some six thousand livres a year. Much obliged! If you have influence, you may possibly be public prosecutor by the time you are thirty; with a salary of a thousand crowns, you could look to marry the mayor's daughter. Some petty piece of political trickery, such as mistaking Villèle for Manuel in a bulletin (the names rhyme, and that quiets your conscience), and you will probably be procureur général by the time you are forty, with a chance of becoming a deputy. Please to observe, my dear boy, that our conscience will have been a little damaged in the process, and that we shall endure twenty years of drudgery and hidden poverty, and that our sisters are wearing Dian's livery. I have the honor to call your attention to another fact, to wit:

that there are but twenty procureurs généraux at a time in all France, while there are some twenty thousand of you young men who aspire to that elevated position; that there are some mountebanks among you who would sell their family to screw their fortunes a peg higher. If this sort of thing sickens you, try another course. The Baron de Rastignac thinks of becoming an advocate, does he? There's a nice prospect for you! Ten years of drudgery straight away. You are obliged to live at the rate of a thousand francs a month; you must have a library of law-books, live in chambers, go into society, go down on your knees to ask a solicitor for briefs, lick the dust off the floor of the Palais de Justice. If this kind of business led to anything, I should not say no; but just give me the names of five advocates here in Paris who by the time that they are fifty are making fifty thousand francs a year! Bah! I would sooner turn pirate on the high-seas than have my soul shrivel up inside me like that. How will you find the capital? There is but one way, marry a woman who has money. There is no fun in it. Have you a mind to marry? You hang a stone round your neck; for if you marry for money, what becomes of our exalted notions of honor and so forth? You might as well fly in the face of social conventions at once. Is it nothing to crawl like a serpent before your wife, to lick her mother's feet, to descend to dirty actions that would sicken swine—faugh!—never mind if you at least make your fortune. But you will be as doleful as a dripstone if you marry for money. It is better to wrestle with men than to wrangle at home with your wife. You are at the crossway of the roads of life, my boy; choose your way.

"But you have chosen already. You have gone to see your cousin of Beauséant, and you have had an inkling of luxury; you have been to Madame de Restaud's house, and in Father Goriot's daughter you have seen a glimpse of the Parisienne for the first time. That day you came back with a word written upon your forehead. I knew it, I could read it—

'*Success!*' Yes, success at any price. 'Bravo,' said I to myself, 'here is the sort of fellow for me.' You wanted money. Where was it to come from? You have drained your sisters' little hoards (all brothers sponge more or less on their sisters). Those fifteen hundred francs of yours (got together, God knows how! in a country where there are more chestnuts than five-franc pieces) will slip away like soldiers after pillage. And, then, what will you do? Shall you begin to work? Work, or what you understand by work at this moment, means, for a man of Poiret's calibre, an old age in Mamma Vauquer's lodging-house. There are fifty thousand young men in your position at this moment, all bent as you are on solving one and the same problem—how to acquire a fortune rapidly. You are but a unit in that aggregate. You can guess, therefore, what efforts you must make, how desperate the struggle is. There are not fifty thousand good positions for you; you must fight and devour one another like spiders in a pot. Do you know how a man makes his way here? By brilliant genius or by skillful corruption. You must either cut your way through these masses of men like a cannon-ball or steal among them like a plague. Honesty is nothing to the purpose. Men bow before the power of genius; they hate it, and try to slander it, because genius does not divide the spoil; but if genius persists, they bow before it. To sum it all up in a phrase, if they fail to smother genius in the mud, they fall on their knees and worship it. Corruption is a great power in the world, and talent is scarce. So corruption is the weapon of superfluous mediocrity; you will be made to feel the point of it everywhere. You will see women who spend more than ten thousand francs a year on dress, while their husband's salary (his whole income) is but six thousand francs. You will see officials buying estates on twelve hundred francs a year. You will see women who sell themselves body and soul to drive in a carriage belonging to a son of a peer of France, who has a right to drive in the middle rank at Longchamp. You have seen that poor simpleton of a Goriot obliged to meet a bill with his daughter's name at the back of it, though her husband has fifty thousand francs a year. I defy you to walk a couple of yards anywhere in Paris without stumbling on some infernal complication. I'll bet my head to a head of that salad that you will stir up a hornet's nest by taking a fancy to the first young, rich, and pretty woman you meet. They are all dodging the law, all at loggerheads with their husbands. If I were to begin to tell you all that vanity or necessity (virtue is not often mixed up in it, you may be sure), all that vanity and necessity drive them to do for lovers, finery, housekeeping, or children, I should never come to an end. So an honest man is the common enemy.

"But do you know what an honest man is? Here, in Paris, an honest man is the man who keeps his own counsel, and will not divide the plunder. I am not speaking now of those poor bond-slaves who do the work of the world without a reward for their toil—God Almighty's outcasts, I call them. Among them, I grant you, is virtue in all the flower of its stupidity, but poverty is no less their portion. At this moment, I think I see the long faces those good folk would pull if God played a practical joke on them and stayed away at the last judgment.

"Well, then, if you mean to make a fortune quickly, you must either be rich to begin with, or make people believe that you are rich. It is no use playing here except for high stakes; once take to low play, it is all up with you. If in the scores of professions that are open to you, there are ten men who rise very rapidly, people are sure to call them thieves. You can draw your own conclusions. Such is life. It is no cleaner than a kitchen; it reeks like a kitchen; and if you mean to cook your dinner, you must expect to soil your hands; the real art is in getting them clean again, and therein lies the whole morality of our epoch. If I take this tone in speaking of the world to you, I have the right to do so; I know it well. Do you think that I am blaming it? Far from it; the world has always been as it is now. Moralists' strictures will never change it. Mankind is not perfect, but one age is more or less hypocritical than another, and then simpletons say that its morality is high or low. I do not think that the rich are any worse than the poor; man is much the same, high or low, or wherever he is. In a million of these human cattle there may be half a score of bold spirits who rise above the rest, above the laws; I am one of them. And you, if you are cleverer than your fellows, make straight to your end, and hold your head high. But you must lay your account with envy and slander and mediocrity, and every man's hand will be against you. Napoleon met with a minister of war, Aubry by name, who all but sent him to the colonies.

"Feel your pulse. Think whether you can get up morning after morning, strengthened in yesterday's purpose. In that case I will make you an offer that no one would decline. Listen attentively. You see, I have an idea of my own. My idea is to live a patriarchal life on a vast estate, say a hundred thousand acres, somewhere in the Southern States of America. I mean to be a planter, to have slaves, to make a few snug millions by selling my cattle, timber, and tobacco; I want to live an absolute monarch, and to do just as I please; to lead such a life as no one here in these squalid dens of lath and plaster ever imagines. I am a great poet; I do not write my poems, I feel them, and act them. At this moment I have fifty thousand francs, which might possibly buy forty negroes. I want two hundred thousand francs, because I want to have two hundred negroes to carry out my notions of the patriarchal life properly. Negroes, you see, are like a sort of family ready grown, and there are no inquisitive public prosecutors out there to interfere with you. That investment in ebony ought to mean three or four million francs in ten years' time. If I am successful, no one will ask me who I am. I shall be

Mr. Four Millions, an American citizen. I shall be fifty years old by then, and sound and hearty still; I shall enjoy life after my own fashion. In two words, if I find you an heiress with a million, will you give me two hundred thousand francs? Twenty per cent. commission, eh? Is that too much? Your little wife will be very much in love with you. Once married, you will show signs of uneasiness and remorse; for a couple of weeks you will be depressed. Then, some night, after sundry grimacings, comes the confession, between two kisses, 'Two hundred thousand francs of debts, my darling!' This sort of farce is played every day in Paris, and by young men of the highest fashion. When a young wife has given her heart, she will not refuse her purse. Perhaps you are thinking that you will lose the money for good? Not you. You will make two hundred thousand francs again by some stroke of business. With your capital and your brains you should be able to accumulate as large a fortune as you could wish. *Ergo*, in six months you will have made your own fortune, and your old friend Vautrin's, and made an amiable woman very happy, to say nothing of your people at home, who must blow on their fingers to warm them, in the winter, for lack of firewood. You need not be surprised at my proposal, nor at the demand I make. Forty-seven out of every sixty great matches here in Paris are made after just such a bargain as this. The Chamber of Notaries compels my gentlemen to——"

"What must I do?" said Rastignac, eagerly interrupting Vautrin's speech.

"Next to nothing," returned the other, with a slight involuntary movement, the suppressed exultation of the angler when he feels a bite at the end of his line. "Follow me carefully! The heart of a girl whose life is wretched and unhappy is a sponge that will thirstily absorb love; a dry sponge that swells at the first drop of sentiment. If you pay court to a young girl whose existence is a compound of loneliness, despair, and poverty, and who has no suspicion that she will come into a fortune, good Lord! it is quint and quatorze at piquet; it is knowing the numbers of the lottery beforehand; it is speculating in the funds when you have news from a sure source; it is building up a marriage on an indestructible foundation. The girl may come in for millions, and she will fling them, as if they were so many pebbles, at your feet. 'Take it, my beloved! Take it, Alfred, Adolphe, Eugène!' or whoever it was that showed his sense by sacrificing himself for her. And as for sacrificing himself, this is how I understand it. You sell a coat that is getting shabby, so that you can take her to the *Cadran bleu*, treat her to mushrooms on toast, and then go to the *Ambigu-Comique* in the evening; you pawn your watch to buy her a shawl. I need not remind you of the fiddle-faddle sentimentality that goes down so well with all women; you spill a few drops of water on your stationery, for instance; those are the tears you shed while far away from her. You look to me as if you were perfectly acquainted with the argot of the heart. Paris, you see, is like a forest in the New World, where you have to deal with a score of varieties of savages—Iroquois and Hurons— who live on the proceeds of their social hunting. You are a hunter of millions; you set your snares; you use lures and nets; there are many ways of hunting. Some hunt heiresses, others a legacy; some fish for souls, yet others sell their clients, bound hand and foot. Every one who comes back from the chase with his game-bag well filled meets with a warm welcome in good society. In justice to this hospitable part of the world, it must be said that you have to do with the most easy and good-natured of great cities. If the proud aristocracies of the rest of Europe refuse admittance among their ranks to a disreputable millionaire, Paris stretches out a hand to him, goes to his banquets, eats his dinners, and hobnobs with his infamy."

"But where is such a girl to be found?" asked Eugène.

"Under your eyes; she is yours already."

"Mlle. Victorine?"

"Precisely."

"And what was that you said?"

"She is in love with you already, your little Baronne de Rastignac!"

"She has not a penny," Eugène continued, much mystified.

"Ah! now we are coming to it! Just another word or two, and it will all be clear enough. Her father, Taillefer, is an old scoundrel; it is said that he murdered one of his friends at the time of the Revolution. He is one of your comedians that sets up to have opinions of his own. He is a banker—senior partner in the house of Frédéric Taillefer and Company. He has one son, and means to leave all he has to the boy, to the prejudice of Victorine. For my part, I don't like to see injustice of this sort. I am like Don Quixote, I have a fancy for defending the weak against the strong. If it should please God to take that youth away from him, Taillefer would only have his daughter left; he would want to leave his money to some one or other; an absurd notion, but it is only human nature, and he is not likely to have any more children, as I know. Victorine is gentle and amiable; she will soon twist her father round her fingers, and set his head spinning like a German top by plying him with sentiment! She will be too much touched by your devotion to forget you; you will marry her. I mean to play Providence for you, and Providence is to do my will. I have a friend whom I have attached closely to myself, a colonel in the Army of the Loire, who has just been transferred into the *garde royale*. He has taken my advice and turned ultra-royalist; he is not one of those fools who never change their opinions. Of all pieces of advice, my cherub, I would give you this—don't stick to your opinions any more than to your words. If any one asks you for them, let him have them—at a price. A man who prides himself on going in a straight line through life is an idiot who believes in infallibility. There are no such things as principles; there are only events, and there are no laws but those of expediency: a man of talent accepts events and the circumstances in which he finds himself, and turns everything to his own ends. If laws and principles were fixed and invariable, nations would not change them as readily as we change our shirts. The individual is not obliged to be more particular than the nation. A man whose services to France have been of the very slightest is a fetich looked on with superstitious awe because he has always seen everything in red; but he is good, at the most, to be put into the Museum of Arts and Crafts, among the automatic machines, and labeled La Fayette; while the prince at whom everybody flings a stone, the man who despises humanity so much that he spits as many oaths as he is asked for in the face of humanity, saved France from being torn in pieces at the Congress of Vienna; and they who should have given him laurels fling mud at him. Oh! I know something of affairs, I can tell you; I have the secrets of many men! Enough. When I find three minds in agreement as to the application of a principle, I shall have a fixed and immovable opinion—I shall have to wait a long while first. In the Tribunals you will not find three judges of the same opinion on a single point of law. To return to the man I was telling you of. He would crucify Jesus Christ again, if I bade him. At a word from his old chum Vautrin he will pick a quarrel with a scamp that will not send so much as five francs to his sister, poor girl, and "—(here Vautrin rose to his feet and stood like a fencing-master about to lunge)—" turn him off into the dark!" he added.

"How frightful!" said Eugène. "You do not really mean it? M. Vautrin, you are joking! I cannot believe that you are sincere in what your are saying."

"There! there! Keep cool!" said the other. "Don't behave like a baby. But if you find any amusement in it, be indignant, flare up! Say that I am a scoundrel, a rascal, a rogue, a bandit; but do not call me a blackleg nor a spy! There, out with it, fire away! I forgive you; it is quite natural at your age. I was like that myself once. Only remember this, you will do worse things yourself some day. You will flirt with some pretty woman and take her money. You have thought of that, of course," said Vautrin, "for how are you to succeed unless love is laid under contribution? There are no two ways about virtue, my dear student; it either is or it is not. Talk of doing penance for your sins! It is a nice system of business, when you pay for your crime by an act of contrition! You seduce a woman that you may set your foot on such and such a rung of the social ladder; you sow dissension among the children of a family; you descend, in short, to every base action that can be committed at home or abroad to gain your own ends for your own pleasure or your profit; and can you imagine that these are acts of faith, hope, or charity? How is it that a dandy, who in a night has robbed a boy of half his fortune, gets only a couple of months in prison; while a poor devil who steals a bank-note for a thousand francs, with aggravating circumstances, is condemned to penal servitude? Those are your laws. Not a single provision but lands you in some absurdity. That man with yellow gloves and a golden tongue commits many a murder; he sheds no blood, but he drains his victim's veins as surely; a desperado forces open a door with a crowbar, dark deeds both of them! You yourself will do every one of the things that I suggest to you to-day, bar the bloodshed. Do you believe that there is any absolute standard in this world? Despise mankind and find out the meshes that you can slip through in the net of the Code. The secret of a great success for which you are at a loss to account is a crime that has never been found out, because it was properly executed."

"Silence, sir! I will not hear any more; you make me

doubt myself. At this moment my sentiments are all my science."

"Just as you please, my fine fellow; I did not think you were so weak-minded," said Vautrin, "I shall say no more about it. One last word, however"—and he looked hard at the student—"you have my secret," he said.

"A young man who refuses your offer knows that he must forget it."

"Quite right, quite right; I am glad to hear you say so. Somebody else might not be so scrupulous, you see. Keep in mind what I want to do for you. I will give you a fortnight. The offer is still open."

"What a head of iron the man has!" said Eugène to himself as he watched Vautrin walk unconcernedly away with his cane under his arm. "Yet Mme. de Beauséant said as much more gracefully; he has only stated the case in cruder language. He would tear my heart with claws of steel. What made me think of going to Mme. de Nucingen? He guessed my motives before I knew them myself. To sum it up, that outlaw has told me more about virtue than all I have learned from men and books. If virtue admits of no compromises, I have certainly robbed my sisters," he said, throwing down the bags on the table.

He sat down again and fell, unconscious of his surroundings, into deep thought.

"To be faithful to an ideal of virtue! A heroic martyrdom! Pshaw! every one believes in virtue, but who is virtuous? Nations have made an idol of liberty, but what nation on the face of the earth is free? My youth is still like a blue and cloudless sky. If I set myself to obtain wealth or power, does it not mean that I must make up my mind to lie, and fawn, and cringe, and swagger, and flatter, and dissemble? To consent to be the servant of others who have likewise fawned, and lied, and flattered? Must I cringe to them before I can hope to be their accomplice? Well, then, I decline. I mean to work nobly and with a single heart. I will work day and night; I will owe my fortune to nothing but my own exertions. It may be the slowest of all roads to success, but I shall lay my head on the pillow at night untroubled by evil thoughts. Is there a greater or a better thing than this—to look back over your life and know that it is stainless as a lily! I and my life are like a young man and his betrothed. Vautrin has put before me all that comes after ten years of marriage. The devil! my head is swimming. I do not want to think at all; the heart is a sure guide."

Eugène was roused from his musings by the voice of the stout Sylvie, who announced that the tailor had come, and Eugène therefore made his appearance before the man with the two money-bags, and was not ill pleased that it should be so. When he had tried on his dress suit, he put on his new morning costume, which completely metamorphosed him.

"I am quite equal to M. de Trailles," he said to himself. "In short, I look like a gentleman."

"You asked me, sir, if I knew the houses where Mme. de Nucingen goes," Father Goriot's voice spoke from the doorway of Eugène's room.

"Yes."

"Very well then, she is going to the Duchesse de Carigliano's ball on Monday. If you can manage to be there, I shall hear from you whether my two girls enjoyed themselves, and how they were dressed, and all about it, in fact."

"How did you find that out, my good Goriot?" said Eugène, putting a chair by the fire for his visitor.

"Her maid told me. I hear all about their doings from Thérèse and Constance," he added gleefully.

The old man looked like a lover who is still young enough to be made happy by the discovery of some little stratagem which brings him information of his lady-love without her knowledge.

"*You* will see them both!" he said, giving artless expression to a pang of jealousy.

"I do not know," answered Eugène. "I will go to Mme. de Beauséant and ask her to give me an introduction to the Duchesse."

Eugène felt a thrill of pleasure at the thought of appearing before the Vicomtesse, dressed as henceforward he always meant to be. The "abysses of the human heart," in the moralists' phrase, are only insidious thoughts, involuntary promptings of personal interest. The instinct of enjoyment turns the scale; those rapid changes of purpose which have furnished the text for so much rhetoric are calculations prompted by the hope of pleasure. Rastignac, beholding himself well dressed and impeccable as to gloves and boots, forgot his virtuous resolutions. Youth, moreover, when bent upon wrong-doing does not dare to behold itself in the mirror of consciousness; mature age has seen itself; and therein lies the whole difference between these two phases of life.

A friendship between Eugène and his neighbor, Father Goriot, had been growing up for several days past. This secret friendship and the antipathy that the student had begun to entertain for Vautrin arose from the same psychological causes. The bold philosopher who shall investigate the effects of mental action upon the physical world will doubtless find more than one proof of the material nature of our sentiments in the relations which they create between human beings and other animals. What physiognomist is as quick to discern character as a dog is to discover from a stranger's face whether this is a friend or no? Those by-words—"atoms," "affinities"—are facts surviving in modern languages for the confusion of philosophic wiseacres who amuse themselves by winnowing the chaff of language to find its grammatical roots. We *feel* that we are loved. Our sentiments make themselves felt in everything, even at a great distance. A letter is a living soul, and so faithful an echo of the voice that speaks in it that finer natures look upon a letter as one of love's most precious treasures. Father Goriot's affection was of the instinctive order, a canine affection raised to a sublime pitch; he had scented compassion in the air, and the kindly respect and youthful sympathy in the student's heart. This friendship had, however, scarcely reached the stage at which confidences are made. Though Eugène had spoken of his wish to meet Mme. de Nucingen, it was not because he counted on the old man to introduce him to her house, for he hoped that his own audacity might stand him in good stead. All that Father Goriot had said as yet about his daughters had referred to the remarks that the student had made so freely in public on that day of the two visits.

"How could you think that Mme. de Restaud bore you a grudge for mentioning my name?" he had said on the day following that scene at dinner. "My daughters are very fond of me; I am a happy father; but my sons-in-law have behaved badly to me, and rather than make trouble between my darlings and their husbands, I choose to see my daughters secretly. Fathers who can see their daughters at any time have no idea of all the pleasure that this mystery gives me; I cannot always see mine when I wish, do you understand? So when it is fine I walk out in the Champs-Élysées, after finding out from their waiting-maids whether my daughters mean to go out. I wait near the entrance; my heart beats fast when the carriages begin to come; I admire them in their dresses, and as they pass they give me a little smile, and it seems that everything was lighted up for me by a ray of bright sunlight. I wait, for they always go back the same way, and then I see them again; the fresh air has done them good and brought color into their cheeks; all about me, people say, 'What a beautiful woman that is!' and it does my heart good to hear them.

"Are they not my own flesh and blood? I love the very horses that draw them; I envy the little lap-dog on their knees. Their happiness is my life. Every one loves after his own fashion, and mine does no one any harm; why should people trouble their heads about me? I am happy in my own way. Is there any law against my going to see my girls in the evening when they are going out to a ball? And what a disappointment it is when I get there too late, and am told that 'madame has gone out!' Once I waited till three o'clock in the morning for Nasie; I had not seen her for two whole days. I was so pleased that it was almost too much for me! Please do not speak of me unless it is to say how good my daughters are to me. They are always wanting to heap presents upon me, but I will not have it. 'Just keep your money,' I tell them. 'What should I do with it? I want nothing.' And what am I, sir, after all? An old carcass, whose soul is always where my daughters are. When you have seen Mme. de Nucingen, tell me which you like the most," said the old man after a moment's pause, while Eugène put the last touches to his toilet. The student was about to go out to walk in the Garden of the Tuileries until the hour when he could venture to appear in Mme. de Beauséant's drawing-room.

That walk was a turning-point in Eugène's career. Several women noticed him; he looked so handsome, so young, and so well dressed. This almost admiring attention gave a new turn to his thoughts. He forgot his sisters and the aunt who had robbed herself for him; he no longer remembered his own virtuous scruples. He had seen hovering above his head the fiend so easy to mistake for an angel, the devil with rainbow wings, who scatters rubies, and aims his golden shafts at palace fronts, who invests women with purple, and thrones with a glory that dazzles the eyes of fools till they forget the simple origins of royal dominion; he had heard the rustle of that vanity whose tinsel seems to us to be the symbol of power. However cynical Vautrin's words had been, they had made an impression on his mind, as the sordid features of the old crone who whispers, "A lover, and gold in torrents, remain engraven on a young girl's memory."

Eugène lounged about the walks till it was nearly five o'clock, then he went to Mme. de Beauséant's, and received one of the terrible blows against which young hearts are defenseless. Hitherto the Vicomtesse had received him with the kindly urbanity, the bland grace of manner that is the result of fine breeding, but is only complete when it comes from the heart.

To-day Mme. de Beauséant bowed constrainedly, and spoke curtly—

"M. de Rastignac, I cannot possibly see you, at least not at this moment. I am engaged——"

An observer, and Rastignac instantly became an observer, could read the whole history, the character and customs of caste, in the phrase, in the tones of her voice, in her glance and bearing. He caught a glimpse of the iron hand beneath the velvet glove—the personality, the egoism beneath the manner, the wood beneath the varnish. In short, he heard that unmistakable I THE KING that issues from the plumed canopy of the throne, and finds its last echo under the crest of the simplest gentleman.

Eugène had trusted too implicitly to the generosity of a woman; he could not believe in her haughtiness. Like all the unfortunate, he had subscribed, in all good faith, the generous compact which should bind the benefactor to the recipient, and the first article in that bond, between two large-hearted natures, is a perfect equality. The kindness which knits two souls together is as rare, as divine, and as little understood as the passion of love, for both love and kindness are the lavish generosity of noble natures. Rastignac was set upon going to the Duchesse de Carigliano's ball, so he meekly swallowed down this rebuff, and concealed any manifestation of his disappointment.

"Madame," he faltered out, "I would not have come to

trouble you about a trifling matter; be so kind as to permit me to see you later, I can wait."

"Very well, come and dine with me," she said, a little confused by the harsh way in which she had spoken, for this lady was as genuinely kind-hearted as she was high-born.

Eugène was touched by this sudden relenting, but none the less he said to himself as he went away, "Crawl in the dust, put up with every kind of treatment. What must the rest of the world be like when one of the kindest of women forgets all her promises of befriending me in a moment, and tosses me aside like an old shoe? So it is every one for himself? It is true that her house is not a shop, and I have put myself in the wrong by needing her help. You should cut your way through the world like a cannon-ball, as Vautrin said."

But the student's bitter thoughts were soon dissipated by the pleasure which he promised himself in this dinner with the Vicomtesse. Fate seemed to determine that the smallest accidents in his life should combine to urge him into a career, which the terrible sphinx of the Maison Vauquer had described as a field of battle where you must either slay or be slain, and cheat to avoid being cheated. You leave your conscience and your heart at the barriers, and wear a mask on entering into this game of grim earnest, where, as in ancient Sparta, you must snatch your prize without being detected if you would deserve the crown.

On his return he found the Vicomtesse gracious and kindly, as she had always been to him. They went together to the dining-room, where the Vicomte was waiting for his wife. In the time of the Restoration the luxury of the table was carried, as is well known, to the highest degree, and M. de Beauséant, like many jaded men of the world, had few pleasures left but those of good-cheer; in this matter, in fact, he was a gourmand of the schools of Louis XVIII. and of the Duc d'Escars, and luxury was supplemented by splendor. Eugène dining for the first time in a house where the traditions of grandeur had descended through many generations, had never seen any spectacle like this that at this time met his eyes.

In the time of the Empire, balls had always ended with a supper, because the officers who took part in them must be fortified for immediate service, and even in Paris might be called upon to leave the ballroom for the battlefield. This arrangement had gone out of fashion under the Monarchy, and Eugène had so far only been asked to dances. The self-possession which pre-eminently distinguished him in later life already stood him in good stead, and he did not betray his amazement. Yet as he saw for the first time the finely wrought silver-plate, the completeness of every detail, the sumptuous dinner, noiselessly served, it was difficult for such an ardent imagination not to prefer this life of studied and refined luxury to the hardships of the life which he had chosen only that morning.

His thoughts went back for a moment to the lodging-house, and, with a feeling of profound loathing, he vowed to himself that at New Year he would go; prompted at least as much by a desire to live among cleaner surroundings as by a wish to shake off Vautrin, whose huge hand he seemed to feel on his shoulder at that moment. When you consider the numberless forms, clamorous or mute, that corruption takes in Paris, common-sense begins to wonder what mental aberration prompted the state to establish great colleges and schools there, and assemble young men in the capital; how it is that pretty women are respected, or that the gold coin displayed in the money-changer's wooden saucers does not take to itself wings in the twinkling of an eye; and when you come to think further, how comparatively few cases of crime there are, and to count up the misdemeanors committed by youth, is there not a certain amount of respect due to these patient Tantaluses who wrestle with themselves and nearly always come off victorious? The struggles of the poor student in

Paris, if skillfully drawn, would furnish a most dramatic picture of modern civilization.

In vain Mme. de Beauséant looked at Eugène as if asking him to speak; the student was tongue-tied in the Vicomte's presence.

"Are you going to take me to the Italiens this evening?" the Vicomtesse asked her husband.

"You cannot doubt that I should obey you with pleasure," he answered, and there was a sarcastic tinge in his politeness which Eugène did not detect, "but I ought to go to meet some one at the Variétés."

"His mistress," said she to herself.

"Then is not Ajuda coming for you this evening?" inquired the Vicomte.

"No," she answered, petulantly.

"Very well, then, if you really must have an arm, take that of M. de Rastignac."

The Vicomtesse turned to Eugène with a smile.

"That would be a very compromising step for you," she said.

"'A Frenchman loves danger, because in danger there is glory,' to quote M. de Chateaubriand," said Rastignac, with a bow.

A few moments later he was sitting beside Mme. de Beauséant in a brougham, that whirled them through the streets of Paris to a fashionable theatre. It seemed to him that some fairy magic had suddenly transported him into a box facing the stage. All the lorgnettes of the house were pointed at him as he entered, and at the Vicomtesse in her charming toilet. He went from enchantment to enchantment.

"You must talk to me, you know," said Mme. de Beauséant. "Ah! look! There is Mme. de Nucingen in the third box from ours. Her sister and M. de Trailles are on the other side."

The Vicomtesse glanced as she spoke at the box where

Mlle. de Rochefide should have been; M. d'Ajuda was not there, and Mme. de Beauséant's face lighted up in a marvelous way.

"She is charming," said Eugène, after looking at Mme. de Nucingen.

"She has white eyelashes."

"Yes, but she has such a pretty slender figure!"

"Her hands are large."

"Such beautiful eyes!"

"Her face is long."

"Yes, but length gives distinction."

"It is lucky for her that she has some distinction in her face. Just see how she fidgets with her opera-glass! The Goriot blood shows itself in every movement," said the Vicomtesse, much to Eugène's astonishment.

Indeed, Mme. de Beauséant seemed to be engaged in making a survey of the house, and to be unconscious of Mme. Nucingen's existence; but no movement made by the latter was lost upon the Vicomtesse. The house was full of the loveliest women in Paris, so that Delphine de Nucingen was not a little flattered to receive the undivided attention of Mme. de Beauséant's young, handsome, and well-dressed cousin, who seemed to have no eyes for any one else.

"If you look at her so persistently, you will make people talk, M. de Rastignac. You will never succeed if you fling yourself at any one's head like that."

"My dear cousin," said Eugène, "you have protected me indeed so far, and now if you would complete your work, I only ask of you a favor which will cost you but little, and be of very great service to me. I have lost my heart."

"Already!"

"Yes."

"And to that woman!"

"How could I aspire to find any one else to listen to me?" he asked, with a keen glance at his cousin. "Her grace the

Duchesse de Carigliano is a friend of the Duchesse de Berri," he went on, after a pause; "you are sure to see her, will you be so kind as to present me to her, and to take me with you to her ball on Monday? I shall meet Mme. de Nucingen there, and enter upon my first skirmish."

"Willingly," she said. "If you have a liking for her already, your affairs of the heart are likely to prosper. That is de Marsay over there in the Princesse Galathionne's box. Mme. de Nucingen is racked with jealousy. There is no better time for approaching a woman, especially if she happens to be a banker's wife. All those ladies of the Chaussée-d'Antin love revenge."

"Then what would you do yourself in such a case?"

"I should suffer in silence."

At this point the Marquis d'Ajuda appeared in Mme. de Beauséant's box.

"I have made a muddle of my affairs to come to you," he said, "and I am telling you about it, so that it may not be a sacrifice."

Eugène saw the glow of joy on the Vicomtesse's face, and knew that this was love, and learned the difference between love and the affectations of Parisian coquetry. He admired his cousin, grew mute, and yielded his place to M. d'Ajuda with a sigh.

"How noble, how sublime a woman is when she loves like that!" he said to himself. "And *he* could forsake her for a doll! Oh! how could any one forsake her?"

There was a boy's passionate indignation in his heart. He could have flung himself at Mme. de Beauséant's feet; he longed for the power of the devil if he could snatch her away and hide her in his heart, as an eagle snatches up some white yeanling from the plains and bears it to his eyrie. It was humiliating to him to think that in all this gallery of fair pictures he had not one picture of his own. "To have a mistress and an almost royal position is a sign of power," he said to himself. And he looked at Mme. de Nucingen as a man measures another who has insulted him.

The Vicomtesse turned to him, and the expression of her eyes thanked him a thousand times for his discretion. The first act came to an end just then.

"Do you know Mme. de Nucingen well enough to present M. de Rastignac to her?" she asked of the Marquis d'Ajuda.

"She will be delighted," said the Marquis. The handsome Portuguese rose as he spoke and took the student's arm, and in another moment Eugène found himself in Mme. de Nucingen's box.

"Madame," said the Marquis, "I have the honor of presenting to you the Chevalier Eugène de Rastignac; he is a cousin of Mme. de Beauséant's. You have made so deep an impression upon him, that I thought I would fill up the measure of his happiness by bringing him nearer to his divinity."

Words spoken half-jestingly to cover their somewhat disrespectful import; but such an implication, if carefully disguised, never gives offense to a woman. Mme. de Nucingen smiled, and offered Eugène the place which her husband had just left.

"I do not venture to suggest that you should stay with me, monsieur," she said. "Those who are so fortunate as to be in Mme. de Beauséant's company seldom desire to soon leave it."

"Madame," Eugène said, lowering his voice, "I think that to please my cousin I should remain with you. Before my Lord Marquis came we were speaking of you and of your exceedingly distinguished appearance," he added aloud.

M. d'Ajuda turned and left them.

"Are you really going to stay with me, monsieur?" asked the Baroness. "Then we shall make each other's acquaintance. Mme. de Restaud told me about you, and has made me anxious to meet you."

"She must be very insincere, then, for she has shut her door on me."

"What?"

"Madame, I will tell you honestly the reason why; but I must crave your indulgence before confiding such a secret to you. I am your father's neighbor; I had no idea that Mme. de Restaud was his daughter. I was rash enough to mention his name; I meant no harm, but I annoyed your sister and her husband very much. You cannot think how severely the Duchesse de Langeais and my cousin blamed this apostasy on a daughter's part, as a piece of bad taste. I told them all about it, and they both burst out laughing. Then Mme. de Beauséant made some comparison between you and your sister, speaking in high terms of you, and saying how very fond you were of my neighbor, M. Goriot. And, indeed, how could you help loving him? He adores you so passionately that I am jealous already. We talked about you this morning for two hours. So this evening I was quite full of all that your father had told me, and while I was dining with my cousin I said that you could not be as beautiful as affectionate. Mme. de Beauséant meant to gratify such warm admiration, I think, when she brought me here, telling me, in her gracious way, that I should see you."

"Then, even now, I owe you a debt of gratitude, monsieur," said the banker's wife. "We shall be quite old friends in a little while."

"Although a friendship with you could only be like an ordinary friendship," said Rastignac; "I should ever wish to be your friend."

Such stereotyped phrases as these, in the mouths of beginners, possess an unfailing charm for women, and are insipid only when read coldly; for a young man's tone, glance, and attitude give a surpassing eloquence to the banal phrases. Mme. de Nucingen thought that Rastignac was adorable. Then, woman-like, being at a loss how to reply to the student's outspoken admiration, she answered a previous remark.

"Yes, it is very wrong of my sister to treat our poor father as she does," she said; "he has been a providence to us. It was not until M. de Nucingen positively ordered me only to receive him in the mornings that I yielded the point. But I have been unhappy about it for a long while; I have shed many tears over it. This violence to my feelings, with my husband's brutal treatment, have been the two causes of my unhappy married life. There is certainly no woman in Paris whose lot seems more enviable than mine, and yet, in reality, there is not one so much to be pitied. You will think I must be out of my senses to talk to you like this; but you know my father, and I cannot very well regard you as a stranger."

"You will find no one," said Eugène, "who longs as eagerly as I do to be yours. What do all women seek? Happiness." (He answered his own question in low, vibrating tones.) "And if happiness for a woman means that she is to be loved and adored, to have a friend to whom she can pour out her wishes, her fancies, her sorrows and joys; to whom she can lay bare her heart and soul, and all her fair defects and her gracious virtues, without fear of a betrayal; believe me, the devotion and the warmth that never fail can only be found in the heart of a young man who, at a bare sign from you, would go to his death, who neither knows nor cares to know anything as yet of the world, because you will be all the world to him. I myself, you see (you will laugh at my simplicity), have just come from a remote country district; I am quite new to this world of Paris; I have only known true and loving hearts; and I made up my mind that here I should find no love. Then I chanced to meet my cousin, and to see my cousin's heart from very near; I have divined the inexhaustible treasures of passion, and, like Cherubino, I am the lover of all women, until the day comes when I find *the* woman to whom I may devote myself. As soon as I saw you, as soon as I came into the theatre this evening, I felt myself borne towards you as if by the current of a stream. I had so often thought of you already, but I had never dreamed that you would be so beautiful! Mme. de Beauséant told me that I must not look so much at you. She does not know the charm of your red lips, your fair face, nor see how soft your eyes are—— I also am beginning to talk nonsense; but let me talk."

Nothing pleases women better than to listen to such whispered words as these; the most puritanical among them listens even when she ought not to reply to them; and Rastignac, having once begun, continued to pour out his story, dropping his voice, that she might lean and listen; and Mme. de Nucingen, smiling, glanced from time to time at de Marsay, who still sat in the Princesse Galathionne's box.

Rastignac did not leave Mme. de Nucingen till her husband came to take her home.

"Madame," Eugène said, "I shall have the pleasure of calling upon you before the Duchesse de Carigliano's ball."

"If matame infites you to come," said the Baron, a thick-set Alsatian, with indications of a sinister cunning in his full-moon countenance, "you are quide sure of being well receifed."

"My affairs seem to be in a promising way," said Eugène to himself. "'Can you love me?' I asked her, and she did not resent it. The bit is in the horse's mouth, and I have only to mount and ride;" and with that he went to pay his respects to Mme. de Beauséant, who was leaving the theatre on d'Ajuda's arm.

The student did not know that the Baroness' thoughts had been wandering; that she was even then expecting a letter from de Marsay, one of those letters that bring about a rupture that rends the soul; so, happy in his delusion, Eugène went with the Vicomtesse to the peristyle, where people were waiting till their carriages were announced.

"That cousin of yours is hardly recognizable for the same man," said the Portuguese laughingly to the Vicomtesse, when Eugène had taken leave of them. "He will break the bank. He is as supple as an eel; he will go a long way, of that I am sure. Who else could have picked out a woman for him, as you did, just when she needed consolation?"

"But it is not certain that she does not still love the faithless lover," said Mme. de Beauséant.

The student meanwhile walked back from the Théâtre-Italien to the Rue Neuve-Sainte-Geneviève, making the most delightful plans as he went. He had noticed how closely Mme. de Restaud had scrutinized him when he appeared in the Vicomtesse's box, and again when he sat beside Mme. de Nucingen, and inferred that the Countess' doors would not be closed in future. Four important houses were now open to him—for he meant to stand well with the Duchesse; he had four supporters in the inmost circle of society in Paris. Even now it was clear to him that, once involved in this intricate social machinery, he must attach himself to a spoke of the wheel that was to turn and raise his fortunes; he would not examine himself too curiously as to the methods, but he was certain of the end, and conscious of the power to gain and keep his hold.

"If Mme. de Nucingen takes an interest in me, I will teach her how to manage her husband. That husband of hers is a great speculator; he might put me in the way of making a fortune by a single stroke."

He did not say this bluntly in so many words; as yet, indeed, he was not sufficient of a diplomatist to sum up a situation, to see its possibilities at a glance, and calculate the chances in his favor. These were nothing but hazy ideas that floated over his mental horizon; they were less cynical than Vautrin's notions; but if they had been tried in the crucible of conscience, no very pure result would have issued from the test. It is by a succession of such like transactions that men sink at last to the level of the relaxed morality of this epoch, when there have never been so few of those who square their courses with their theories, so few of those noble characters who do not yield to temptation, for whom the slightest deviation from the line of rectitude is a crime. To these magnificent types of uncompromising right we owe two masterpieces—the Alceste of Molière, and, in our own day, the characters of Jeanie Deans and her father in Sir Walter Scott's novel. Perhaps a work which should chronicle the opposite course, which should trace out all the devious courses through which a man of the world, a man of ambitions, drags his conscience, just steering clear of crime that he may gain his end and yet save appearances, such a chronicle would be no less edifying and no less dramatic.

Rastignac went home. He was fascinated by Mme. de Nucingen; he seemed to see her before him, slender and graceful as a swallow. He recalled the intoxicating sweetness of her eyes, her fair hair, the delicate silken tissue of the skin, beneath which it almost seemed to him that he could see the blood coursing; the tones of her voice still exerted a spell over him; he had forgotten nothing; his walk perhaps heated his imagination by sending a glow of warmth through his veins. He knocked unceremoniously at Goriot's door.

"I have seen Mme. Delphine, neighbor," said he.

"Where?"

"At the Italiens."

"Did she enjoy it?—— Just come inside," and the old man left his bed, unlocked the door, and promptly returned again.

It was the first time that Eugène had been in Father Goriot's room, and he could not control his feeling of amazement at the contrast between the den in which the father lived and the costume of the daughter whom he had just beheld. The window was curtainless, the walls were damp, in places the varnished wall-paper had come away and gave glimpses of the grimy yellow plaster beneath. The wretched bed on which the old man lay boasted but one thin blanket, and a wadded quilt made out of large pieces of Mme. Vauquer's old dresses. The floor was damp and gritty. Opposite the window stood a chest of drawers made of rosewood, one of the old-fashioned kind with a curving front and brass handles, shaped like rings of twisted vine stems covered with flowers and leaves. On a venerable piece of furniture with a wooden shelf stood an ewer and basin and shaving apparatus. A pair of shoes stood in one corner; a night-table by the bed had neither a door nor marble slab. There was not a trace of a fire in the empty grate; the square walnut table with the cross-bar against which Father Goriot had crushed and twisted his posset-dish stood near the hearth. The old man's hat was lying on a broken-down bureau. An arm-chair stuffed with straw and a couple of chairs completed the list of ramshackle furniture. From the tester of the bed, tied to the ceiling by a piece of rag, hung a strip of some cheap material in large red and black checks. No poor drudge in a garret could be worse lodged than Father Goriot in Mme. Vauquer's lodging-house. The mere sight of the room sent a chill through you and a sense of oppression; it was like the worst cell in a prison. Luckily, Goriot could not see the effect that his surroundings produced on Eugène as the latter deposited his candle on the night-table. The old man turned round, keeping the bed-clothes huddled up to his chin.

"Well," he said, "and which do you like the best, Mme. de Restaud or Mme. de Nucingen?"

"I like Mme. Delphine the best," said the law student, "because she loves you the best."

At the words so heartily spoken the old man's hand slipped out from under the bedclothes and eagerly grasped that of Eugène.

"Thank you, thank you," he said, gratefully. "Then what did she say about me?"

The student repeated the Baroness' remarks with some embellishments of his own, the old man listening the while as though he heard a voice from heaven.

"Dear child!" he said. "Yes, yes, she is very fond of me. But you must not believe all that she tells you about Anastasie. The two sisters are jealous of each other, you see, another proof of their affection. Mme. de Restaud is very fond of me too. I know she is. A father sees his children as God sees all of us; he looks into the very depths of their hearts; he knows their intentions; and both of them are so loving. Oh! if I only had good sons-in-law, I should be too happy, and I dare say there is no perfect happiness here below. If I might live with them—simply hear their voices, know that they are there, see them go and come as I used to do at home when they were still with me; why, my heart bounds at the thought—— Were they nicely dressed?"

"Yes," said Eugène. "But, M. Goriot, how is it that your daughters have such fine houses, while you live in such a den as this?"

"Dear me, why should I want anything better?" he replied, with seeming carelessness. "I can't quite explain to you how it is; I am not used to stringing words together properly, but it all lies there——" he said, tapping his heart.

"My real life is in my two girls, you see; and so long as they are happy and smartly dressed, and have soft carpets under their feet, what does it matter what clothes I wear or where I lie down of a night? I shall never feel cold so long as they are warm; I shall never feel dull if they are laughing. I have no troubles but theirs. When you, too, are a father, and you hear your children's little voices, you will say to yourself, 'That has all come from me.' You will feel that those little ones are akin to every drop in your veins, that they are the very flower of your life (and what else are they?);

you will cleave so closely to them that you seem to feel every movement that they make. Everywhere I hear their voices sounding in my ears. If they are sad, the look in their eyes freezes my blood. Some day you will find out that there is far more happiness in another's happiness than in your own. It is something that I cannot explain, something within that sends a glow of warmth all through you. In short, I live my life three times over. Shall I tell you something funny? Well, then, since I have been a father, I have come to understand God. He is everywhere in the world, because the whole world comes from Him. And it is just the same with my children, monsieur. Only, I love my daughters better than God loves the world, for the world is not so beautiful as God Himself is, but my children are more beautiful than I am. Their lives are so bound up with mine that I felt somehow that you would see them this evening! Great heaven! If any man would make my little Delphine as happy as a wife is when she is loved, I would black his boots and run on his errands. That miserable M. de Marsay is a cur; I know all about him from her maid. A longing to wring his neck comes over me now and then. He does not love her! does not love a pearl of a woman, with a voice like a nightingale and shaped like a model. Where can her eyes have been when she married that great lump of an Alsatian? They ought both of them to have married young men, good-looking and good-tempered—but, after all, they had their own way."

Father Goriot was sublime. Eugène had never yet seen his face light up as it did now with the passionate fervor of a father's love. It is worthy of remark that strong feeling has a very subtle and pervasive power; the roughest nature, in the endeavor to express a deep and sincere affection, communicates to others the influence that has put resonance into the voice, and eloquence into every gesture, wrought a change in the very features of the speaker; for under the inspiration of passion the stupidest human being attains to the highest eloquence of ideas, if not of language, and seems to move in some sphere of light. In the old man's tones and gesture there was something just then of the same spell that a great actor exerts over his audience. But does not the poet in us find expression in our affections?

"Well," said Eugène, "perhaps you will not be sorry to hear that she is pretty sure to break with de Marsay before long. That sprig of fashion has left her for the Princesse Galathionne. For my own part, I fell in love with Mme. Delphine this evening."

"Stuff!" said Father Goriot.

"I did, indeed; and she did not regard me with aversion. For a whole hour we talked of love, and I am to go to call on her on Saturday, the day after to-morrow."

"Oh! how I should love you, if she should like you. You are kind-hearted; you would never make her miserable. If you were to forsake her, I would cut your throat at once. A woman does not love twice, you see! Good heavens! what nonsense I am talking, M. Eugène! It is cold; you ought not to stay here. *Mon Dieu!* so you have heard her speak? What message did she give you for me?"

"None at all," said Eugène to himself; aloud he answered, "She told me to tell you that your daughter sends you a good kiss."

"Good-night, neighbor! Sleep well, and pleasant dreams to you! I have mine already made for me by that message from her. May God grant you all your desires! You have come in like a good angel on me to-night, and brought with you the air that my daughter breathes."

"Poor old fellow!" said Eugène as he lay down. "It is enough to melt a heart of stone. His daughter no more thought of him than of the Grand Turk."

Ever after this conference Goriot looked upon his neighbor as a friend, a confidant such as he had never hoped to find;

and there was established between the two the only relationship that could attach this old man to another man. The passions never miscalculate. Father Goriot felt that this friendship brought him closer to his daughter Delphine; he thought that he should find a warmer welcome for himself if the Baroness should care for Eugène. Moreover, he had confided one of his troubles to the younger man. Mme. de Nucingen, for whose happiness he prayed a thousand times daily, had never known the joys of love. Eugène was certainly (to make use of his own expression) one of the nicest young men that he had ever seen, and some prophetic instinct seemed to tell him that Eugène was to give her the happiness which had not been hers. These were the beginnings of a friendship that grew up between the old man and his neighbor; but for this friendship the catastrophe of the drama must have remained a mystery.

The affection with which Father Goriot regarded Eugène, by whom he seated himself at breakfast, the change in Goriot's face, which, as a rule, looked as expressionless as a plaster cast, and a few words that passed between the two, surprised the other lodgers. Vautrin, who saw Eugène for the first time since their interview, seemed as if he would fain read the student's very soul. During the night Eugène had had some time in which to scan the vast field that lay before him; and now, as he remembered yesterday's proposal, the thought of Mlle. Taillefer's dowry came, of course, to his mind, and he could not help thinking of Victorine as the most exemplary youth may think of an heiress. It chanced that their eyes met. The poor girl did not fail to see that Eugène looked very handsome in his new clothes. So much was said in the glance thus exchanged, that Eugène could not doubt but that he was associated in her mind with the vague hopes that lie dormant in a girl's heart and gather round the first attractive new-comer. "Eight hundred thousand francs!" a voice cried in his ears, but suddenly he took refuge in the memories of yesterday evening, thinking that his extemporized passion for Mme. de Nucingen was a talisman that would preserve him from this temptation.

"They gave Rossini's 'Barber of Seville' at the Italiens yesterday evening," he remarked. "I never heard such delicious music. Good gracious! how lucky people are to have a box at the Italiens!"

Father Goriot drank in every word that Eugène let fall, and watched him as a dog watches his master's slightest movement.

"You men are like fighting-cocks," said Mme. Vauquer; "you do what you like."

"How did you get back?" inquired Vautrin.

"I walked," answered Eugène.

"For my own part," remarked the tempter, "I do not care about doing things by halves. If I want to enjoy myself that way, I should prefer to go in my carriage, sit in my own box, and do the thing comfortably. Everything or nothing; that is my motto."

"And a good one too," commented Mme. Vauquer.

"Perhaps you will see Mme. de Nucingen to-day," said Eugène, addressing Goriot in an undertone. "She will welcome you with open arms, I am sure; she would want to ask you for all sorts of little details about me. I have found out that she would do anything in the world to be known by my cousin Mme. de Beauséant; don't forget to tell her that I love her too well not to think of trying to arrange this."

Rastignac went at once to the École de droit. He had no mind to stay a moment longer than was necessary in that odious house. He wasted his time that day; he had fallen a victim to that fever of the brain that accompanies the too vivid hopes of youth. Vautrin's arguments had set him meditating on social life, and he was deep in these reflections when he happened on his friend Bianchon in the Jardin du Luxembourg.

"What makes you look so solemn?" said the medical student, putting an arm through Eugène's as they went towards the Palais.

"I am tormented by temptations."

"What kind? There is a cure for temptation."

"What?"

"Yielding to it."

"You laugh, but you don't know what it is all about. Have you read Rousseau?"

"Yes."

"Do you remember that he asks the reader somewhere what he would do if he could make a fortune by killing an old mandarin somewhere in China by mere force of wishing it, and without stirring from Paris?"

"Yes."

"Well, then?"

"Pshaw! I am at my thirty-third mandarin."

"Seriously, though. Look here, suppose you were sure that you could do it, and had only to give a nod. Would you do it?"

"Is he well stricken in years, this mandarin of yours? Pshaw! after all, young or old, paralytic, or well and sound, my word for it—— Well, then. Hang it, no!"

"You are a good fellow, Bianchon. But suppose you loved a woman well enough to lose your soul in hell for her, and that she wanted money, lots of money for dresses and a carriage, and all her whims, in fact?"

"Why, here you are taking away my reason, and want me to reason!"

"Well, then, Bianchon, I am mad; bring me to my senses. I have two sisters as beautiful and innocent as angels, and I want them to be happy. How am I to find two hundred thousand francs a piece for them in the next five years? Now and then in life, you see, you must play for heavy stakes, and it is no use wasting your luck on low play."

"But you are only stating the problem that lies before every one at the outset of his life, and you want to cut the Gordian knot with a sword. If that is the way of it, dear boy, you must be an Alexander, or to the hulks you go. For my own part, I am quite contented with the little lot I mean to make for myself somewhere in the country, when I mean to step into my father's shoes and plod along. A man's affections are just as fully satisfied by the smallest circle as they can be by a vast circumference. Napoleon himself could only dine once, and he could not have more mistresses than a house-student at the Capucins. Happiness, old man, depends on what lies between the sole of your foot and the crown of your head; and whether it costs a million or a hundred louis, the actual amount of pleasure that you receive rests entirely with you, and is just exactly the same in any case. I am for letting that Chinaman live."

"Thank you, Bianchon; you have done me good. We will always be friends."

"I say," remarked the medical student, as they came to the end of a broad walk in the Jardin des Plantes, "I saw the Michonneau and Poiret a few minutes ago on a bench chatting with a gentleman whom I used to see in last year's troubles hanging about the Chamber of Deputies; he seems to me, in fact, to be a detective dressed up like a decent retired tradesman. Let us keep an eye on that couple; I will tell you why some time. Good-by; it is nearly four o'clock, and I must be in to answer to my name."

When Eugène reached the lodging-house, he found Father Goriot waiting for him.

"Here!" cried the old man, "here is a letter from her. Pretty handwriting, eh?"

Eugène broke the seal and read—

"Sir:—I have heard from my father that you are fond of Italian music. I shall be delighted if you will do me the pleasure of accepting a seat in my box. La Fodor and Pellegrini will sing on Saturday, so I am sure that you will not refuse me. M. de Nucingen and I shall be pleased if you will dine with us; we shall be quite by ourselves. If you will come and be my escort, my husband will be glad to be relieved from his conjugal duties. Do not answer, but simply come. Yours sincerely,

"D. DE N."

"Let me see it," said Father Goriot, when Eugène had read the letter. "You are going, aren't you?" he added, when he had smelt the writing-paper. "How nice it smells! Her fingers have touched it, that is certain."

"A woman does not fling herself at a man's head in this way," the student was thinking. "She wants to use me to bring back de Marsay; nothing but pique makes a woman do a thing like this."

"Well," said Father Goriot, "what are you thinking about?"

Eugène did not know the fever of vanity that possessed some women in those days; how should he imagine that to open a door in the Faubourg Saint-Germain a banker's wife would go to almost any length. For the coterie of the Faubourg Saint-Germain was a charmed circle, and the women who moved in it were at that time the queens of society; and among the greatest of these *Dames du Petit-Château,* as they were called, were Mme. de Beauséant and her friends the Duchesse de Langeais and the Duchesse de Maufrigneuse. Rastignac was alone in his ignorance of the frantic efforts made by women who lived in the Chausée-d'Antin to enter this seventh heaven and shine among the brightest constellations of their sex. But his cautious disposition stood him in good stead, and kept his judgment cool, and the not altogether enviable power of imposing instead of accepting conditions.

"Yes, I am going," he replied.

So it was curiosity that drew him to Mme. de Nucingen; while, if she had treated him disdainfully, passion, perhaps, might have brought him to her feet. Still he waited almost impatiently for to-morrow, and the hour when he could go to her. There is almost as much charm for a young man in a first flirtation as there is in first love, The certainty of success is a source of happiness to which men do not confess, and all the charm of certain women lies in this. The desire of conquest springs no less from the easiness than from the difficulty of triumph, and every passion is excited or sustained by one or other of these two motives which divide the empire of love. Perhaps this division is one result of the great question of temperaments; which, after all, dominates social life. The melancholic temperament may stand in need of the tonic of coquetry, while those of nervous or sanguine complexion withdraw if they meet with a too stubborn resistance. In other words, the lymphatic temperament is essentially despondent and the rhapsodic is bilious.

Eugène lingered over his toilet with an enjoyment of all its little details that is grateful to a young man's self-love, though he will not own to it for fear of being laughed at. He thought, as he arranged his hair, that a pretty woman's glances would wander through the dark curls. He indulged in childish tricks like any young girl dressing for a dance, and gazed complacently at his graceful figure while he smoothed out the creases of his coat.

"There are worse figures, that is certain," he said to himself.

Then he went downstairs, just as the rest of the household were sitting down to dinner, and took with good-humor the boisterous applause excited by his elegant appearance. The amazement with which any attention to dress is regarded in a lodging-house is a very characteristic trait. No one can put on a new coat but every one else must say his say about it.

"Clk! clk! clk!" cried Bianchon, making the sound with his tongue against the roof of his mouth, like a driver urging on a horse.

"He holds himself like a duke and a peer of France," said Mme. Vauquer.

"Are you going a-courting?" inquired Mlle. Michonneau.

"Cock-a-doodle-doo?" cried the artist.

"My compliments to my lady, your wife," from the employé at the Muséum.

"Your wife; have you a wife?" interposed the redoubtable Poiret.

"Yes, in compartments, water-tight and floats, guaranteed fast color, all prices from twenty-five to forty sous, neat check patterns in the latest fashion and best taste, will wash, half-linen, half-cotton, half-wool; a certain cure for toothache and other complaints under the patronage of the Royal College of Physicians! children like it! a remedy for headache, indigestion, and all other diseases affecting the throat, eyes, and ears!" cried Vautrin, with the comical imitation of the volubility of a quack at a fair. "And how much shall we say for this marvel, gentlemen? Twopence? No. Nothing of the sort. All that is left in stock after supplying the Great Mogul. All the crowned heads of Europe, including the Gr-r-r-rand Duke of Baden, have been anxious to get a sight of it. Walk up! walk up! gentlemen! Pay at the desk as you go in! Strike up the music there! Brooum, la, la, trinn! la, la, boum! boum! Mister Clarinette, there you are out of tune!" he added gruffly; "I will rap your knuckles for you!"

"Goodness! what an amusing man!" said Mme. Vauquer to Mme. Couture; "I should never feel dull with him in the house."

This burlesque of Vautrin's was the signal for an outburst of merriment, and under cover of jokes and laughter Eugène caught a glance from Mlle. Taillefer; she had leaned over to say a few words in Mme. Couture's ear.

"The cab is at the door," announced Sylvie.

"But where is he going to dine?" asked Bianchon.

"With Madame la Baronne de Nucingen."

"M. Goriot's daughter," said the law student.

At this, all eyes turned to the old vermicelli-maker; he was gazing at Eugène with something like envy in his eyes.

Rastignac reached the house in the Rue Saint-Lazare, one of those many-windowed houses with a mean-looking portico and slender columns, which are considered the thing in Paris; a typical banker's house, decorated in the most ostentatious fashion; the walls lined with stucco, the landings of marble mosaic. Mme. de Nucingen was sitting in a little drawing-room; the room was painted in the Italian fashion, and decorated like a restaurant. The Baroness seemed depressed. The effort that she made to hide her feelings aroused Eugène's interest; it was plain that she was not playing a part. He had expected a little flutter of excitement at his coming, and he found her dispirited and sad. The disappointment piqued his vanity.

"My claim to your confidence is very small, madame," he said, after rallying her on her abstracted mood; "but if I am in the way, please tell me so frankly; I count on your good faith."

"No, stay with me," she said; "I shall be all alone if you go. Nucingen is dining in town, and I do not want to be alone; I want to be taken out of myself."

"But what is the matter?"

"You are the very last person whom I should tell," she exclaimed.

"Then I am connected in some way with this secret. I wonder what it is."

"Perhaps. Yet, no," she went on; "it is a domestic quarrel, which ought to be buried in the depths of the heart.

"AM I TO YOUR TASTE?"

I am very unhappy; did I not tell you so the day before yesterday? Golden chains are the heaviest of all fetters."

When a woman tells a young man that she is very unhappy, and when the young man is clever, and well-dressed, and has fifteen hundred francs lying idle in his pocket, he is sure to think as Eugène said, and he becomes a coxcomb.

"What can you have left to wish for?" he answered. "You are young, beautiful, beloved, and rich."

"Do not let us talk of my affairs," she said, shaking her head mournfully. "We will dine together *tête-à-tête*, and afterwards we will go to hear the most exquisite music. Am I to your taste?" she went on, rising and displaying her gown of white cashmere, covered with Persian designs in the most superb taste.

"I wish that you were altogether mine," said Eugène; "you are charming."

"You would have a forlorn piece of property," she said, smiling bitterly. "There is nothing about me that betrays my wretchedness; and yet, in spite of appearances, I am in despair. I cannot sleep; my troubles have broken my night's rest; I shall grow ugly."

"Oh! that is impossible," cried the law student; "but I am curious to know what these troubles can be that a devoted love cannot efface."

"Ah! if I were to tell you about them, you would shun me," she said. "Your love for me as yet is only the conventional gallantry that men use to masquerade in; and, if you really loved me, you would be driven to despair. I must keep silent, you see. Let us talk of something else for pity's sake," she added. "Let me show you my rooms."

"No; let us stay here," answered Eugène; he sat down on the sofa before the fire, and boldly took Mme. de Nucingen's hand in his. She surrendered it to him; he even felt the pressure of her fingers in one of the spasmodic clutches that betray terrible agitation.

"Listen," said Rastignac; "if you are in trouble, you ought to tell me about it. I want to prove to you that I love you for yourself alone. You must speak to me frankly about your troubles, so that I can put an end to them, even if I have to kill half-a-dozen men; or I shall go, never to return."

"Very well," she cried, putting her hand to her forehead in an agony of despair, " I will put you to the proof, and this very moment. Yes," she said to herself, "I have no other resource left."

She rang the bell.

"Are the horses put in for the master?" she asked of the servant.

"Yes, madame."

"I shall take his carriage myself. He can have mine and my horses. Serve dinner at seven o'clock."

"Now, come with me," she said to Eugène, who thought as he sat in the banker's carriage beside Mme. de Nucingen that he must surely be dreaming.

"To the Palais-Royal," she said to the coachman; "stop near the Théâtre-Français."

She seemed to be too troubled and excited to answer the innumerable questions that Eugène put to her. He was at a loss what to think of her mute resistance, her obstinate silence.

"Another moment and she will escape me," he said to himself.

When the carriage stopped at last, the Baroness gave the law student a glance that silenced his wild words, for he was almost beside himself.

"Is it true that you love me?" she asked.

"Yes," he answered, and in his manner and tone there was no trace of the uneasiness that he felt.

"You will not think ill of me, will you, whatever I may ask of you?"

"No."

"Are you ready to do my bidding?"

"Blindly."

"Have you ever been to a gaming-house?" she asked in a tremulous voice.

"Never."

"Ah! now I can breathe. You will have luck. Here is my purse," she said. "Take it! there are a hundred francs in it, all that such a fortunate woman as I can call her own. Go up into one of the gaming-houses—I do not know where they are, but there are some near the Palais-Royal. Try your luck with the hundred francs at a game they call roulette; lose it all, or bring me back six thousand francs. I will tell you about my troubles when you come back."

"Devil take me, I'm sure, if I have a glimmer of a notion of what I am about, but I will obey you," he added, with inward exultation, as he thought, "She has gone too far to draw back—she can refuse me nothing now!"

Eugène took the dainty little purse, inquired the way of a second-hand clothes-dealer, and hurried to number 9, which happened to be the nearest gaming-house. He mounted the staircase, surrendered his hat, and asked the way to the roulette-table, whither the attendant took him, not a little to the astonishment of the regular comers. All eyes were fixed on Eugène as he asked, without bashfulness, where he was to deposit his stakes.

"If you put a louis on one only of those thirty-six numbers, and it turns up, you will win thirty-six louis," said a respectable-looking, white-haired old man in answer to his inquiry.

Eugène staked the whole of his money on the number 21 (his own age). There was a cry of surprise; before he knew what he had done, he had won.

"Take your money off, sir," said the old white-haired gentleman; "you don't often win twice running by that system of playing."

Eugène took the rake that the old man handed to him, and drew in his three thousand six hundred francs, and, still perfectly ignorant of what he was about, staked again on the red. The bystanders watched him enviously as they saw him continue to play. The disc turned, and again he won; the banker threw him three thousand six hundred francs once more.

"You have seven thousand two hundred francs of your own," the old gentleman said in his ear. "Take my advice and go away with your winnings; red has turned up eight times already. If you are charitable, you will show your gratitude for sound counsel by giving a trifle to an old préfect of Napoleon's who is down on his luck and without the means to stake anew."

Rastignac's head was swimming; he saw ten of his louis pass into the white-haired man's possession, and went downstairs with his seven thousand francs; he was still ignorant of the game, and stupefied by his luck.

"So that is over; and now where will you take me?" he asked, as soon as the door was closed, and he showed the seven thousand francs to Mme. de Nucingen.

Delphine flung her arms about him, but there was no passion in that wild embrace.

"You have saved me!" she cried, and tears of joy flowed fast.

"I will tell you everything, my friend. For you will be my friend, will you not? I am rich, you think, very rich; I have everything I want, or I seem as if I had everything. Very well, you must know that M. de Nucingen does not allow me the control of a single penny; he pays all the bills for the house expenses; he pays for my carriages and opera box; he does not give me enough to pay for my dress, and he reduces me to poverty in secret on purpose. I am too proud to beg from him. I should be the vilest of women if I could take his money at the price at which he offers it. Do you ask how I, with seven hundred thousand francs of my own, could let myself be robbed? It is because I was proud, and scorned to speak. We are so young, so artless when our married life begins! I never could bring myself to ask my husband for money; the words would have made my lips bleed, I did not dare to ask; I spent my savings first, and then the money that my poor father gave me, then I ran into debt. Marriage for me is a hideous farce; I cannot talk about it; let it suffice to say that Nucingen and I have separate rooms, and that I would fling myself out of the window sooner than consent to any other manner of life. I suffered agonies when I had to confess to my girlish extravagance, my debts for jewelry and trifles (for our poor father had never refused us anything, and spoiled us), but at last I found courage to tell him about them. After all, I had a fortune of my own. Nucingen flew into a rage; he said that I should be the ruin of him, and used frightful language; I wished myself a hundred feet down in the earth. He had my dowry, so he paid my debts, but he stipulated at the same time that my expenses in the future must not exceed a certain fixed sum, and I gave way for the sake of peace. And then," she went on, "I wanted to gratify the self-love of some one whom you know. He may have deceived me, but I should do him the justice to say that there was nothing petty in his character. But, after all, he threw me over disgracefully. If, at a woman's utmost need, *somebody* heaps gold upon her, he ought never to forsake her; that love should last for ever! But you, at one-and-twenty, you, the soul of honor, with the unsullied conscience of youth, will ask me how a woman can bring herself to accept money in such a way. *Mon Dieu!* is it not natural to share everything with the one to whom we owe our happiness? When all has been given, why should we pause and hesitate over a part? Money is as nothing between us until the moment when the sentiment that bound us together ceases to exist. Were we not bound to each other for life? Who that believes in love foresees such an end of love? You swear to love us eternally; how, then, can our interests be separate?

"You do not know how I suffered to-day when Nucingen refused to give me six thousand francs; he spends as much as that every month on his mistress, an opera dancer! I thought of killing myself. The wildest thoughts came into my head. There have been moments in my life when I have envied my servants, and would have changed places with my maid. It was madness to think of going to our father, Anastasie and I have bled him dry; our poor father would have sold himself if he could have raised six thousand francs that way. I should have driven him frantic to no purpose. You have saved me from shame and death; I was beside myself with anguish. Ah! monsieur, I owed you this explanation after my mad ravings. When you left me just now, as soon as you were out of sight, I longed to escape, to run away—— where, I did not know. Half the women in Paris lead such lives as mine; they live in apparent luxury, and in their souls are tormented by anxiety. I know of poor creatures even more miserable than I; there are women who are driven to ask their tradespeople to make out false bills, women who rob their husbands. Some men believe that an India shawl worth a hundred louis only cost five hundred francs, others that a shawl costing five hundred francs is worth a hundred louis. There are women, too, with narrow incomes, who scrape and save and starve their children to pay for a dress. I am innocent of these base meannesses. But this is the last extremity of my torture. Some women will sell themselves to their husbands, and so obtain their way, but I, at any rate, am free. If I chose, Nucingen would cover me with gold, but I would rather weep on the breast of a man whom I can respect. Ah! to-night, M. de Marsay will no longer have a right to think of me as a woman whom he has paid." She tried to conceal her tears from him, hiding her face in her hands; Eugène drew them away and looked at her; she seemed to him sublime at that moment.

"It is hideous, is it not," she cried, "to speak in a breath of money and affection? You cannot love me after this," she added.

The incongruity between the ideas of honor which make women so great and the errors in conduct which are forced upon them by the constitution of society had thrown Eugène's thoughts into confusion; he uttered soothing and consoling words, and wondered at the beautiful woman before him, and at the artless imprudence of her cry of pain.

"You will not remember this against me?" she asked; "promise me that you will not."

"Ah! madame, I am incapable of doing so," he said. She took his hand and held it to her heart, a movement full of grace that expressed her deep gratitude.

"I am free and happy once more, thanks to you," she said. "Oh! I have felt lately as if I were in the grasp of an iron hand. But after this I mean to live simply and to spend nothing. You will think me just as pretty, will you not, my friend? Keep this," she went on, as she took only six of the bank-notes. "In conscience I owe you a thousand crowns, for I really ought to go halves with you."

Eugène's maiden conscience resisted; but when the Baroness said, "I am bound to look on you as an accomplice or as an enemy," he took the money.

"It shall be a last stake in reserve," he said, "in case of misfortune."

"That was what I was dreading to hear," she cried, turning pale. "Oh, if you would that I should be anything to you, swear to me that you will never re-enter a gaming-house. Great heaven! that I should corrupt you! I should die of sorrow!"

They had reached the Rue Saint-Lazare by this time. The contrast between the ostentation of wealth in the house and the wretched condition of its mistress dazed the student; and Vautrin's cynical words began to ring in his ears.

"Seat yourself there," said the Baroness, pointing to a low chair beside the fire. "I have a difficult letter to write," she added. "Tell me what to say."

"Say nothing," Eugène answered her. "Put the bills in an envelope, direct it, and send it by your maid."

"Why, you are a love of a man," she said. "Ah! see what it is to have been well brought up. That is the Beauséant through and through," she went on, smiling at him.

"She is charming," thought Eugène, more and more in love. He looked round him at the room; there was an ostentatious character about the luxury, a meretricious taste in the splendor.

"Do you like it?" she asked, as she rang for her maid.

"Thérèse, take this to M. de Marsay, and give it into his hands yourself. If he is not at home, bring the letter back to me."

Thérèse went, but not before she had given Eugène a spiteful glance.

Dinner was announced. Rastignac gave his arm to Mme. de Nucingen, she led the way into a pretty dining-room, and again he saw the luxury of the table which he had admired in his cousin's house.

"Come and dine with me on opera evenings, and we will go to the Italiens afterwards," she said.

"I should soon grow used to the pleasant life if it could last, but I am a poor student, and I have my way to make."

"Oh! you will succeed," she said, laughing. "You will see. All that you wish will come to pass. *I* did not expect to be so happy."

It is the wont of women to prove the impossible by the possible, and to annihilate facts by presentiments. When Mme. de Nucingen and Rastignac took their places in her box at the Bouffons, her face wore a look of happiness that made her so lovely that every one indulged in those small slanders against which women are defenseless; for the scandal that is uttered lightly is often seriously believed. Those who know Paris believe nothing that is said, and say nothing of what is done there.

Eugène took the Baroness' hand in his, and by some light pressure of the fingers, or a closer grasp of the hand, they found a language in which to express the sensations which the music gave them. It was an evening of intoxicating delight for both; and when it ended, and they went out together, Mme. de Nucingen insisted on taking Eugène with her as far as the Pont Neuf, he disputing with her the whole of the way for a single kiss after all those that she had showered upon him so passionately at the Palais-Royal; Eugène reproached her with inconsistency.

"That was gratitude," she said, "for devotion that I did not dare to hope for, but now it would be a promise."

"And will you give me no promise, ingrate?"

He grew vexed. Then, with one of those impatient gestures that fill a lover with ecstasy, she gave him her hand to kiss, and he took it with a discontented air that delighted her.

"I shall see you at the ball on Monday," she said.

As Eugène went home in the moonlight, he fell to serious reflections. He was satisfied, and yet dissatisfied. He was pleased with an adventure which would probably give him his desire, for in the end one of the prettiest and best-dressed women in Paris would be his; but, as a set-off, he saw his hopes of fortune brought to nothing; and, as soon as he realized this fact, the vague thoughts of yesterday evening began to take a more decided shape in his mind. A check is sure to reveal to us the strength of our hopes. The more Eugène learned of the pleasures of life in Paris, the more impatient he felt of poverty and obscurity. He crumpled the bank-note in his pocket, and found any quantity of plausible excuses for appropriating it.

He reached the Rue Neuve-Sainte-Geneviève at last, and from the stairhead he saw a light in Goriot's room; the old man had lighted a candle, and set the door ajar, lest the student should pass him by, and go to his room without "telling him all about his daughter," to use his own expression. Eugène, accordingly, told him everything that transpired and without reserve.

"Then they think that I am ruined!" cried Father Goriot, in an agony of jealousy and desperation. "Why, I have still thirteen hundred livres a year! *Mon Dieu!* Poor little girl! why did she not come to me? I would have sold my *rentes;* she should have had some of the principal, and I would have bought a life-annuity with the rest. My good neighbor, why did *you* not come to tell me of her difficulty? How had you the heart to go and risk her poor little hundred francs at play? This is heart-breaking work. You see what it is to have sons-in-law. Oh! if I had hold of them, I would wring their necks. *Mon Dieu! crying!* Did you say she was crying?"

"With her head on my waistcoat," said Eugène.

"Oh! give it to me," said Father Goriot. "What! my daughter's tears have fallen there—my darling Delphine, who never used to cry when she was a little girl! Oh! I will buy you another; do not wear it again; let me have it. By the terms of her marriage-contract she ought to have the use of her property. To-morrow morning I will go and see Derville; he is an attorney. I will demand that her money should be invested in her own name. I know the law. I am an old wolf; I will show my teeth."

"Here, father; this is a bank-note for a thousand francs that she wanted me to keep out of our winnings. Keep them for her, in the pocket of the waistcoat."

Goriot looked hard at Eugène, reached out and took the law-student's hand, and Eugène felt a tear fall on it.

"You will succeed," the old man said. "God is just, you see. I know an honest man when I see him, and I can tell you, there are not many men like you. I am to have another dear child in you, am I? There, go to sleep; you can sleep, you are not yet a father. She was crying! and I have to be told about it!—and I was quietly eating my dinner, like an idiot, all the time—I, who would sell my soul to save one tear to either of them."

"An honest man!" said Eugène to himself as he lay down. "Upon my word, I think I will be an honest man all my life; it is so pleasant to obey the voice of conscience." Perhaps none but believers in God do good in secret; and Eugène believed in a God.

The next day Rastignac went at the appointed time to Mme. de Beauséant, who took him with her to the Duchesse de Carigliano's ball. The Duchesse received Eugène most graciously. Mme. de Nucingen was there. Delphine's dress seemed to suggest that she wished for the admiration of others, so that she might shine the more in Eugène's eyes; she was eagerly expecting a glance from him, hiding, as she thought, this eagerness from all beholders. This moment is full of charm for the one who can guess all that passes in a woman's mind. Who has not refrained from giving his opinion, to prolong her suspense, concealing his pleasure from a desire to tantalize, seeking a confession of love in her uneasiness, enjoying the fears that he can dissipate by a smile? In the course of the evening the law student suddenly comprehended his position; he saw that, as the cousin of Mme. de Beauséant, he was a personage in this world. He was already credited with the conquest of Mme. de Nucingen, and for this reason was a conspicuous figure; he caught the envious glances of other young men, and experienced the earliest pleasures of coxcombry. People wondered at his luck, and scraps of these conversations came to his ears as he went from room to room; all the women prophesied his success; and Delphine, in her dread of losing him, promised that this evening she would not refuse the kiss that all his entreaties could scarcely win yesterday.

Rastignac received several invitations. His cousin presented him to other women who were present; women who could claim to be of the highest fashion; whose houses were looked upon as pleasant; and this was the loftiest and most fashionable society in Paris into which he was launched. So this evening had all the charm of a brilliant *début;* it was an evening that he was to remember even in old age, as a woman looks back on her first ball and the memories of her girlish triumphs.

The next morning at breakfast, he related the story of his success for the benefit of Father Goriot and the lodgers. Vautrin began to smile in a diabolical fashion.

"And do you suppose," cried that cold-blooded logician, "that a young man of fashion can live here in the Rue Neuve-Sainte-Geneviève, in the Maison Vauquer—an exceedingly respectable boarding-house in every way, I grant you, but an establishment that, none the less, falls short of being fashionable? The house is comfortable, it is lordly in its abundance; it is proud to be the temporary abode of a Rastignac; but, after all, it is in the Rue Neuve-Sainte-Geneviève, and luxury would be out of place here, where we only aim at the purely *patriarchalorama*. If you mean to cut a figure in Paris, my young friend," Vautrin continued, with half-paternal jocularity, "you must have three horses, a tilbury for the mornings, and a closed carriage for the evenings; you should spend altogether about nine thousand francs on your stables. You would show yourself unworthy of your destiny if you spent no more than three thousand francs with your tailor, six hundred in perfumery, a hundred crowns to your shoemaker, and a hundred more to your hatter. As for your laundress, there goes another thousand francs; a young man of fashion must of necessity make a great point of his linen; if your linen comes up to the required standard, people often do not look any farther. Love and the church demand a fair altarcloth. That is fourteen thousand francs. I am saying nothing of losses at play, bets, and presents; it is impossible to allow less than two thousand francs for pocket money. I have led that sort of life, and I know all about these expenses. Add the cost of necessaries next; three hundred louis for provender, a thousand francs for a place to roost in. Well, my boy, for all these little wants of ours we had need to have twenty-five thousand francs every year in our purse, or we shall find ourselves in the kennel, and people laughing at us, and our career is cut short, good-by to success, and good-by to your mistress. I am forgetting your valet and your groom! Is Christophe going to carry your *billets-doux* for you? And do you mean to employ the stationery you use at present? Suicidal policy! Hearken to the wisdom of your elders!" he went on, his bass voice growing louder at each syllable. "Either take up your quarters in a garret, live virtuously, and wed your work, or set about the thing in a different way."

Vautrin winked and leered in the direction of Mlle. Taillefer to enforce his remarks by a look which recalled the late tempting proposals by which he had sought to corrupt the student's mind.

Several days went by, and Rastignac lived in a whirl of gaiety. He dined almost every day with Mme. de Nucingen, and went wherever she went, only returning to the Rue Neuve-Sainte-Geneviève in the small hours. He rose at mid-day, and dressed to go into the Bois with Delphine if the day was fine, squandering in this way time that was worth far more than he knew. He turned as eagerly to learn the lessons of luxury, and was as quick to feel its fascination as the flowers of the date palm to receive the fertilizing pollen. He played high, lost and won large sums of money, and at last became accustomed to the extravagant life that young men lead in Paris. He sent fifteen hundred francs out of his first winnings to his mother and sisters, sending handsome presents as well as the money, He had given out that he meant to leave the Maison Vauquer; but January came and went, and he was still there, still unprepared to go.

One rule holds good of most young men—whether rich or poor. They never have money for the necessaries of life, but they always have money to spare for their caprices—an anomaly which finds its explanation in their youth and in the almost frantic eagerness with which youth grasps at pleasure. They are reckless with anything obtained on credit, while everything for which they must pay in ready money is made to last as long as possible; if they cannot have all that they want, they make up for it, it would seem, by squandering what they have. To state the matter simply—a student is far more careful of his hat than of his coat, because the latter being a comparatively costly article of dress, it is in the nature of things that a tailor should be a creditor; but it is otherwise with the hatter; the sums of money spent with him are so modest that he is the most independent and unmanageable of his tribe, and it is almost impossible to bring him to terms. The young man in the balcony of a theatre who displays a gorgeous waistcoat for the benefit of the fair owners of opera glasses has very probably no socks in his wardrobe, for the hosier is another of the genus of weevils that nibble at the purse. This was Rastignac's condition. His purse was always empty for Mme. Vauquer, always full at the demand of vanity; there was a periodical ebb and flow in his fortunes, which was seldom favorable to the payment of just debts. If he was to leave that unsavory and mean abode, where from time to time his pretensions met with humiliation, the first step was to pay his hostess for a month's board and lodging, and the second to purchase furniture worthy of the new lodgings he must take in his quality of dandy, a course that remained impossible. Rastignac, out of his winnings at cards, could pay his jeweler exorbitant prices for gold watches and chains, and, then to meet the exigencies of play, would carry them to the pawnbroker, that discreet and forbidding-looking friend of youth; but when it was a question of paying for board or lodging, or for the necessary implements for the cultivation of his Elysian fields, his imagination and pluck alike deserted him. There was no inspiration to be found in vulgar necessity, in debts contracted for past requirements. Like most of those who trust to their luck, he put off till the last moment the payment of debts that among the bourgeoisie are regarded as sacred engagements, acting on the plan of Mirabeau, who never settled his baker's bill until it underwent a formidable transformation into a bill of exchange.

It was about this time, when Rastignac was down on his luck and fell into debt, that it became clear to the law-student's mind that he must have some more certain source of income if he meant to live as he had been doing. But while he groaned over the thorny problems of his precarious situation, he felt that he could not bring himself to renounce the pleasures of this extravagant life, and decided that he must continue it at all costs. His dreams of obtaining a fortune appeared more and more chimerical, and the real obstacles grew more formidable. His initiation into the secrets of the Nucingen household had revealed to him that if he were to attempt to use this love affair as a means of mending his fortunes, he must swallow down all sense of decency, and renounce all the generous ideas which redeem the sins of youth. He had chosen this life of apparent splendor, but secretly gnawed by the canker-worm of remorse, a life of fleeting pleasure dearly paid for by persistent pain; like "Le Distrait" of La Bruyère, he had descended so far as to make his bed in a ditch; but (also like "Le Distrait") he himself was uncontaminated as yet by the mire that stained his garments.

"So we have killed our mandarin, have we?" said Bianchon one day as they left the dinner table.

"Not yet," he answered, "but he is at the last gasp."

The medical student took this for a joke, but it was not a jest. Eugène had dined in the house that night for the first time in a long while, and had looked thoughtful during the meal. He had taken his place beside Mlle. Taillefer, and stayed through the dessert, giving his neighbor an expressive glance from time to time. A few of the boarders discussed the walnuts at the table, and others walked about the room, still taking part in a conversation which had begun among them. People usually went when they chose; the amount of time that they lingered being determined by the amount of interest that the conversation possessed for them, or by the difficulty of the process of digestion. In winter-time the room was seldom empty before eight o'clock, when the four women had it all to themselves, and made up for the silence previously imposed upon them by the preponderating masculine element. This evening Vautrin had noticed Eugène's abstractedness, and stayed in the room, though he had seemed to be in a hurry to finish his dinner and go. All through the talk afterwards he had kept out of sight of the law student, who quite believed that Vautrin had left the room. He now took up his position cunningly in the sitting-room instead of going when the last boarders went. He had fathomed the young man's thoughts, and felt that a crisis was at hand. Rastignac was, in fact, in a dilemma, which many another young man under similar circumstances must have most readily understood.

Mme. de Nucingen might love him, or might merely be playing with him, but in either case Rastignac had been made to experience all the alternations of hope and despair of genuine passion, and all the diplomatic arts of a Parisienne had been employed on him. After compromising herself by continually appearing in public with Mme. de Beauséant's cousin she still hesitated, and would not give him the lover's privileges which he appeared to enjoy. For a whole month she had so wrought on his senses, that at last she had made an impression on his heart. If in the earliest days the student had fancied himself to be the master, Mme. de Nucingen had since become the stronger of the two, for she had skillfully roused and played upon every instinct, good or bad, in the two or three men comprised in a young student in Paris. This was not the result of deep design on her part, nor was she playing a part, for women are in a manner true to themselves even through their grossest deceit, because their actions are prompted by a natural impulse. It may have been that Delphine, who had allowed this young man to gain such an ascendency over her, conscious that she had been too demonstrative, was obeying a sentiment of dignity, and either repented of her concessions, or it pleased her to suspend them. It is so natural to a Parisienne, even when passion has almost mastered her, to hesitate and pause before taking the plunge; to probe the heart of him to whom she intrusts her future. And once already Mme. de Nucingen's hopes had been betrayed, and her loyalty to a selfish young lover had been despised. She had good reason to be suspicious. Or it may have been that something in Eugène's manner (for his rapid success was making a coxcomb of him) had warned her that the grotesque nature of their position had lowered her somewhat in his eyes. She doubtless wished to assert her dignity; he was young, and she would be great in his eyes; for the lover who had forsaken her had so underestimated her that she was determined that Eugène should not think her an easy conquest, and for this very reason—he knew that de Marsay had been his predecessor. Finally, after the degradation of submission to the pleasure of a heartless young rake, it was so sweet for her to wander in the flower-strewn realms of love, that it was not wonderful that she should wish to dwell a while on the prospect, to tremble with the vibrations of love, to feel the freshness of the breath of its dawn. The true lover was suffering for the sins of the false. This inconsistency is unfortunately only to be expected so long as men do not know how many flowers are mown down in a young woman's soul by the first stroke of treachery.

Whatever her reasons may have been, Delphine was playing with Rastignac, and took pleasure in playing with him, doubtless because she felt sure of his love, and confident that she could put an end to the torture as soon as it was her royal pleasure to do so. Eugène's self-love was engaged; he could not suffer his first passage of love to end in a defeat, and persisted in his suit, like a sportsman determined to bring down at least one partridge to celebrate his first Feast of Saint Hubert. The pressure of anxiety, his wounded self-love, his despair, real or feigned, drew him nearer and nearer to this woman. All Paris credited him with this conquest, and yet he was conscious that he had made no progress since the day when he saw Mme. de Nucingen for the first time. He did not know as yet that a woman's coquetry is sometimes more delightful than the pleasure of secure possession of her love, and was possessed with helpless rage. If, at this time, while she denied herself to love, Eugène gathered the springtide spoils of his life, the fruit, somewhat sharp and green, and dearly bought, was no less delicious to the taste. There were moments when he had not a *sou* in his pockets, and at such times he thought in spite of his conscience of Vautrin's offer and the possibility of fortune by a marriage with Mlle. Taillefer. Poverty would clamor so loudly that more than once he was on the point of yielding to the cunning temptations of the terrible sphinx, whose glance had so often exerted a strange spell over him. His dilemma, in short, at this time proved most perplexing, and he felt greatly depressed in spirit.

Poiret and Mlle. Michonneau went up to their rooms; and Rastignac, thinking that he was alone with the women in the dining-room, sat between Mme. Vauquer and Mme. Couture, who was nodding over the woolen cuffs that she was knitting by the stove, and looked at Mlle. Taillefer so tenderly that she lowered her eyes.

"Can you be in trouble, M. Eugène?" Victorine said after a pause.

"Who has not his troubles?" answered Rastignac. "If we men were sure of being loved, sure of a devotion which would be our reward for the sacrifices which we are always ready to make, then perhaps we should have no troubles."

For answer Mlle. Taillefer only gave him a glance, but it was impossible to mistake its meaning.

"You, for instance, mademoiselle; you feel sure of your heart to-day, but are you sure that it will never change?"

A smile flitted over the poor girl's lips; it seemed as if a ray of light from her soul had lighted up her face. Eugène was dismayed at the sudden explosion of feeling caused by his words.

"Ah! but suppose," he said, "that you should be rich and happy to-morrow, suppose that a vast fortune dropped down from the clouds for you, would you still love the man whom you loved in your days of poverty?"

A charming movement of the head was her only answer to the question propounded.

"Even if he were very poor?"

Again the same mute answer.

"What nonsense you are talking, you two?" exclaimed Mme. Vauquer.

"Never mind," answered Eugène; "we understand each other."

"So there is to be an engagement of marriage between M. le Chevalier Eugène de Rastignac and Mlle. Victorine Taillefer, is there!" The words were uttered in Vautrin's deep voice, and Vautrin appeared at the door as he spoke.

"Oh! how you startled me!" Mme. Couture and Mme. Vauquer exclaimed together.

"I might make a worse choice," said Rastignac, laughing. Vautrin's voice had thrown him into the most painful agitation that he had yet known.

"No bad jokes, gentlemen!" said Mme. Couture. "My dear, let us go upstairs."

Mme. Vauquer followed the two ladies, meaning to pass the evening in their room, an arrangement that economized fire and candlelight. Eugène and Vautrin were left alone.

"I felt sure you would come round to it," said the elder man with the coolness that nothing seemed to shake. "But stay a moment. I have as much delicacy as anybody else. Don't make up your mind on the spur of the moment; you are a little thrown off your balance just now. You are in debt, and I want you to come over to my way of thinking after sober reflection, and not in a fit of passion or desperation. Perhaps you want a thousand crowns. There, you can have them if you like."

The tempter took out a pocket-book, and drew thence three bank-notes, which he fluttered before the student's eyes. Eugène was in a most painful dilemma. He had debts, debts of honor. He owed a hundred louis to the Marquis d'Ajuda and to the Comte de Trailles; he had not the money, and for this reason had not dared to go to Mme. de Restaud's house, where he was expected that evening. It was one of those informal gatherings where tea and little cakes are handed round, but where it is possible to lose six thousand francs at whist in the course of a night.

"You must see," said Eugène, struggling to hide a convulsive tremor, "that after what has passed between us, I cannot possibly lay myself under any obligation to you."

"Quite right; I should be sorry to hear you speak otherwise," answered the tempter. "You are a fine young fellow, honorable, brave as a lion, and as gentle as a young girl. You would be a fine haul for the devil! I like youngsters of your sort. Get rid of one or two more prejudices, and you will see the world as it is. Make a little scene now and then, and act a virtuous part in it, and a man with a head on his shoulders can do exactly as he likes amid deafening applause

from the fools in the gallery. Ah! a few days yet, and you
will be with us; and if you would only be tutored by me, I
would put you in the way of achieving all your ambitions.
You should no sooner form a wish than it should be realized
to the full; you should have all your desires—honors, wealth,
or women. Civilization should flow with milk and honey for
you. You should be our pet and favorite, our Benjamin. We
would all work ourselves to death for you with pleasure; every
obstacle should be removed from your path. You have a few
prejudices left; so you think that I am a scoundrel, do you?
Well, M. de Turenne, quite as honorable a man as you take
yourself to be, had some little private transactions with bandits,
and did not feel that his honor was tarnished. You would
rather not lay under any obligation to me, eh? You need not
draw back on that account," Vautrin went on, and a smile
stole over his lips. "Take those bits of paper and write
across this," he added, producing a piece of stamped paper,
"*Accepted the sum of three thousand five hundred francs due this
day twelvemonth*, and fill in the date. The rate of interest is
stiff enough to silence any scruples on your part; it gives you
the right to call me a Jew. You can call quits with me on
the score of gratitude. I am quite willing that you should
despise me to-day, because I am sure that you will have a
kindlier feeling towards me later on. You will find out
fathomless depths in my nature, enormous and concentrated
forces that weaklings call vices, but you will never find me
base or ungrateful. In short, I am neither a pawn nor a
bishop, but a castle, a tower of strength, my boy."

"What manner of man are you?" cried Eugène. "Were
you created to torment me?"

"Why, no; I am a good-natured fellow, who is willing to do
a dirty piece of work to put you high and dry above the mire
for the rest of your days. Do you ask the reason of this
devotion? All right; I will tell you that some of these days.
A word or two in your ear will explain it. I have begun by

shocking you, by showing you the way to ring the changes, and giving you a sight of the mechanism of the social machine; but your first fright will go off like a conscript's terror on the battlefield. You will grow used to regarding men as common soldiers who have made up their minds to lose their lives for some self-constituted king. Times have altered strangely. Once you could say to a bravo, ' Here are a hundred crowns; go and kill Monsieur So-and-so for me,' and you could sup quietly after turning some one off into the dark for the least thing in the world. But nowadays I propose to put you in the way of a handsome fortune: you have only to nod your head, it won't compromise you in any way, and you hesitate. 'Tis an effeminate age."

Eugène accepted the draft, and received the bank-notes in exchange for it.

"Well, well. Come, now, let us talk rationally," Vautrin continued. "I mean to leave this country in a few months' time for America, and set about planting tobacco. I will send you the cigars of friendship. If I make money at it, I will help you in your career. If I have no children—which will probably be the case, for I have no anxiety to raise slips of myself here—you shall inherit my fortune. That is what you may call standing by a man; but I myself have a liking for you. I have a mania, too, for devoting myself to some one else. I have done it before. You see, my boy, I live in a loftier sphere than other men do; I look on all actions as means to an end, and the end is all that I look at. What is a man's life to me? Not *that*," he said, and he snapped his thumb-nail against his teeth. "A man, in short, is everything to me, or just nothing at all. Less than nothing if his name happens to be Poiret; you can crush him like a bug, he is flat and he is offensive. But a man is a god when he is like you; he is not a machine covered with a skin, but a theatre in which the greatest sentiments are displayed—great thoughts and feelings—and for these, and these only, I live. A sentiment—what is that but the whole world in a thought? Look at Father Goriot. For him, his two girls are the whole universe; they are the clue by which he finds his way through creation. Well, for my own part, and I have fathomed the depths of life, there is only one real sentiment—comradeship between man and man. Pierre and Jaffier, that is my passion. I know "Venice Preserved" by heart. Have you met many men plucky enough when a comrade says, ' Let us bury a dead body!' to go and do it without a word or plaguing him by taking a high moral tone? I have done it myself. I should not talk like this to just everybody, but you are not like an ordinary man; one can talk to you, you can understand things. You will not dabble about much longer among the tadpoles in these swamps. Well, then, it is all settled. You will marry. Both of us carry our point. Mine is made of iron, and will never soften, he! he!"

Vautrin went out. He would not wait to hear the student's repudiation, he wished to put Eugène at his ease. He seemed to understand the secret springs of the faint resistance still made by the younger man; the struggles in which men seek to preserve their self-respect by justifying their blameworthy actions to themselves.

"He may do as he likes; I shall not marry Mlle. Taillefer, that is certain," said Eugène to himself.

He regarded this man with abhorrence, and yet the very cynicism of Vautrin's ideas, and the audacious way in which he used other men for his own ends, raised him in the student's eyes; but the thought of a compact threw Eugène into a fever of apprehension, and not until he had recovered somewhat did he dress, call for a cab, and go to Mme. de Restaud's.

For some days the Countess had paid more and more attention to a young man whose every step seemed a triumphal progress in the great world; it seemed to her that he might be a formidable power before long. He paid Messieurs de Trailles and d'Ajuda, played at whist for part of the evening, and made good his losses. Most men who have their way to make are more or less fatalists, and Eugène was superstitious; he chose to consider that his luck was heaven's reward for his perseverance in the right way. As soon as possible on the following morning he asked Vautrin whether the bill that he had given was still in the other's possession; and on receiving a reply in the affirmative, he repaid the three thousand francs with a not unnatural relief.

"Everything is going on well," said Vautrin.

"But I am not your accomplice," said Eugène.

"I know, I know," Vautrin broke in. "You are still acting like a child. You are making mountains out of molehills at the outset."

Two days later, Poiret and Mlle. Michonneau were sitting together on a bench in the sun. They had chosen a little frequented alley in the Jardin des Plantes, and a gentleman was chatting with them, the same person, as a matter of fact, about whom the medical student had, not without good reason, his own suspicions.

"Mademoiselle," this M. Gondureau was saying, "I do not see any cause for your scruples. His excellency monseigneur the minister of police——"

"Ah!" echoed Poiret, "His excellency monseigneur the minister of police!"

"Yes, his excellency is taking a personal interest in the matter," said Gondureau.

Who would think it probable that Poiret, a retired clerk, doubtless possessed of some notions of civic virtue, though there might be nothing else in his head—who would think it likely that such a man would continue to lend an ear to this supposed independent gentleman of the Rue de Buffon, when the latter dropped the mask of a decent citizen by that word "police," and gave a glimpse of the features of a detective from the Rue de Jérusalem? And yet nothing was more natural. Perhaps the following remarks from the hitherto unpublished records made by certain observers will throw a light on the particular species to which Poiret belonged in the great family of fools. There is a race of quill-drivers, confined in the columns of the budget between the first degree of latitude (a kind of administrative Greenland where the salaries begin at twelve hundred francs) to the third degree, a more temperate zone, where incomes grow from three to six thousand francs, a climate where the *bonus* flourishes like a half-hardy annual in spite of some difficulties of culture. A characteristic trait that best reveals the feeble narrow-mindedness of these inhabitants of petty officialdom is a kind of involuntary, mechanical, and instinctive reverence for the Grand Lama of every ministry, known to the rank and file only by his signature (an illegible scrawl) and by his title—" His excellency monseigneur le minister," five words which produce as much effect as the *il Bondo Cani* of the *Calife de Bagdad*, five words which in the eyes of this low order of intelligence represent a sacred power from which there is no appeal. The minister is administratively infallible for the clerks in the employ of the government, as the pope is infallible for good Catholics. Something of his peculiar radiance invests everything he does or says, or that is said or done in his name ; the robe of office covers everything and legalizes everything done by his orders ; does not his very title—his excellency—vouch for the purity of his intentions and the righteousness of his will, and serve as a sort of passport and introduction to ideas that otherwise would not be entertained for a moment ? Pronounce the words "his excellency," and these poor folk will forthwith proceed to do what they would not do for their own interests. Passive obedience is as well known in a government department as in the army itself ; and the administrative system silences consciences, annihilates the individual, and ends (give it time enough) by fashioning a man into a vice or a thumbscrew, and he becomes part of the machinery of government. Wherefore, M. Gondureau, who seemed to know something of human nature, recognized Poiret at once as one of these dupes of officialdom, and brought out for his benefit, at the proper moment, the *deus ex machinâ*, the magical words "his excellency," so as to dazzle Poiret just as he himself unmasked his batteries, for he took Poiret and the Michonneau for the male and female of the same species.

"If his excellency himself, his excellency the minister—— Ah! that is quite another thing," said Poiret.

"You seem to be guided by this gentleman's opinion, and you hear what he says," said the man of independent means, addressing Mlle. Michonneau. "Very well, his excellency is at this moment absolutely certain that the so-called Vautrin, who lodges at the Maison Vauquer, is a convict who escaped from penal servitude at Toulon, where he is known by the nickname *Trompe-la-Mort.*"

"Trompe-la-Mort?" said Poiret. "Dear me, he is very lucky if he deserves that nickname."

"Well, yes," said the detective. "They call him so because he has been so lucky as not to lose his life in the very risky businesses that he has carried through. He is a dangerous man, you see! He has qualities that are out of the common; the thing he is wanted for, in fact, was a matter which gained him no end of credit with his own set——"

"Then he is a man of honor?" asked Poiret.

"Yes, according to his notions. He agreed to take another man's crime upon himself—a forgery committed by a very handsome young fellow that he had taken a great fancy to, a young Italian, a bit of a gambler, who has since gone into the army, where his conduct has been unexceptionable."

"But if his excellency the minister of police is certain that M. Vautrin is this *Trompe-la-Mort*, why should he want me?" asked Mlle. Michonneau.

"Oh, yes," said Poiret, "if the minister, as you have been so obliging as to tell us, really knows for a certainty that——"

"Certainty is not the word; he only suspects. You will soon understand how things are. Jacques Collin, nicknamed *Trompe-la-Mort*, is in the confidence of every convict in the three prisons; he is their man of business and their banker. He makes a very good thing out of managing their affairs, which want a *man of mark* to see about them."

"Ha! ha! do you see the pun, mademoiselle?" asked Poiret. "This gentleman calls him a *man of mark* because he is a *marked man*—branded, you know."

"This so-called Vautrin," said the detective, "receives the money belonging to my lords the convicts, invests it for them, and holds it at the disposal of those who escape, or hands it over to their families if they leave a will, or to their mistresses when they draw upon him for their benefit."

"Their mistresses! You mean their wives," remarked Poiret.

"No, sir. A convict's wife is usually an illegitimate connection. We call them concubines."

"Then they all live in a state of concubinage?"

"Naturally."

"Why, these are abominations that his excellency ought not to allow. Since you have the honor of seeing his excellency, you, who seem to have philanthropic ideas, ought really to enlighten him as to their immoral conduct—they are setting a shocking example to the rest of society."

"But the government does not hold them up as models of all the virtues, my dear sir."

"Of course not, sir; but still——"

"Just let the gentleman say what he has to say, dearie," said Mlle. Michonneau.

"You see how it is, mademoiselle," Gondureau continued. "The government may have the strongest reasons for getting this illicit hoard into its hands; it mounts up to something considerable, by all that we can make out. Trompe-la-Mort not only holds very large sums for his friends the convicts, but he has other amounts which are paid over to him by the Society of the Ten Thousand——"

"Ten Thousand Thieves!" cried Poiret at this, in the utmost alarm.

"No. The Society of the Ten Thousand is not an association of petty offenders, but of people who set about their work on a large scale—they won't touch a matter unless there are ten thousand francs in it. It is composed of the most distinguished of the men who are sent straight to the assize courts when they come up for trial. They know the Code too well to risk their necks when they are nabbed. Collin is their confidential agent and legal adviser. By means of the large sums of money at his disposal he has established a sort of detective system of his own; it is widespread, and mysterious in its workings. We have had spies all about him for a twelvemonth, and yet we could not manage to fathom his games. His capital and his cleverness are at the service of vice and crime; this money furnishes the necessary funds for a regular army of blackguards in his pay who wage incessant war against society. If we can catch Trompe-la-Mort, and take possession of his funds, we should strike at the root of this evil. So this job is a kind of government affair—a state secret—and likely to redound to the honor of those who bring the thing to a successful conclusion. You, sir, for instance, might very well be taken into a government department again; they might make you secretary to a commissary of police; you could accept that post without prejudice to your retiring pension."

Mlle. Michonneau interposed at this point with, "What is there to hinder Trompe-la-Mort from making off with the money?"

"Oh!" said the detective, "a man is told off to follow him everywhere he goes, with orders to kill him if he were to rob the convicts. Then it is not quite as easy to make off with a lot of money as it is to run away with a young lady of family.

Besides, Collin is not the sort of fellow to play such a trick; he would be disgraced, according to his notions."

"You are quite right, sir," said Poiret, "utterly disgraced he would be."

"But none of all this explains why you do not come and take him without more ado," remarked Mlle. Michonneau.

"Very well, mademoiselle, I will explain—but," he added in her ear, "keep your companion quiet, or I shall never have done. The old boy ought to pay people handsomely for listening to him. Trompe-la-Mort, when he came back here," he went on aloud, "slipped into the skin of an honest man; he turned up disguised as a decent Parisian citizen, and took up his quarters in an unpretending lodging-house. He is cunning, that he is! You won't catch him napping. Then M. Vautrin is a man of consequeuce, who transacts a good deal of business."

"Naturally," said Poiret to himself.

"And suppose that the minister were to make a mistake and get hold of the real Vautrin, he would put every one's back up among the business men in Paris, and public opinion would be against him. M. le préfet de police is on slippery ground; he has enemies. They would take advantage of any mistake. There would be a fine outcry and fuss made by the Opposition, and he would be sent packing. We must set about this just as we did about the Cogniard affair, the sham Comte de Sainte-Hélène; if he had been the real Comte de Sainte-Hélène, we should have been in the wrong box. We want to be quite sure what we are about."

"Yes, but what you want is a pretty woman," said Mlle. Michonneau briskly.

"Trompe-la-Mort would not let a woman come near him," said the detective. "I will tell you a secret—he does not like them."

"Still, I do not see what I can do, supposing that I did agree to identify him for two thousand francs."

"Nothing simpler," said the stranger. "I will send you a little bottle containing a dose that will send a rush of blood to the head; it will do him no harm whatever, but he will fall down as if he were in a fit. The drug can be put into wine or coffee; either will do equally well. You carry your man to bed at once, and undress him to see that he is not dying. As soon as you are alone, you give him a slap on the shoulder, and, *presto!* the letters will appear."

"Why, that is just nothing at all," said Poiret, very complacently.

"Well, do you agree?" said Gondureau, addressing the old maid.

"But, my dear sir, suppose there are no letters at all," said Mlle. Michonneau; am I to have the two thousand francs all the same?"

"No."

"What will you give me, then?"

"Five hundred francs."

"It is quite a thing to do for so little! It lies on your conscience just the same, and I must quiet my conscience, sir."

"I assure you," said Poiret, "that mademoiselle has a great deal of conscience, and not only so, she is a very amiable person, and very intelligent."

"Well, now," Mlle. Michonneau went on, "make it three thousand francs if he is Trompe-la-Mort, and nothing at all if he is an ordinary man."

"Done!" said Gondureau, "but on condition that the thing is settled to-morrow."

"Not quite so soon, my dear sir; I must consult my confessor first."

"You are a sly one," said the detective as he rose to his feet. "Good-by till to-morrow, then. And if you should want to see me in a hurry, go to the Petite Rue Sainte-Anne at the bottom of the Cour de la Sainte-Chapelle. There is only one door under the archway. Ask there for M. Gondureau."

Bianchon, on his way back from Cuvier's lecture, overheard the sufficiently striking nickname of *Trompe-la-Mort,* and caught the celebrated chief detective's "*Done!*"

"Why didn't you close with him? It would be three hundred francs a year," said Poiret to Mlle. Michonneau.

"Why didn't I?" she asked. "Why, it wants thinking over. Suppose that M. Vautrin is this Trompe-la-Mort, perhaps we might do better for ourselves with him. Still, on the other hand, if you ask him for money, it would put him on his guard, and he is just the man to clear out without paying, and that would be an abominable sell."

"And suppose you did warn him," Poiret went on, "didn't that gentleman say that he was closely watched? You would spoil everything."

"Anyhow," thought Mlle. Michonneau, "I can't abide him. He says nothing but disagreeable things to me."

"But you can do better than that," Poiret resumed. "As that gentleman said (and he seemed to me to be a very good sort of man, besides being very well got up), it is an act of obedience to the laws to rid society of a criminal, however virtuous he may be. Once a thief, always a thief. Suppose he were to take it into his head to murder us all? The deuce! We should be guilty of manslaughter, and be the first to fall victims into the bargain!"

Mlle. Michonneau's musings did not permit her to listen very closely to the remarks that fell one by one from Poiret's lips like water dripping from a leaky tap. When once this elderly babbler began to talk, he would go on like clockwork unless Mlle. Michonneau stopped him. He started on some subject or other, and wandered on through parenthesis after parenthesis till he came to regions as remote as possible from his premises without coming to any conclusions by the way. By the time they reached the Maison Vauquer he had tacked together a whole string of examples and quotations more or less irrelevant to the subject in hand, which led him to give a full account of his own deposition in the case of the Sieur Ragoulleau *versus* Dame Morin, when he had been summoned as a witness for the defense.

As they entered the dining-room, Eugène de Rastignac was talking apart with Mlle. Taillefer; the conversation appeared to be of such thrilling interest that the pair never noticed the two older lodgers as they passed through the room. None of this was thrown away on Mlle. Michonneau.

"I knew how it would end," remarked that lady, addressing Poiret. "They have been making eyes at each other in a heart-rending way for a week past."

"Yes," he answered. "So she was found guilty."

"Who?"

"Mme. Morin."

"I am talking about Mlle. Victorine," said Mlle. Michonneau, as she entered Poiret's room with an absent air, "and you answer, ' Mme. Morin.' Who may Mme. Morin be?"

"What can Mlle. Victorine be guilty of?" demanded Poiret.

"Guilty of falling in love with M. Eugène de Rastignac, and going farther and farther without knowing exactly where she is going, poor innocent!"

That morning Mme. de Nucingen had driven Eugène to despair. In his own mind he had completely surrendered himself to Vautrin, and deliberately shut his eyes to the motive for the friendship which that extraordinary man professed for him, nor would he look to the consequences of such an alliance. Nothing short of a miracle could extricate him now out of the gulf into which he had walked an hour ago, when he exchanged vows in the softest whispers with Mlle. Taillefer. To Victorine it seemed as if she heard an angel's voice, that heaven was opening above her; the Maison Vauquer took

VAUTRIN CAME IN IN HIGH SPIRITS.

strange and wonderful hues, like a stage fairy palace. She loved and she was beloved; at any rate, she believed that she was loved; and what woman would not likewise have believed after seeing Rastignac's face and listening to the tones of his voice during that hour snatched under the argus eyes of the Maison Vauquer? He had trampled on his conscience; he knew that he was doing wrong, and did it deliberately; he had said to himself that a woman's happiness should atone for this venial sin. The energy of desperation had lent new beauty to his face; the lurid fire that burned in his heart shone from his eyes. Luckily for him, the miracle took place. Vautrin came in in high spirits, and at once read the hearts of these two young creatures whom he had brought together by the combinations of his infernal genius, but his deep voice broke in upon their bliss.

> *"A charming girl is my Fanchette*
> *In her simplicity,"*

he sang mockingly.

Victorine fled. Her heart was more full than it had ever been, but it was full of joy, and not of sorrow. Poor child! A pressure of the hand, the light touch of Rastignac's hair against her cheek, a word whispered in her ear so closely that she felt the student's warm breath on her, the pressure of a trembling arm about her waist, a kiss upon her throat—such had been her betrothal. The near neighborhood of the stout Sylvie, who might invade that glorified room at any moment, only made these first tokens of love more ardent, more eloquent, more entrancing than the noblest deeds done for love's sake in the most famous romances. This *plain-song* of love, to use the pretty expression of our forefathers, seemed almost criminal to the devout young girl who went to confession every fortnight. In that one hour she had poured out more of the treasures of her soul than she could give in later days of wealth and happiness, when her whole self followed the gift.

"The thing is arranged," Vautrin said to Eugène, who remained. "Our two dandies have fallen out. Everything was done in proper form. It is a matter of opinion. Our pigeon has insulted my hawk. They will meet to-morrow in the redoubt at Clignancourt. By half-past eight in the morning Mlle. Taillefer, calmly dipping her bread and butter in her coffee-cup, will be sole heiress of her father's fortune and affections. A funny way of putting it, isn't it? Taillefer's youngster is an expert swordsman, and quite cocksure about it, but he will be bled; I have just invented a thrust for his benefit, a way of raising your sword-point and driving it at the forehead. I must show you that thrust; it is an uncommonly handy thing to know."

Rastignac heard him in dazed bewilderment; he could not find a word in reply. Just then Goriot came in, and Bianchon and a few of the boarders likewise appeared.

"That is just as I intended," Vautrin said. "You know quite well what you are about. Good, my little eaglet! You are born to command, you are strong, you stand firm on your feet, you are game! I respect you."

He made as though he would take Eugène's hand, but Rastignac hastily withdrew it, sank into a chair, and turned ghastly pale; it seemed to him that there was a sea of blood before his eyes.

"Oh! so we have still a few dubious tatters of the swaddling-clothes of virtue about us!" murmured Vautrin. "But Papa Doliban has three millions; I know the amount of his fortune. Once have her dowry in your hands, and your character will be as white as the bride's white dress, even in your own eyes."

Rastignac hesitated no longer. He made up his mind that he would go that evening to warn the Taillefers, father and son. But just as Vautrin left him, Father Goriot came up and said in his ear, "You look melancholy, my boy; I will cheer you up. Come with me."

The old vermicelli-dealer lighted his dip at one of the lamps as he spoke. Eugène went with him, his curiosity had been aroused.

"Let us go up to your room," the worthy soul remarked, when he had asked Sylvie for the law-student's key. "This morning," he resumed, "you thought that *she* did not care about you, did you not, eh? She would have nothing to say to you, and you went away out of humor and out of heart. Stuff and rubbish! She wanted you to go because she was expecting *me!* Now do you understand? We were to complete the arrangements for taking some chambers for you, a jewel of a place, you are to move into it in three days' time. Don't split upon me. She wants it to be a surprise; but I couldn't bear to keep the secret from you. You will be in the Rue d'Artois, only a step or two from the Rue Saint-Lazare, and you are to be housed like a prince! Any one might have thought we were furnishing the house for a bride. Oh! we have done a lot of things in the last month, and you knew nothing about it. My attorney has appeared on the scene, and my daughter is to have thirty-six thousand francs a year, the interest on her money, and I shall insist on having her eight hundred thousand francs invested in sound securities, landed property that won't run away."

Eugène was dumb. He folded his arms and paced up and down his cheerless, untidy room. Father Goriot waited till the student's back was turned, and seized the opportunity to go to the chimney-piece and set upon it a little red morocco case with Rastignac's arms stamped in gold on the leather.

"My dear boy," said the kind soul, "I have been up to the eyes in this business. You see, there was plenty of selfishness on my part; I have an interested motive in helping you to change lodgings. You will not refuse me if I ask you something; will you, eh?"

"What is it?"

"There is a room on the fifth floor, up above your rooms,

that is to let along with them; that is where I am going to live, isn't that so? I am getting old; I am too far from my girls. I shall not be in the way, but I shall be there, that is all. You will come and talk to me about her every evening. It will not put you about, will it? I shall have gone to bed before you come in, but I shall hear you come up, and I shall say to myself, 'He has just seen my little Delphine. He has been to a dance with her, and she is happy, thanks to him.' If I were ill, it would do my heart good to hear you moving about below, to know when you leave the house and when you come in. It is only a step to the Champs-Élysées, where they go every day, so I shall be sure of seeing them, whereas now I am sometimes too late. And then—perhaps she may come to see you! I shall hear her, I shall see her in her soft quilted pelisse tripping about as daintily as a kitten. In this one month she has become my little girl again, so light-hearted and gay. Her soul is recovering, and her happiness is owing to you. Oh! I would do impossibilities for you. Only just now she said to me, 'I am very happy, papa!' When they say 'father' stiffly, it sends a chill through me; but when they call me 'papa,' it is as if they were little girls again, and it brings all the old memories back. I feel most their father then; I even believe that they belong to me, and to no one else."

The good man wiped his eyes, he was crying.

"It is a long while since I have heard them talk like that, a long, long time since she took my arm as she did to-day. Yes, indeed, it must be quite ten years since I walked side by side with one of my girls. How pleasant it was to keep step with her, to feel the touch of her gown, the warmth of her arm! Well, I took Delphine everywhere this morning; I went shopping with her, and I brought her home again. Oh! you must let me live near you. You may want some one to do you a service some of these days, and I shall be on the spot to do it. Oh! if only that great dolt of an Alsatian would die, if his gout would have the sense to attack his stomach, how happy my poor child would be! You would be my son-in-law; you would be her husband in the eyes of the world. Bah! she has known no happiness, that excuses everything. Our Father in heaven is surely on the side of fathers on earth who love their children. How fond of you she is!" he said, raising his head after a pause. "All the time we were going about together she chatted away about you. 'He is nice-looking, papa; isn't he? He is kind-hearted! Does he talk to you about me?' Pshaw! she said enough about you to fill whole volumes; between the Rue d'Artois and the Passage des Panoramas she poured her heart out into mine. I did not feel old once during that delightful morning; I felt as light as a feather. I told her how you had given that bank-note to me; it moved my darling to tears. But what can this be on your chimney-piece!" said Father Goriot at last. Rastignac had showed no sign, and he was dying of impatience.

Eugène stared at his neighbor in dumb and dazed bewilderment. He thought of Vautrin, of that duel to be fought tomorrow morning, and of this realization of his dearest hopes, and the violent contrast between the two sets of ideas gave him all the sensations of nightmare. He went to the chimney-piece, saw the little square case, opened it, and found a watch of Bréguet's make wrapped in paper, on which these words were written:

"I want you to think of me every hour, *because*——
"DELPHINE."

That last word doubtless contained an allusion to some scene that had taken place between them. Eugène felt touched. Inside the gold watch-case his arms had been wrought in enamel. The chain, the key, the workmanship, and design of the trinket were all such as he had imagined, for he had long coveted such a possession. Father Goriot was radiant. Of course he had promised to tell his daughter every little detail of the scene and of the effect produced upon Eugène by her present; he shared in the pleasure and excitement of the young people, and seemed to be not the least happy of the three. He loved Rastignac already for his own as well as for his daughter's sake.

"You must go and see her; she is expecting you this evening. That great lout of an Alsatian is going to have supper with his opera-dancer. Aha! he looked very foolish when my attorney let him know where he was. He says he idolizes my daughter, does he? He had better let her alone, or I will kill him. To think that my Delphine is his"—he heaved a sigh—"it is enough to make me murder him, but it would not be manslaughter to kill that animal; he is a pig with a calf's brains. You will take me with you, will you not?"

"Yes, dear Father Goriot; you know very well how fond I am of you——"

"Yes, I do know very well. You are not ashamed of me, are you! Not you! Let me embrace you," and he flung his arms round the student's neck.

"You will make her very happy; promise me that you will! You will go to her this evening, will you not?"

"Oh! yes. I must go out; I have some urgent business on hand."

"Can I be of any use?"

"My word, yes! Will you go to old Taillefer's while I go to Mme. de Nucingen. Ask him to make an appointment with me some time this evening; it is a matter of life and death."

"Really, young man!" cried Father Goriot, with a change of countenance; "are you really paying court to his daughter, as those simpletons were saying down below?—— *Tonnerre de Dieu!* you have no notion what a tap *à la Goriot* is like, and if you are playing a double game, I shall put a stop to it by one blow of the fist—— Oh! the thing is impossible!"

"I swear to you that I love but one woman in the world," said the student. "I only knew it a moment ago."

"Oh! what happiness!" cried Goriot.

"But young Taillefer has been called out; the duel comes off to-morrow morning, and I have heard it said that he may lose his life in it."

"But what business is it of yours?" said Goriot.

"Why, I ought to tell him so, that he may prevent his son from putting in an appearance——"

Just at that moment Vautrin's voice broke in upon them; he was standing at the threshold of his door and singing—

> "*Oh! Richard, oh my king!*
> *All the world abandons thee!*
> *Broum! broum! broum! broum! broum!*
>
> "*The same old story everywhere,*
> *A roving heart and a—— tra la la.*"

"Gentlemen!" shouted Christophe, "the soup is ready, and every one is waiting for you."

"Here," Vautrin called down to him, "come and take a bottle of my Bordeaux."

"Do you think your watch is pretty?" asked Goriot. "She has good taste, hasn't she, eh?"

Vautrin, Father Goriot, and Rastignac came downstairs in company, and, all three of them being late, were obliged to sit together.

Eugène was as distant as possible in his manner to Vautrin during dinner; but the other, so charming in Mme. Vauquer's opinion, had never been so witty. His lively sallies and sparkling talk put the whole table in good-humor. His assurance and great coolness filled Eugène with the utmost consternation.

"Why, what has come to you to-day?" inquired Mme. Vauquer. "You are as merry as a skylark."

"I am always in spirits after I have made a good bargain."

"Bargain?" asked Eugène.

"Well, yes, bargain. I have just delivered a lot of goods, and I shall be paid a handsome commission on them. Mlle. Michonneau," he went on, seeing that the elderly spinster was scrutinizing him intently, "have you any objection to some feature in my face, that you are making those lynx-eyes at me? Just let me know, and I will have it changed to oblige you—— We shall not fall out about it, Poiret, I daresay?" he added, winking at the superannuated clerk.

"Bless my soul, you ought to stand as model for a burlesque Hercules," said the young painter.

"I will, upon my word! if Mlle. Michonneau will consent to sit as the Venus of Père-Lachaise," replied Vautrin.

"There's Poiret," suggested Bianchon.

"Oh! Poiret shall pose as Poiret. He can be a garden god!" cried Vautrin; "his name means a pear——"

"A sleepy pear!" Bianchon put in. "You will come in between the pear and the cheese."

"What stuff you are all talking!" said Mme. Vauquer; "you would do better to treat us to your Bordeaux; I see a glimpse of a bottle there. It would keep us all in a good-humor, and it is good for the stomach besides."

"Gentlemen," said Vautrin, "the lady president calls us to order. Mme. Couture and Mlle. Victorine will take your jokes in good part, but respect the innocence of the aged Goriot. I propose a glass or two of Bordeauxrama, rendered twice illustrious by the name of Laffitte, no political allusions intended. Come, you Turk!" he added, looking at Christophe, who did not offer to stir. "Christophe! Here! What, you don't answer to your own name? Bring us some liquor, Turk!"

"Here it is, sir," said Christophe, holding out the bottle.

Vautrin filled Eugène's glass and Goriot's likewise, then he deliberately poured out a few drops into his own glass, and sipped it while his two neighbors drank their wine. All at once he made a grimace.

"Corked!" he cried. "The devil! You can drink the rest of this, Christophe, and go and find another bottle; take from the right-hand side, you know. There are sixteen of us; take down eight bottles."

"If you are going to stand treat," said the painter, "I will pay for a hundred chestnuts."

"Oh! oh!"

"Booououh!"

"Prrrr!"

These exclamations came from all parts of the table like squibs from a set firework.

"Come, now, Mamma Vauquer, a couple of bottles of champagne," called Vautrin.

"*Quien!* just like you! Why not ask for the whole house at once? A couple of bottles of champagne; that means twelve francs! I shall never see the money back again, I know! But if M. Eugène has a mind to pay for it, I have some currant cordial."

"That currant cordial of hers is as bad as a black draught," muttered the medical student.

"Shut up, Bianchon," exclaimed Rastignac; "the very mention of black draught makes me feel—— Yes, champagne, by all means; I will pay for it," he added.

"Sylvie," called Mme. Vauquer, "bring in some biscuits and the little cakes."

"Those little cakes are moldy graybeards," said Vautrin. "But trot out the biscuits."

The Bordeaux wine circulated; the dinner table became a livelier scene than ever, and the fun grew fast and furious. Imitations of the cries of various animals mingled with the loud laughter; the Muséum official having taken it into his head to mimic a cat-call rather like the caterwauling of the animal in question, eight voices simultaneously struck up with the following variations:

"Scissors to grind!"

"Chick-weed for singing bir-ds!"

"Brandy-snaps, ladies!"

"China to mend!"

"Boat ahoy!"

"Sticks to beat your wives or your clothes!"

"Old clo'!"

"Cherries all ripe!"

But the palm was awarded to Bianchon for the nasal accent with which he rendered the cry of "Umbrellas to me-end!"

A few seconds later, and there was a head-splitting racket in the room, a storm of tomfoolery, a sort of cats' concert, with Vautrin as conductor of the orchestra, the latter keeping an eye the while on Eugène and Father Goriot. The wine seemed to have gone to their heads already. They leaned back in their chairs, looking at the general confusion with an air of gravity, and drank but little; both of them were absorbed in the thought of what lay before them to do that evening, and yet neither of them felt able to rise and go. Vautrin gave a side glance at them from time to time, and watched the change that came over their faces, choosing the moment when their eyes drooped and seemed about to close to bend over Rastignac and to say in his ear:

"My little lad, you are not quite shrewd enough to outwit Papa Vautrin yet, and he is too fond of you to let you make a mess of your affairs. When I have made up my mind to do a thing, no one short of Providence can put me off. Aha! we were for going round to warn old Taillefer, telling tales out of school! The oven is hot, the dough is kneaded, the bread is ready for the oven; to-morrow we will eat it up and whisk away the crumbs; and we are not going to spoil the baking?—— No, no, it is all as good as done! We may suffer from a few conscientious scruples, but they will be digested along with the bread. While we are having our forty winks, Colonel Count Franchessini will clear the way to Michel Taillefer's inheritance with the point of his sword. Victorine will come in for her brother's money, a snug fifteen thousand francs a year. I have made inquiries already, and I know that her late mother's property amounts to more than three hundred thousand——"

Eugène heard all this, and could not answer a word; his tongue seemed to be glued to the roof of his mouth, an irresistible drowsiness was creeping over him. He still saw the table and the faces round it, but it was through a bright mist. Soon the noise began to subside, one by one the boarders went. At last, when their numbers had so dwindled that the party consisted of Mme. Vauquer, Mme. Couture, Mlle. Victorine, Vautrin, and Father Goriot, Rastignac watched as though in a dream how Mme. Vauquer busied herself by collecting the bottles, and drained the remainder of the wine out of each to fill others.

"Oh! how uproarious they are! what a thing it is to be young!" said the widow.

These were the last words that Eugène heard and understood.

"There is no one like M. Vautrin for a bit of fun like this," said Sylvie. "There, just hark at Christophe, he is snoring like a top."

"Good-by, mamma," said Vautrin; "I am going to a theatre on the Boulevard to see M. Marty in 'Le Mont Sauvage,' a fine play taken from 'Le Solitaire'—— If you like, I will take you and these two ladies——"

"Thank you; I must decline," said Mme. Couture.

"What! my good lady!" cried Mme. Vauquer, "decline to see a play founded on the 'Le Solitaire,' a work by Atala de Chateaubriand. We were so fond of that book that we cried over it like Magdalens under the *line trees* last summer, and then it is an improving work that might edify your young lady."

"We are forbidden to go to the play," answered Victorine.

"Just look, those two yonder have dropped off where they sit," said Vautrin, shaking the heads of the two sleepers in a comical way.

He altered the sleeping student's position, settled his head more comfortably on the back of his chair, kissed him warmly on the forehead, and began to sing—

> "*Sleep, little darlings;*
> *I watch while you slumber.*"

"I am afraid he may be ill," said Victorine.

"Then stop and take care of him," returned Vautrin. "'Tis your duty as a meek and obedient wife," he whispered in her ear. "The young fellow worships you, and you will be his little wife—there's your fortune for you. In short," he added aloud, "they lived happily ever afterwards, were much looked up to in all the countryside, and had a numerous family. That is how all the romances end. Now, mamma," he went on, as he turned to Mme. Vauquer and put his arm round her waist, "put on your bonnet, your best flowered silk, and the countess' scarf, while I go out to call a cab—all my ownself."

And he started out, singing as he went—

> "*Oh! sun! divine sun!*
> *Ripening the pumpkins every one.*"

"My goodness! Well, I'm sure! Mme. Couture, I could live happily in a garret with a man like that! There now," she added, looking round for the old vermicelli-maker, "there is that Father Goriot half-seas over. *He* never thought of taking me anywhere, the old skinflint. But he will measure his length somewhere. My word! it is disgraceful to lose his senses like that, at his age! You will be telling me that he couldn't lose what he hadn't got—Sylvie! just take him up to his room!"

Sylvie took him by the arm, supported him upstairs, and flung him, just as he was, like a package, across the bed.

"Poor young fellow!" said Mme. Couture, putting back Eugène's hair that had fallen over his eyes; he is like a young girl, he does not know what dissipation is."

"Well, I can tell you this, I know," said Mme. Vauquer, "I have taken lodgers these thirty years, and a good many have passed through my hands, as the saying is, but I have never seen a nicer nor a more aristocratic-looking young man than M. Eugène. How handsome he looks sleeping! Just let his head rest on your shoulder, Mme. Couture. Pshaw! he falls over towards Mlle. Victorine. There's a special providence for young things. A little more, and he would have broken his head against the knob of the chair. They'd make a pretty pair, those two would!"

"Hush! my good neighbor," cried Mme. Couture, "you are saying such things——"

"Pooh!" put in Mme. Vauquer, "he does not hear. Here, Sylvie! come and help me to dress. I shall put on my best stays."

"What! your best stays just after dinner, madame?" said Sylvie. "No, you can get some one else to lace you. I am not going to be your murderer. It's a rash thing to do, and might cost you your life."

"I don't care, I must do honor to M. Vautrin."

"Are you so fond of your heirs as all that?"

"Come, Sylvie, don't argue," said the widow, as she left the room.

"At her age, too!" said the cook to Victorine, pointing to her mistress as she spoke.

Mme. Couture and her ward were left in the dining-room,

and Eugène slept on on Victorine's shoulder. The sound of Christophe's snoring echoed through the silent house; Eugène's quiet breathing seemed all the quieter by force of contrast, he was sleeping as peacefully as a child. Victorine was very happy; she was free to perform one of those acts of charity which form an innocent outlet for all the overflowing sentiments of a woman's nature; he was so close to her that she could feel the throbbing of his heart; there was a look of almost maternal protection and a conscious pride in Victorine's face. Among the countless thoughts that crowded up in her young innocent heart, there was a wild flutter of joy at this close contact.

"Poor, dear child!" said Mme. Couture, squeezing her hand.

The old lady looked at the girl. Victorine's innocent, pathetic face, so radiant with the new happiness that had befallen her, called to mind some naïve work of mediæval art, when the painter neglected the accessories, reserving all the magic of his brush for the quiet, austere outlines and ivory tints of the face, which seems to have caught something of the golden glory of heaven.

"After all, he only took two glasses, mamma," said Victorine, as she lovingly passed her fingers through Eugène's hair.

"Indeed, if he had been a dissipated young man, child, he would have carried his wine like the rest of them. His drowsiness does him credit."

There was a sound of wheels outside in the street.

"There is M. Vautrin, mamma," said the girl. "Just take M. Eugène. I would rather not have that man see me like this; there are some ways of looking at you that seem to sully your soul and make you feel as though you had nothing on."

"Oh, no, you are wrong!" said Mme. Couture. "M. Vautrin is a worthy man; he reminds me a little of my late husband, poor dear M. Couture, rough but kind-hearted; his bark is worse than his bite."

Vautrin came in while she was speaking; he did not make a sound, but looked for a while at the picture of the two young faces—the lamplight falling full upon them seemed to caress them.

"Well," he remarked, folding his arms, " here is a picture! It would have suggested some pleasing pages to Bernardin de Saint-Pierre (good soul), who wrote 'Paul et Virginie.' Youth is very charming, Mme. Couture! Sleep on, poor boy," he added, looking at Eugène, " luck sometimes comes while we are sleeping. There is something touching and attractive to me about this young man, madame," he continued; "I know that his nature is in harmony with his face. Just look, the head of a cherub on an angel's shoulder! He deserves to be loved. If I were a woman I would die (no—not such a fool), I would live for him." He bent lower and spoke in the widow's ear. "When I see those two together, madame, I cannot help thinking that Providence meant them for each other; He works by secret ways, and tries the reins and the heart," he said in a loud voice. "And when I see you, my children, thus united by a like purity and by all human affections, I say to myself that it is quite impossible that the future should separate you. God is just." He turned to Victorine. "It seems to me," he said, " that I have seen the line of success in your hand. Let me look at it, Mlle. Victorine; I am well up in palmistry, and I have told fortunes many a time. Come, now, don't be frightened. Ah! what do I see? Upon my word, you will be one of the richest heiresses in Paris before very long. You will heap riches on the man who loves you. Your father will want you to go and live with him. You will marry a young and handsome man with a title, and he will idolize you."

The heavy footsteps of the coquettish widow, who was coming down the stairs, interrupted Vautrin's fortune-telling.

"Here is Mamma Vauquer, fair as a starr-r-r, dressed within an inch of her life. Aren't we a trifle pinched for room?" he inquired, with his arm round the lady; "we are screwed up very tightly about the bust, mamma! If we are much agitated, there may be an explosion; but I will pick up the fragments with all the care of an antiquary."

"There is a man who can talk the language of French gallantry!" said the widow, bending to speak in Mme. Couture's ear.

"Good-by, little ones!" said Vautrin, turning to Eugène and Victorine. "Bless you both!" and he laid a hand on either head. "Take my word for it, young lady, an honest man's prayers are worth something; they should bring you happiness, for God hears them."

"Good-by, dear," said Madame Vauquer to her lodger. "Do you think that M. Vautrin means to run away with me?" she added, lowering her voice.

"Lack-a-day!" said the widow.

"Oh! mamma dear, suppose it should really happen as that kind M. Vautrin said!" said Victorine with a sigh, as she looked at her hands. The two women were alone together.

"Why, it wouldn't take much to bring it to pass," said the elder lady; "just a fall from his horse, and your monster of a brother——"

"Oh! mamma."

"Good Lord! Well, perhaps it is a sin to wish bad luck to an enemy," the widow remarked. "I will do penance for it. Still, I would strew flowers on his grave with the greatest pleasure, and that is the truth. Black-hearted, that he is! The coward couldn't speak up for his own mother, and cheats you out of your share by deceit and trickery. My cousin had a pretty fortune of her own, but, unluckily for you, nothing was said in the marriage contract about anything that she might come in for."

"It would be very hard if my good-fortune is to cost some

one else his life," said Victorine. "If I cannot be happy unless my brother is to be taken out of the world, I would rather stay here all my life."

"*Mon Dieu!* it is just as that good M. Vautrin says, and he is full of piety, you see," Mme. Couture remarked. "I am very glad to find that he is not an unbeliever like the rest of them that talk of the Almighty with less respect than they do of the devil. Well, as he was saying, who can know the ways by which it may please Providence to lead us?"

With Sylvie's help the two women at last succeeded in getting Eugène up to his room; they laid him on the bed, and the cook unfastened his clothes to make him more comfortable. Before they left the room, Victorine snatched an opportunity when her guardian's back was turned, and pressed a kiss on Eugène's forehead, feeling all the joy that this stolen pleasure could give her. Then she looked round the room, and gathering up, as it were, into one single thought, all the untold bliss of that day, she made a picture of her memories, and dwelt upon it until she slept, the happiest creature in Paris.

That evening's merrymaking, in the course of which Vautrin had given the drugged wine to Eugène and Father Goriot, was his own ruin. Bianchon, flustered with wine, forgot to open the subject of Trompe-la-Mort with Mlle. Michonneau. The mere mention of the name would have set Vautrin on his guard; for Vautrin, or, to give him his real name, Jacques Collin, was in fact the notorious escaped convict.

But it was the joke about the Venus of Père-Lachaise that finally decided his fate. Mlle. Michonneau had very nearly made up her mind to warn the convict and to throw herself on his generosity, with the idea of making a better bargain for herself by helping him to escape that night; but as it was, she went out escorted by Poiret in search of the famous chief of detectives in the Petite Rue Saint-Anne, still thinking that it was the district superintendent—one Gondureau—with whom she had to do. The head of the department received his visitors courteously. There was a little talk, and the details were definitely arranged. Mlle. Michonneau asked for the draught that she was to administer in order to set about her investigation. But the great man's evident satisfaction set Mlle. Michonneau thinking; and she began to see that this business involved something more than the mere capture of a runaway convict. She racked her brains while he looked in a drawer in his desk for the little phial, and it dawned upon her that in consequence of the treacherous revelations made by the prisoners the police were hoping to lay their hands on a considerable sum of money. But on hinting her suspicions to the old fox of the Petite Rue Saint-Anne, that officer began to smile, and tried to put her off the scent.

"A delusion," he said. "Collin's *sorbonne* is the most dangerous that has yet been found among the dangerous classes. That is all, and the rascals are quite aware of it. They rally round him; he is the backbone of the federation, its Bonaparte, in short; he is very popular with them all. The rogue will never leave his *chump* in the Place de Grève."

As Mlle. Michonneau seemed mystified, Gondureau explained the two slang words for her benefit. *Sorbonne* and *chump* are two forcible expressions borrowed from thieves' Latin, thieves, of all people, being compelled to consider the human head in its two aspects. A *sorbonne* is the head of a living man, his faculty of thinking—his council; a *chump* is a contemptuous epithet that implies how little a human head is worth after the axe has done its work.

"Collin is playing us off," he continued. "When we come across a man like a bar of steel tempered in the English fashion, there is always one resource left—we can kill him if he takes it into his head to make the least resistance. We are reckoning on several methods of killing Collin to-morrow morning. It saves a trial, and society is rid of him without all the expense of guarding and feeding him. What with getting up the case, summoning witnesses, paying their expenses, and carrying out the sentence, it costs a lot to go through all the proper formalities before you can get quit of one of these good-for-nothings, over and above the three thousand francs that you are going to have. There is a saving in time as well. One good thrust of the bayonet into Trompe-la-Mort's paunch will prevent scores of crimes, and save fifty scoundrels from following his example; they will be very careful to keep themselves out of the police courts. That is doing the work of the police thoroughly, and true philanthropists will tell you that it is better to prevent crime than to punish it."

"And you do a service to our country," said Poiret.

"Really, you are talking in a very sensible manner to-night, that you are," said the head of the department. "Yes, of course, we are serving our country, and we are very hardly used too. We do society very great services that are not recognized. In fact, a superior man must rise above vulgar prejudices, and a Christian must resign himself to the mishaps that doing right entails, when right is done in an out-of-the-way style. Paris is Paris, you see! That is the explanation of my life. I have the honor to wish you a good-evening, mademoiselle. I shall bring my men to the Jardin du Roi in the morning. Send Christophe to the Rue du Buffon, tell him to ask for M. Gondureau in the house where you saw me before. Your servant, sir. If you should ever have anything stolen from you, come to me, and I will do my best to get it back for you."

"Well, now," Poiret remarked to Mlle. Michonneau, "there are idiots who are scared out of their wits by the word police. That was a very pleasant-spoken gentleman, and what he wants you to do is as easy as saying 'Good-day.'"

The next day was destined to be one of the most extraordinary in the annals of the Maison Vauquer. Hitherto the most startling occurrence in its tranquil existence had been the portentous, meteor-like apparition of the sham Comtesse de l'Ambermesnil. But the catastrophes of this great day were to cast all previous events into the shade, and supply an inexhaustible topic of conversation for Mme. Vauquer and her boarders so long as she lived.

In the first place, Goriot and Eugène de Rastignac both slept until close upon eleven o'clock. Mme. Vauquer, who came home about midnight from the Gaîté lay abed till half-past ten. Christophe, after a prolonged slumber (he had finished Vautrin's first bottle of wine), was behindhand with his work, but Poiret and Mlle. Michonneau uttered no complaint, though breakfast was delayed. As for Victorine and Mme. Couture, they also lay late. Vautrin went out before eight o'clock, and only came back just as breakfast was ready. Nobody protested, therefore, when Sylvie and Christophe went up at a quarter-past eleven, knocked at all the doors, and announced that breakfast was waiting. While Sylvie and the man were upstairs, Mlle. Michonneau, who came down first, poured the contents of the phial into the silver cup belonging to Vautrin—it was standing with the others in the bain-marie that kept the cream hot for the morning coffee. The spinster had reckoned on this custom of the house to do her stroke of business. The seven lodgers were at last collected together, not without some difficulty. Just as Eugène came downstairs, stretching himself and yawning, a commissionaire handed him a letter from Mme. de Nucingen. It ran thus:

"I feel neither false vanity nor anger where you are concerned, my friend. Till two o'clock this morning I waited for you. Oh, that waiting for one whom you love! No one that had passed through that torture could inflict it on another. I know now that you could have never loved before. What can have happened? Anxiety has taken hold of me. I would have come myself to find out what had happened, if I had not feared to betray the secrets of my heart? How can I walk or drive out at this time of day? Would it not be ruin? I have felt to the full how wretched it is to be a woman. Send a word to reassure me, and explain how it is that you have not come after what my father told you. I shall be angry, but I will forgive you. One word, for pity's sake. You will come to me very soon, will you not? If you are busy, a word will be enough. Say, 'I will hasten to you,' or else 'I am ill.' But if you were ill my father would have come immediately to tell me so. What can have happened?——"

"Yes, indeed, what has happened?" exclaimed Eugène, and, hurrying down to the dining-room, he crumpled up the letter without reading any more. "What time is it?"

"Half-past eleven," said Vautrin, dropping a lump of sugar into his coffee.

The escaped convict cast a glance at Eugène, a cold and fascinating glance; men gifted with this magnetic power can quell furious lunatics in a madhouse by such a glance, it is said. Eugène shook in every limb. There was the sound of wheels in the street, and in another moment a man with a scared face rushed into the room. It was one of M. Taillefer's servants; Mme. Couture recognized the livery at once.

"Mademoiselle," he cried, "your father is asking for you —something terrible has happened! M. Frédéric has had a sword thrust in the forehead in a duel, and the doctors have given him up. You will scarcely be in time to say good-by to him! he is unconscious."

"Poor young fellow!" exclaimed Vautrin. "How can people brawl when they have a certain income of thirty thousand livres? Young people have bad manners, and that is a fact."

"Sir!" cried Eugène.

"Well, what then, you big baby!" said Vautrin, swallowing down his coffee imperturbably, an operation which Mlle. Michonneau watched with such close attention that she had no emotion to spare for the dreadful news that had struck the others dumb with amazement. "Are there not duels every morning in Paris?" added Vautrin, with the utmost calmness and deliberation.

"I will go with you, Victorine," said Mme. Couture, and the two women hurried away at once without either hats or shawls. But before she went, Victorine, with her eyes full of tears, gave Eugène a glance that said—"How little I thought that our happiness should cost me tears!"

"Dear me, you are a prophet, M. Vautrin," said Mme. Vauquer.

"I am all sorts of things," said Vautrin.

"Queer, isn't it?" said Mme. Vauquer, stringing together a succession of commonplaces suited to the occasion. "Death takes us off without asking us about it. The young often go before the old. It is a lucky thing for us women that we are not liable to fight duels, but we have other complaints that men don't suffer from. We bear children, and it takes a long time to get over it. What a windfall for Victorine! Her father will have to acknowledge her now!"

"There!" said Vautrin, looking at Eugène, "yesterday she had not a penny; this morning she has several millions to her fortune."

"I say, M. Eugène!" cried Mme. Vauquer, "you have landed on your feet!"

At this exclamation, Father Goriot looked at the student, and saw the crumpled letter still in his hand.

"You have not read it through! What does this mean? Are you going to be like the rest of them?" he asked.

"Madame, I shall never marry Mlle. Victorine," said Eugène, turning to Mme. Vauquer with an expression of terror and loathing that surprised the onlookers at this scene.

Father Goriot caught the student's hand and grasped it warmly. He could have kissed it.

"Oh, ho!" said Vautrin, "the Italians have a good proverb—*Col tempo.*"

"Is there any answer?" said Mme. de Nucingen's messenger, addressing Eugène.

"Say that I will come directly."

The man went. Eugène was in a state of such violent excitement that he could not be prudent.

"What is to be done?" he exclaimed aloud. "There are no proofs!"

Vautrin began to smile. Though the drug he had taken was doing its work, the convict was so vigorous that he rose to his feet, gave Rastignac a look, and said in hollow tones, "Luck comes to us while we sleep, young man," and fell stiff and stark, as if he were struck dead.

"So there is a Divine justice!" said Eugène.

"Well, if ever! What has come to that poor dear M. Vautrin?"

"A stroke!" cried Mlle. Michonneau.

"Here, Sylvie! girl, run for the doctor," called the widow. "Oh, M. Rastignac, just go for M. Bianchon, and be as quick as you can; Sylvie might not be in time to catch our doctor, M. Grimprel."

Rastignac was glad of an excuse to leave that den of horrors, his departure for the doctor was nothing less than a hurried flight.

"Here, Christophe, go round to the chemist's and ask for something that's good for the apoplexy."

Christophe likewise went.

"Father Goriot, just help us to get him upstairs."

Vautrin was taken up among them, carried carefully up the narrow staircase, and laid upon his bed.

"I can do no good here, so I shall go to see my daughter," said M. Goriot.

"Selfish old thing!" cried Mme. Vauquer. "Yes, go; I wish you may die like a dog."

"Just go and see if you can find some ether," said Ml l. Michonneau to Mme. Vauquer; the former, with some help from Poiret, had unfastened the sick man's clothes.

Mme. Vauquer went down to her room, and left Mlle. Michonneau mistress of the situation.

"Now! just pull down his shirt and turn him over, quick! You might be of some use in sparing my modesty," she said to Poiret, "instead of standing there like a stock."

Vautrin was turned over; Mlle. Michonneau gave his shoulder a sharp slap, and the two portentous letters appeared, white against the red.

"There, you have earned your three thousand francs very easily," exclaimed Poiret, supporting Vautrin while Mlle. Michonneau slipped on the shirt again. "Oh! how heavy he is," he added, as he laid the convict down.

"Hush! Suppose there is a strong box here!" said the old maid briskly; her glances seemed to pierce the walls, she scrutinized every article of the furniture with greedy eyes. "Could we find some excuse for opening that desk?"

"It mightn't be quite right," responded Poiret to this.

"Where is the harm? It is money stolen from all sorts of people, so it doesn't belong to any one now. But we haven't time, there is the Vauquer."

"Here is the ether," said that lady. "I must say that this is an eventful day. Lord! that man can't have had a stroke; he is as white as curds."

"White as curds?" echoed Poiret.

"And his pulse is steady," said the widow, laying her hand on his breast.

"Steady?" said the astonished Poiret.

"He is all right."

"Do you think so?" asked Poiret.

"Lord! Yes, he looks as if he were sleeping. Sylvie has

gone for a doctor. I say, Mlle. Michonneau, he is sniffing the ether. Pooh! it is only a spasm. His pulse is good. He is as strong as a Turk. Just look, mademoiselle, what a fur tippet he has on his chest; that is the sort of man to live till he is a hundred. His wig holds on tightly, however. Dear me! it is glued on, and his own hair is red; that is why he wears a wig. They always say that red-haired people are either the worst or the best. Is he one of the good ones, I wonder!"

"Good to hang," said Poiret.

"Round a pretty woman's neck, you mean," said Mlle. Michonneau, hastily. "Just go away, M. Poiret. It is a woman's duty to nurse you men when you are ill. Besides, for all the good you are doing, you may as well take yourself off," she added. "Mme. Vauquer and I will take great care of dear M. Vautrin."

Poiret went out on tiptoe without a murmur, like a dog kicked out of the room by his master.

Rastignac had gone out for the sake of physical exertion; he wanted to breathe the air, he felt stifled. Yesterday evening he had meant to prevent the murder arranged for half-past eight that morning. What had happened? What ought he to do now? He trembled to think that he himself might be implicated. Vautrin's coolness still further dismayed him.

"Yet, how if Vautrin should die without saying a word?" Rastignac asked himself.

He hurried along the alleys of the Luxembourg Gardens as if the hounds of justice were after him, and he already heard the baying of the pack.

"Well," shouted Bianchon, "have you seen the *Pilote?*"

The *Pilote* was a Radical sheet, edited by M. Tissot. It came out several hours later than the morning papers, and was meant for the benefit of country subscribers; for it brought the morning's news into provincial districts twenty-four hours sooner than the ordinary local journals.

"There is a wonderful history in it," said the house student of the Hôpital Cochin. "Young Taillefer called out Count Franchessini, of the Old Guard, and the Count put a couple of inches of steel into his forehead. And here is little Victorine one of the richest heiresses in Paris! If we had known that, eh? What a game of chance death is! They said Victorine was sweet on you; was there any truth in it?"

"Shut up, Bianchon; I shall never marry her. I am in love with a charming woman, and she is in love with me, so——"

"You said that as if you were screwing yourself up to be faithful to her. I should like to see the woman worth the sacrifice of Master Taillefer's money!"

"Are all the devils of hell at my heels," cried Rastignac.

"What is the matter with you? Are you mad? Give us your hand," said Bianchon, "and let me feel your pulse. You are feverish."

"Just go to Mother Vauquer's," said Rastignac; "that scoundrel Vautrin has dropped down like one dead."

"Aha!" said Bianchon, leaving Rastignac to his reflections, "you confirm my suspicions, and now I mean to make sure for myself."

The law-student's long walk was a memorable one for him. He made in some way a survey of his conscience. After a close scrutiny, after hesitation and self-examination, his honor at any rate came out scathless from this sharp and terrible ordeal, like a bar of iron tested in the English fashion. He remembered Father Goriot's confidences of the evening before; he recollected the rooms taken for him in the Rue d'Artois, so that he might be near Delphine; and then he thought of his letter, and read it again and kissed it.

"Such a love is my anchor of safety," he said to himself. "How the old man's heart must have been wrung! He says nothing about all that he has been through; but who could not guess? Well, then, I will be like a son to him; his life shall be made happy. If she cares for me, she will often come to spend the day with him. That grand Comtesse de Restaud is a heartless thing; she would turn her father into her hall porter. Dear Delphine! she is kinder to the old man; she is worthy to be loved. Ah! this evening I shall be very happy!"

He took out his watch and admired it.

"I have had nothing but success! If two people mean to love each other for ever, they may help each other, and I can take this. Besides, I shall succeed, and I will repay her a hundredfold. There is nothing criminal in this *liaison;* nothing that could cause the most austere moralist to frown. How many respectable people contract similar unions! We deceive nobody; it is deception that makes a position humiliating. If you lie, you lower yourself at once. She and her husband have lived apart for a long while. Besides, how if I called upon that Alsatian to resign a wife whom he cannot make happy?"

Rastignac's battle with himself went on for a long while; and though the scruples of youth inevitably gained the day, an irresistible curiosity led him, about half-past four, to return to the Maison Vauquer through the gathering dusk.

Bianchon had given Vautrin an emetic, reserving the contents of the stomach for chemical analysis at the hospital. Mlle. Michonneau's officious alacrity had still further strengthened his suspicions of her. Vautrin, moreover, had recovered so quickly that it was impossible not to suspect some plot against the leader of all frolics at the lodging-house. Vautrin was standing in front of the stove in the dining-room when Rastignac came in. All the lodgers were assembled sooner than usual by the news of young Taillefer's duel. They were anxious to hear any detail about the affair, and to talk over the probable change in Victorine's prospects. Father Goriot alone was absent, but the rest were chatting. No sooner did Eugène come into the room, than his eyes met the inscrutable gaze of Vautrin. It was the same look that had read his thoughts before—the look that had such power to waken evil thoughts in his heart. He shuddered.

"Well, dear boy," said the escaped convict, "I am likely to cheat death for a good while yet. According to these ladies, I have had a stroke that would have felled an ox, and come off with flying colors."

"A bull you might say," cried the widow.

"You really might be sorry to see me still alive," said Vautrin in Rastignac's ear, thinking that he guessed the student's thoughts. "You must be mighty sure of yourself."

"Mlle. Michonneau was talking the day before yesterday about a gentleman nicknamed *Trompe-la-Mort*," said Bianchon; "and, upon my word, that name would do very well for you."

Vautrin seemed thunderstruck. He turned pale, and staggered back. He turned his magnetic glance, like a ray of vivid light, on Mlle. Michonneau; the old maid shrank and trembled under the influence of that strong will, and collapsed into a chair. The mask of good-nature had dropped from the convict's face; from the unmistakable ferocity of that sinister look, Poiret felt that the old maid was in danger, and hastily stepped between them. None of the lodgers understood this scene in the least, they looked on in mute amazement. There was a pause. Just then there was a sound of tramping feet outside; there were soldiers there, it seemed, for there was a ring of several rifles on the pavement of the street. Collin was mechanically looking round the walls for a way of escape, when four men entered by way of the sitting-room.

"In the name of the king and the law!" said an officer, but the words were almost lost in a murmur of astonishment.

Silence fell on the room. The lodgers made way for three of the men, who had each a hand on a cocked pistol in a side pocket. Two policemen, who followed the detectives, kept the entrance to the sitting-room, and two more appeared in the doorway that gave access to the staircase. A sound of footsteps came from the garden, and again the rifles of several soldiers rang on the cobble-stones under the window. All chance of salvation by flight was cut off for Trompe-la-Mort, to whom all eyes instinctively turned. The chief walked straight up to him, and commenced operations by giving him a sharp blow on the head, so that the wig fell off, and Collin's face was revealed in all its ugliness. There was a terrible suggestion of strength mingled with cunning in the short, brick-red crop of hair, the whole head was in harmony with his powerful frame, and at that moment the fires of hell seemed to gleam from his eyes. In that flash the real Vautrin shone forth, revealed at once before them all; they understood his past, his present, and future, his pitiless doctrines, his actions, the religion of his own good pleasure, the majesty with which his cynicism and contempt for mankind invested him, the physical strength of an organization proof against all trials. The blood flew to his face, and his eyes glared like the eyes of a wildcat. He started back with savage energy and a fierce growl which drew exclamations of alarm from the lodgers. At that leonine start the police caught at their pistols under cover of the general clamor. Collin saw the gleaming muzzles of the weapons, saw his danger, and instantly gave proof of a power of the highest order. There was something horrible and majestic in the spectacle of the sudden transformation in his face; he could only be compared to a caldron full of the steam that can send mountains flying, a terrific force dispelled in a moment by a drop of cold water. The drop of water that cooled his wrathful fury was a reflection that flashed across his brain like lightning. He began to smile, and looked down at his wig.

"You are not in the politest of humors to-day," he remarked to the chief, and he held out his hands to the policemen with a jerk of his head.

"Gentlemen," he said, "put on the bracelets or the handcuffs. I call on those present to witness that I make no resistance."

A murmur of admiration ran through the room at the sudden outpouring like fire and lava flood from this human volcano, and its equally sudden cessation.

"There's a sell for you, master crusher," the convict added, looking at the famous director of police.

"Come, strip!" said he of the Petite Rue Saint-Anne, contemptuously.

"Why?" asked Collin. "There are ladies present; I deny nothing, and surrender."

He paused, and looked round the room like an orator who is about to overwhelm his audience.

"Take this down, Daddy Lachapelle," he went on, addressing a little, white-haired old man who had seated himself at the end of the table; and, after drawing a printed form from a portfolio, was proceeding to draw up a document. "I acknowledge myself to be Jacques Collin, otherwise known as Trompe-la-Mort, condemned to twenty years' penal servitude, and I have just proved that I have come fairly by my nickname. If I had as much as raised my hand," he went on, addressing the other lodgers, "those three sneaking wretches yonder would have drawn claret on Mamma Vauquer's domestic hearth. The rogues have laid their heads together to set a trap for me."

Mme. Vauquer felt sick and faint at these words.

"Good Lord!" she cried, "this does give one a turn; and me at the Gaîté with him only last night!" she said to Sylvie.

"Summon your philosophy, mamma," Collin resumed. "Is it a misfortune to have sat in my box at the Gaîté yesterday evening? After all, are you better than we are? The brand upon our shoulders is less shameful than the brand set on your hearts, you flabby members of a society rotten to the core. Not the best man among you could stand up to me." His eyes rested upon Rastignac, to whom he spoke with a pleasant smile that seemed strangely at variance with the savage expression in his eyes. " Our little bargain still holds good, dear boy; you can accept any time you like! Do you understand?" And he sang—

> "*A charming girl is my Fanchette
> In her simplicity.*"

" Don't you trouble yourself," he went on; "I can get in my money. They are too much afraid of me to swindle me."

The convicts' prison, its language and customs, its sudden sharp transitions from the humorous to the horrible, its appalling grandeur, its triviality and its dark depths, were all revealed in turn by the speaker's discourse; he seemed to be no longer a man, but the type and mouthpiece of a degenerate race, a brutal, supple, clear-headed race of savages. In one moment Collin became the poet of an inferno, wherein all thoughts and passions that move human nature (save repentance) find a place. He looked about him like a fallen archangel who is for war to the end. Rastignac lowered his eyes, and acknowledged this kinship claimed by crime as an expiation of his own evil thoughts.

"Who betrayed me?" said Collin, and his terrible eyes traveled round the room. Suddenly they rested on Mlle. Michonneau.

"It was you, old cat!" he said. "That sham stroke of apoplexy was your doing, lynx-eyes!—— Two words from me, and your throat would be cut in less than a week, but I forgive you, I am a Christian. You did not sell me either. But who did?—— Aha! you may rummage upstairs," he shouted, hearing the police officers opening his cupboards and taking possession of his effects. "The nest is empty, the birds flew away yesterday, and you will be none the wiser.

My ledgers are here," he said, tapping his forehead. "Now I know who sold me! It could only be that blackguard Fil-de-Soie. That is who it was, old catchpoll, eh?" he said, turning to the chief. "It was timed so neatly to get the bank-notes up above there. There is nothing left for you—spies! As for Fil-de-Soie, he will be under the daisies in less than a fortnight, even if you were to tell off the whole force to protect him. How much did you give the Michonneau?" he asked of the police officers. "A thousand crowns? Oh you Ninon in decay, Pompadour in tatters, Venus of the graveyard, I was worth more than that! If you had given me warning, you should have had six thousand francs. Ah! you had no suspicion of that, old trafficker in flesh and blood, or I should have had the preference. Yes, I would have given six thousand francs to save myself an inconvenient journey and some loss of money," he said, as they fastened the handcuffs on his wrists. "These folks will amuse themselves by dragging out this business till the end of time to keep me idle! If they were to send me straight to jail, I should soon be back at my old tricks in spite of the duffers at the Quai des Orfévres. Down yonder they would all turn themselves inside out to help their general—their good Trompe-la-Mort—to get clear away. Is there a single one among you that can say as I can, that he has ten thousand brothers ready to do anything for him?" he asked proudly. "There is some good there," he said, tapping his heart; "I have never betrayed any one! Look you here, you slut," he said to the old maid, "they are all afraid of me, do you see? but the sight of you turns them sick. Rake in your gains."

He was silent for a moment, and looked round at the lodgers' faces.

"What dolts you are, all of you! Have you never seen a convict before? A convict of Collin's stamp, whom you see before you, is a man less weak-kneed than others; he lifts up his voice against the colossal fraud of the social contract, as Jean Jacques did, whose pupil he is proud to declare himself. In short, I stand here single-handed against a government and a whole subsidized machinery of tribunals and police, and I am a match for them all."

"Ye gods!" cried the painter, "what a magnificent sketch one might make of him!"

"Look here, you gentlemen-in-waiting to his highness the gibbet, master of ceremonies to the widow" (a nickname full of sombre poetry, given by prisoners to the guillotine), "be a good-fellow, and tell me if it really was Fil-de-Soie who sold me. I don't want him to suffer for some one else, that would not be fair."

But before the chief had time to answer, the rest of the party returned from making their investigations upstairs. Everything had been opened and inventoried. A few words passed between them and the chief, and the official preliminaries were complete.

"Gentlemen," said Collin, addressing the lodgers, "they will take me away directly. You have all made my stay among you very agreeable, and I shall look back upon it with gratitude. Receive my adieux, and permit me to send you figs from Provence."

He advanced a step or two, and then turned to look once more at Rastignac.

"Good-by, Eugène," he said, in a sad and gentle tone, a strange transition from his previous rough and stern manner. "If you should be hard up, I have left you a devoted friend," and, in spite of his shackles, he managed to assume a posture of defense, called, "One! two!" like a fencing-master, and lunged. "If anything goes wrong, apply in that quarter. Man and money, all at your service."

The speaker's strange manner was sufficiently burlesque, so that no one but Rastignac knew that there was a serious meaning underlying the pantomime.

As soon as the police, soldiers, and detectives had left the house, Sylvie, who was rubbing her mistress' temples with vinegar, looked round at the bewildered lodgers.

"Well," said she, "he was a man, he was, for all that."

Her words broke the spell. Every one had been too much excited, too much moved by very various feelings to speak. But now the lodgers began to look at each other, and then all eyes were turned at once on Mlle. Michonneau, a thin, shriveled, dead-alive, mummy-like figure crouching by the stove; her eyes were downcast, as if she feared that the green eyeshade could not shut out the expression of those faces from her. This figure and the feeling of repulsion she had so long excited were explained all at once. A smothered murmur filled the room; it was so unanimous that it seemed as if the same feeling of loathing had pitched all the voices in one key. Mlle. Michonneau heard it, and did not stir. It was Bianchon who was the first to move; he bent over his neighbor, and said in a low voice, "If that creature is going to stop here, and have dinner with us, I shall clear out."

In the twinkling of an eye it was clear that every one in the room, save Poiret, was of the medical student's opinion, so that the latter, strong in the support of the majority, went up to that elderly person.

"You are more intimate with Mlle. Michonneau than the rest of us," he said; "speak to her, make her understand that she must go, and go at once," showing by his manner a most determined spirit.

"At once!" echoed Poiret in amazement.

Then he went across to the crouching figure, and spoke a few words in her ear.

"I have paid beforehand for the quarter; I have as much right to be here as any one else," she said, with a viperous look at the boarders.

"Never mind that! we will club together and pay you the money back," said Rastignac.

"Monsieur is taking Collin's part," she said, with a questioning, malignant glance at the law student; "it is not difficult to guess why."

Eugène started forward at the words, as if he meant to spring upon her and wring her neck. That glance, and the depths of treachery that it revealed, had been a hideous enlightenment.

"Let her alone!" cried the boarders.

Rastignac folded his arms, and was silent.

"Let us have no more of Mlle. Judas," said the painter, turning to Mme. Vauquer. "If you don't show the Michonneau the door, madame, we shall all leave your shop, and wherever we go we shall say that there are only convicts and spies left there. If you do the other thing, we will hold our tongues about the business; for when all is said and done, it might happen in the best society until they brand them on the forehead, when they send them to the hulks. They ought not to let convicts go about Paris disguised like decent citizens, so as to carry on their antics like a set of rascally humbugs, which they are."

At this Mme. Vauquer recovered miraculously. She sat up and folded her arms; her eyes were wide open now, and there was no sign of tears in them.

"Why, do you really mean to be the ruin of my establishment, my dear sir? There is M. Vautrin—— Goodness," she cried, interrupting herself, "I can't help calling him by the name he passed himself off by for an honest man! There is one room to let already, and you want me to turn out two more lodgers in the middle of the season, when no one is moving——"

"Gentlemen, let us take our hats and go and dine at Flicoteaux's in the Place Sorbonne," cried Bianchon.

Mme. Vauquer glanced round, and saw in a moment on which side her interest lay. She waddled across to Mlle. Michonneau.

"Come, now," she said; "you would not be the ruin of

my establishment, would you, eh? There's a dear, kind soul. You see what a pass these gentlemen have brought me to; just go up to your room for this evening."

"Never a bit of it!" cried the boarders. "She must go, and go this minute!"

"But the poor lady has had no dinner," said Poiret, with piteous entreaty.

"She can go and dine where she likes," shouted several voices.

"Turn her out, the spy!"

"Turn them both out! Spies!"

"Gentlemen," cried Poiret, his head swelling with the courage that love gives to the ovine male, "respect the weaker sex."

"Spies are of no sex!" said the painter.

"A precious sexorama!"

"Turn her into the streetorama!"

"Gentlemen, this is not manners! If you turn people out of the house, it ought not to be done so unceremoniously and with no notice at all. We have paid our money, and we are not going," said Poiret, putting on his cap, and taking a chair beside Mlle. Michonneau, with whom Mme. Vauquer was remonstrating.

"Naughty boy!" said the painter, with a comical look; "run away, naughty little boy!"

"Look here," said Bianchon; "if you do not go, all the rest of us will," and the boarders, to a man, made for the sitting-room door.

"Oh! mademoiselle, what is to be done?" cried Mme. Vauquer. "I am a ruined woman. You can't stay here; they will go farther, do something violent."

Mlle. Michonneau rose to her feet.

"She is going! She is not going! She is going! No, she isn't."

These alternate exclamations, and a suggestion of hostile

intentions, borne out by the behavior of the insurgents, compelled Mlle. Michonneau to take her departure. She made some stipulations, speaking in a low voice in her hostess' ear, and then—"I shall go to Mme. Buneaud's," she said, with a threatening look.

"Go where you please, mademoiselle," said Mme. Vauquer, who regarded this choice of an opposition establishment as an atrocious insult. "Go and lodge with the Buneaud; the wine would give a cat the colic, and the food is cheap and nasty."

The boarders stood aside in two rows to let her pass; not a word was spoken. Poiret looked so wistfully after Mlle. Michonneau, and so artlessly revealed that he was in two minds whether to go or stay, that the boarders, in their joy at being quit of Mlle. Michonneau, burst out laughing at the sight of him.

"Hist!—st!—st! Poiret," shouted the painter. "Hallo! I say, Poiret, hallo!" The employé from the Muséum began to sing—

> "*Partant pour la Syrie,*
> *Le jeune at beau Dunois——*"

"Get along with you; you must be dying to go, *trahit sua quemque voluptas!*" said Bianchon.

"Every one to his taste—free rendering from Virgil," said the tutor.

Mlle. Michonneau made a movement as if to take Poiret's arm, with an appealing glance that he could not resist. The two went out together, the old maid leaning upon him, and there was a burst of applause, followed by peals of laughter.

"Bravo, Poiret!"

"Who would have thought it of old Poiret!"

"Apollo Poiret!"

"Mars Poiret!"

"Intrepid Poiret!"

A messenger came in at that moment with a letter for Mme. Vauquer, who read it through, and collapsed in her chair.

"The house might as well be burnt down at once," cried she, "if there are to be any more of these thunderbolts! Young Taillefer died at three o'clock this afternoon. It serves me right for wishing well to those ladies at that poor young man's expense. Mme. Couture and Victorine want me to send their things, because they are going to live with her father. M. Taillefer allows his daughter to keep old Mme. Couture with her as lady companion. Four rooms to let! and five lodgers gone!——"

She sat up, and seemed about to burst into tears.

"Bad luck has come to lodge here, I think," she cried.

Once more there came a sound of wheels from the street outside.

"What! another windfall for somebody!" was Sylvie's comment.

But it was Goriot who came in, looking so radiant, so flushed with happiness, that he seemed to have grown young again.

"Goriot in a cab!" cried the boarders; "the world is coming to an end."

The good soul made straight for Eugène, who was standing rapt in thought in a corner, and laid a hand on the young man's arm.

"Come," he said, with gladness in his eyes.

"Then you haven't heard the news?" said Eugène. "Vautrin was an escaped convict; they have just arrested him; and young Taillefer is dead."

"Very well, but what business is it of ours?" replied Father Goriot. "I am going to dine with my daughter *in your house*, do you understand? She is expecting you. Come!"

He carried off Rastignac with him by main force, and they departed in as great a hurry as a pair of eloping lovers.

"Now, let us have dinner," cried the painter, and every one drew his chair to the table.

"Well, I never?" said the portly Sylvie. "Nothing goes right to-day! The haricot mutton has caught! Bah! you will have to eat it, burnt as it is, more's the pity!"

Mme. Vauquer was so dispirited that she could not say a word as she looked round the table and saw only ten people where eighteen should be; but every one tried to comfort and cheer her. At first the dinner contingent, as was natural, talked about Vautrin and the day's events; but the conversation wound round to such topics of interest as duels, jails, justice, prison life, and alterations that ought to be made in the laws. They soon wandered miles away from Jacques Collin and Victorine and her brother. There might be only ten of them, but they made noise enough for twenty; indeed, there seemed to be more of them than usual; that was the only difference between yesterday and to-day. Indifference to the fate of others is a matter of course in this selfish world, which, on the morrow of a tragedy, seeks among the events of Paris for a fresh sensation for its daily renewed appetite, and this indifference soon gained the upper hand. Mme. Vauquer herself grew calmer under the soothing influence of hope, and the mouthpiece of hope was the portly Sylvie.

That day had gone by like a dream for Eugène, and the sense of unreality lasted into the evening; so that, in spite of his energetic character and clear-headedness, his ideas were a chaos as he sat beside Goriot in the cab. The old man's voice was full of unwonted happiness, but Eugène had been shaken by so many emotions that the words sounded in his ears like works spoken in a dream.

"It was finished this morning! All three of us are going to dine there together, together! Do you understand? I have not dined with my Delphine, my little Delphine, these four years, and I shall have her for a whole evening! We have been at your lodging the whole time since morning.

I have been working like a porter in my shirt sleeves, helping to carry in the furniture. Aha! you don't know what pretty ways she has; at table she will look after me, 'Here, papa, just try this, it is nice.' And I shall not be able to eat. Oh, it is a long while since I have been with her in quiet every-day life as we shall have her."

"It really seems as if the world had been turned upside down."

"Upside down?" repeated Father Goriot. "Why, the world has never been so right-side up. I see none but smiling faces in the streets, people who shake hands cordially and embrace each other, people who all look as happy as if they were going to dine with their daughter, and gobble down a nice little dinner that she went with me to order of the chef at the Café des Anglais. But, pshaw! with her beside you gall and wormwood would be as sweet as honey."

"I feel as if I were coming back to life again," said Eugène.

"Why, hurry up there!" cried Father Goriot, letting down the window in front. "Get on faster; I will give you five francs if you get to the place I told you of in ten minutes' time."

With this prospect before him the cabman crossed Paris with miraculous celerity.

"How that fellow crawls!" said Father Goriot.

"But where are you taking me?" Eugène asked him.

"To your own house," said Goriot.

The cab stopped in the Rue d'Artois. Father Goriot stepped out first and flung ten francs to the man with the recklessness of a widower returning to bachelor ways.

"Come along upstairs," he said to Rastignac. They crossed a courtyard, and climbed up to the third floor of a new and handsome house. Here they stopped before a door; but before Goriot could ring, it was opened by Thérèse, Mme. de Nucingen's maid. Eugène found himself in a charming set of chambers; an ante-room, a little drawing-room, a bed-room, and a study, looking out upon a garden. The furniture and the decoration of the little drawing-room were of the most daintily charming description, the room was full of soft light, and Delphine rose up from a low chair by the fire and stood before him. She set her fire-screen down on the chimney-piece, and spoke with tenderness in every tone of her voice.

"So we had to go in search of you, sir, you who are so slow to understand!"

Thérèsa left the room. The student took Delphine in his arms and held her in a tight clasp, his eyes filled with tears of joy. This last contrast between his present surroundings and the scenes he had just witnessed was too much for Rastignac's overwrought nerves, after the day's strain and excitement that had wearied heart and brain; he was almost overcome by it.

"I felt sure myself that he loved you," murmured Father Goriot, while Eugène lay back bewildered on the sofa, utterly unable to speak a word or to reason out how and why the magic wand had been waved to bring about this final transformation scene.

"But you must see your rooms," said Mme. de Nucingen. She took his hand and led him into a room carpeted and furnished like her own; indeed, down to the smallest details, it was a reproduction in miniature of Delphine's own handsome apartment.

"There is no bed," said Rastignac.

"No, monsieur," she answered, reddening, and pressing his hand. Eugène, looking at her, understood, young though he yet was, how deeply modesty is implanted in the heart of a woman who loves.

"You are one of those beings whom we cannot choose but to adore for ever," he said in her ear. "Yes, the deeper and truer love is, the more mysterious and closely veiled it should be; I can dare to say so, since we understand each other so well. No one shall learn our secret."

"Oh! so I am nobody, I suppose," growled the father.

"You know quite well that 'we' means you."

"Ah! that is what I wanted. You will not mind me, will you? I shall go and come like a good fairy who makes himself felt everywhere without being seen, shall I not? Eh, Delphinette, Ninette, Dedel—was it not a good idea of mine to say to you, 'There are some nice rooms to let in the Rue d'Artois; let us furnish them for him?' And she would not hear of it! Ah! your happiness has been all my doing. I am the author of your happiness and of your existence. Fathers must always be giving if they would be happy themselves; always giving—they would not be fathers else."

"Was that how it happened?" asked Eugène.

"Yes. She would not listen to me. She was afraid that people would talk, as if the rubbish that they say about you were to be compared with happiness! Why, all women dream of doing what she has done——"

Father Goriot found himself without an audience, for Mme. de Nucingen had led Rastignac into the study; he heard a kiss given and taken, low though the sound was.

The study was furnished as elegantly as the other rooms, and nothing was wanting there.

"Have we guessed your wishes rightly?" she asked, as they returned to the drawing-room for dinner.

"Yes," he said, "only too well, alas! For all this luxury so well carried out, this realization of pleasant dreams, the elegance that satisfies all the romantic fancies of youth, appeals to me so strongly that I cannot but feel that it is my rightful possession, but I cannot accept it from you, and I am too poor as yet to——"

"Ah! ah! you say me nay already," she said with arch imperiousness, and a charming little pout of the lips, a woman's way of laughing away scruples.

But Eugène had submitted so lately to that solemn self-questioning, and Vautrin's arrest had so plainly shown him the depths of the pit that lay ready to his feet, that the instincts of generosity and honor had been strengthened in him, and he could not allow himself to be coaxed into abandoning his high-minded determinations. Profound melancholy filled his mind.

"Do you really mean to refuse?" said Mme. de Nucingen. "And do you know what such a refusal means? That you are not sure of yourself, that you do not dare to bind yourself to me. Are you really afraid of betraying my affection? If you love me, if I—love you, why should you shrink back from such a slight obligation? If you but knew what a pleasure it has been to see after all the arrangements of this bachelor establishment, you would not hesitate any longer, you would ask me to forgive you for your hesitation. I had some money that belonged to you, and I have made good use of it, that is all. You mean this for magnanimity, but it is very little of you. You are asking me for far more than this—— ('Ah!' she cried, as Eugène's passionate glance was turned on her), and you are making difficulties about the merest trifles. Oh, if you feel no love whatever for me, refuse, by all means. My fate hangs on a word from you. Speak! Father," she said after a pause, "make him listen to reason. Can he imagine that I am less nice than he is on the point of honor?"

Father Goriot was looking on and listening to this pretty quarrel with a placid smile, as if he had found some balm for all the sorrows of life.

"Child that you are!" she cried again, catching Eugène's hand. "You are just beginning life; you find barriers at the outset that many a man finds insurmountable; a woman's hand opens the way, and you shrink back! Why, you are sure to succeed! You will have a brilliant future. Success is written on that broad forehead of yours, and will you not be able to repay me my loan of to-day? Did not a lady in olden times arm her knight with sword and helmet and coat of mail, and find him a charger, so that he might fight for her in the tournament? Well, then, Eugène, these things that I offer you are the weapons of this age; every one who means to be something must have such tools as these. A pretty place your garret must be if it is like papa's room! See, dinner is waiting all this time. Do you want to make me unhappy? Why don't you answer?" she said, shaking his hand. "*Mon Dieu!* papa, make up his mind for him, or I will go away and never see him any more."

"I will make up your mind," said Goriot, coming down from the clouds. "Now, my dear M. Eugène, the next thing is to borrow money of the Jews, isn't it?"

"There is positively no help for it," said Eugène.

"All right, I will give you credit," said the other, drawing out a cheap leather pocket-book, much the worse for wear. "I have turned Jew myself; I have paid for everything; here are the invoices. You do not owe a penny for anything here. It did not come to very much—five thousand francs at most, and I am going to lend you the money myself. I am not a woman—you cannot refuse me. You shall give me a receipt on a scrap of paper, and you can return it some time or other."

Delphine and Eugène looked at each other in amazement, tears sprang to their eyes. Rastignac held out his hand and grasped Goriot's warmly.

"Well, what is all this about? Are you not my children?"

"Oh! my poor father," said Mme. de Nucingen, "how did you do it?"

"Ah! now you ask me. When I made up my mind to move him nearer to you, and saw you buying things as if they were wedding presents, I said to myself, 'She will never be able to pay for them.' The attorney says that those law proceedings will last quite six months before your husband can be made to disgorge your fortune. Well and good. I sold out my property in the funds that brought in thirteen hundred and fifty livres a year, and bought a safe annuity of twelve hundred francs a year for fifteen thousand francs. Then I paid your tradesmen out of the rest of the capital. As for me, children, I have a room upstairs for which I pay fifty crowns a year; I can live like a prince on two francs a day, and still have something left over. I shall not have to spend anything much on clothes, for I never wear anything out. This fortnight past I have been laughing in my sleeves, thinking to myself, 'How happy they are going to be!' and—well, now, are you not happy?"

"Oh papa! papa!" cried Mme. de Nucingen, springing to her father, who took her on his knee. She covered him with kisses, her fair hair brushed his cheek, her tears fell on the withered face that had grown so bright and radiant.

"Dear father, what a father you are! No, there is not another father like you under the sun. If Eugène loved you before, what must he feel for you now?"

"Why, children! why, Delphinette!" cried Goriot, who had not felt his daughter's heart beat against his breast for ten years, "do you want me to die of joy? My poor heart will break! Come, Monsieur Eugène, we are quits already." And the old man strained her to his breast with such fierce and passionate force that she cried out.

"Oh! you are hurting me!" she said.

"I am hurting you!" He grew pale at the words. The pain expressed in his face seemed greater than it is given to humanity to know. The agony of this Christ of paternity can only be compared with the masterpieces of those princes of the palette who have left for us the record of their visions of an agony suffered for a whole world by the Saviour of men. Father Goriot pressed his lips very gently against the waist that his fingers had grasped too roughly.

. "Oh! no, no," he cried. "I have not hurt you, have I?" and his smile seemed to repeat the question. "*You* have hurt me with that cry just now. The things cost rather more than that," he said in her ear, with another gentle kiss, "but I had to deceive him about it, or he would have been angry."

Eugène sat dumb with amazement in the presence of this inexhaustible love; he gazed at Goriot, and his face betrayed the artless admiration which shapes the beliefs of youth.

"I will be worthy of all this," he cried.

"Oh! my Eugène, that is nobly said," and Mme. de Nucingen kissed the law student on the forehead.

"He gave up Mlle. Taillefer and her millions for you," said Father Goriot. "Yes, the little thing was in love with you, and now that her brother is dead she is as rich as Crœsus."

"Oh! why did you tell her?" cried Rastignac.

"Eugène," Delphine said in his ear, "I have one regret now this evening. Ah! how I will love you! and for ever!"

"This is the happiest day I have had since you two became acquainted!" cried Goriot. "God may send me any suffering, so long as I do not suffer through you, and I can still say, 'In this short month of February I had more happiness than other men have in their whole lives.' Look at me, Fifine!" he said to his daughter. "She is very beautiful, is she not? Tell me, now, have you seen many women with that pretty soft color—that little dimple of hers? No, I thought not. Ah, well, and but for me this lovely woman would never have been. And very soon happiness will make her a thousand times lovelier, happiness through you. I could give up my place in heaven to you, neighbor, if needs be, and go down to hell instead. Come, let us have dinner," he added, scarcely knowing what he said, "everything is ours."

"Poor dear father!"

He rose and went over to her, and took her face in his hands, and set a kiss on the plaits of hair. "If you only knew, little one, how happy you can make me—how little it takes to make me happy! Will you come and see me sometimes? I shall be just above, so it is only a step. Promise me, say that you will!"

"Yes, dear father."

"Say it again."

"Yes, I will, my kind father."

"Hush, hush! I should make you say it a hundred times over if I followed my own wishes. Let us have dinner."

The three behaved like children that evening, and Father Goriot's spirits were certainly not the least wild. He lay at his daughter's feet, kissed them, gazed into her eyes, rubbed his head against her dress; in short, no young lover could have been more extravagant or more tender.

"You see!" Delphine said with a look at Eugène, "so long as my father is with us, he monopolizes me. He will be rather in the way sometimes."

Eugène had himself already felt certain twinges of jealousy, and could not blame this speech that contained the germ of all ingratitude.

"And when will the rooms be ready?" asked Eugène, looking round. "We must all leave them this evening, I suppose."

"Yes, but to-morrow you must come and dine with me," she answered, with an eloquent glance. "It is our night at the Italiens."

"I shall go to the pit," said her father.

It was midnight. Mme. de Nucingen's carriage was waiting for her, and Father Goriot and the student walked back to the Maison Vauquer, talking of Delphine, and warming over their talk till there grew up a curious rivalry between the two violent passions. Eugène could not help seeing that the father's selfish love was deeper and more steadfast than his own. For this worshiper Delphine was always pure and fair, and her father's admiration drew its fervor from a whole past as well as a future of love.

They found Mme. Vauquer by the stove, with Sylvie and

Christophe to keep her company; the old landlady, sitting like Marius among the ruins of Carthage, was waiting for the two lodgers that yet remained to her, and bemoaning her lot with the sympathetic Sylvie. Tasso's lamentations as recorded in Byron's poem are undoubtedly eloquent, but for sheer force of truth they fall far short of the widow's cry from the depths.

"Only three cups of coffee in the morning, Sylvie! Oh, dear! to have your house emptied in this way is enough to break your heart. What is life, now my lodgers are gone? Nothing at all. Just think of it! It is just as if all the furniture had been taken out of the house, and your furniture is your life. How have I offended heaven to draw down all this trouble upon me? And haricot beans and potatoes laid in for twenty people! The police in my house, too! We shall have to live on potatoes now, and Christophe will have to go!"

The Savoyard, who was fast asleep, suddenly woke up at this, and said, "Madame?" questioningly.

"Poor fellow!" said Sylvie, "he is like a dog."

"In the dead season, too! Nobody is moving now. I would like to know where the lodgers are to drop down from. It drives me distracted. And that old witch of a Michonneau goes and takes Poiret with her! What can she have done to him to make him so fond of her? He runs about after her like a little dog."

"Lord!" said Sylvie, flinging up her head, "those old maids are up to all sorts of tricks."

"There's that poor M. Vautrin that they made out to be a convict," the widow went on. "Well, you know that is too much for me, Sylvie; I can't bring myself to believe it. Such a lively man as he was, and paid fifteen francs a month for his coffee of an evening, paid you every penny on the nail too."

"And open-handed he was!" said Christophe.

"There is some mistake," said Sylvie.

"Why, no there isn't! he said so himself!" said Mme.

Vauquer. "And to think that all these things have happened in my house, and in a quarter where you never see a cat go by. On my word as an honest woman, it's like a dream. For, look here, we saw Louis XVI. meet with his mishap; we saw the fall of the Emperor; and we saw him come back and fall again; there was nothing out of the way in all that, but lodging-houses are not liable to revolutions. You can do without a king, but you must eat all the same; and so long as a decent woman, a de Conflans born and bred, will give you all sorts of good things for dinner, nothing short of the end of the world ought to—but there, it is the end of the world, that is just what it is!"

"And to think that Mlle. Michonneau who made all this mischief is to have a thousand crowns a year for it, so I hear," cried Sylvie.

"Don't speak of her, she is a wicked woman!" said Mme. Vauquer. "She is going to the Buneaud, who charges less than cost. But the Buneaud is capable of anything; she must have done frightful things, robbed and murdered people in her time. *She* ought to be put in jail for life instead of that poor dear——"

Eugène and Goriot, reaching the Maison Vauquer, rang the door-bell at that moment.

"Ah! here are my two faithful lodgers," said the widow, sighing.

But the two faithful lodgers, who retained but shadowy recollections of the misfortunes of their lodging-house, announced to their hostess without more ado that they were about to remove to the Chaussée d'Antin.

"Sylvie!" cried the widow, "this is the last straw. Gentlemen, this will be the death of me! It has quite upset me! There's a weight on my chest! I am ten years older for this day! Upon my word, I shall go out of my senses! And what is to be done with the haricots? Oh, well, if I am to be left here all by myself, you shall go to-morrow, Christophe. Good-night, gentlemen," and she went upstairs.

"What is the matter now?" Eugène inquired of Sylvie, in much astonishment.

"Lord! everybody is going about his business, and that has addled her wits. There! she is crying upstairs. It will do her good to snivel a bit. It's the first time she has cried since I've been with her."

By the morning, Mme. Vauquer, to use her own expression, had "made up her mind to it." True, she still wore a doleful countenance, as might be expected of a woman who had lost all her lodgers, and whose manner of life had been suddenly revolutionized, but she had all her wits about her. Her grief was genuine and profound; it was real pain of mind, for her purse had suffered, the routine of her existence had been broken. A lover's farewell glance at his lady-love's window is not more mournful than Mme. Vauquer's survey of the empty places round her table. Eugène administered comfort, telling the widow that Bianchon, whose term of residence at the hospital was about to expire, would doubtless take his (Rastignac's) place; that the official from the Muséum had often expressed a desire to have Mme. Couture's room; and that in a very few days her household would be on the old footing.

"God send it may, my dear sir! but bad luck has come to lodge here. There'll be a death in the house before ten days are out, you'll see," and she gave a lugubrious look around the dining-room. "Whose turn will it be, I wonder?"

"It is just as well that we are moving out," said Eugène to Father Goriot in a low voice.

"Madame," said Sylvie, running in with a scared face, "I have not seen Mistigris these three days."

"Ah! well, if my cat is dead, if *he* has gone and left us, I——"

The poor woman could not finish her sentence; she clasped

her hands and hid her face on the back of her armchair, quite overcome by this dreadful portent.

By twelve o'clock, when the postman reaches that quarter, Eugène received a letter. The dainty envelope bore the Beauséant arms on the seal, and contained an invitation to the Vicomtesse's great ball, which had been talked of in Paris for a month. A little note for Eugène was slipped in with the card.

"I think, monsieur, that you will undertake with pleasure to interpret my sentiments to Mme. de Nucingen, so I am sending the card for which you asked me to you. I shall be delighted to make the acquaintance of Mme. de Restaud's sister. Pray introduce that charming lady to me, and do not let her monopolize all your affection, for you owe me not a little in return for mine.

"VICOMTESSE DE BEAUSÉANT."

"Well," said Eugène to himself, as he read the note a second time, "Mme. de Beauséant says pretty plainly that she does not want the Baron de Nucingen."

He went to Delphine at once in his joy. He had procured this pleasure for her, and doubtless he would receive the price of it. Mme. de Nucingen was dressing. Rastignac waited in her boudoir, enduring as best he might the natural impatience of an eager temperament for the reward desired and withheld for a year. Such sensations are only known once in a life. The first woman to whom a man is drawn, if she is really a woman—that is to say, if she appears to him amid the splendid accessories that form a necessary background to life in the world of Paris—will never have a rival.

Love in Paris is a thing distinct and apart; for in Paris neither men nor women are the dupes of the commonplaces by which people seek to throw a veil over their motives, or to parade a fine affectation of disinterestedness in their sentiments. In this country within a country, it is not merely required of a woman that she should satisfy the senses and the soul; she knows perfectly well that she has still greater obligations to discharge, that she must fulfill the countless demands of a vanity that enters into every fibre of that living organism called society. Love, for her, is above all things, and by its very nature, a vainglorious, brazen-fronted, ostentatious, thriftless charlatan. If at the court of Louis XIV. there was not a woman but envied Mlle. de la Vallière the reckless devotion of passion that led the grand monarch to tear the priceless ruffles at his wrists in order to assist the entry of a Duc de Vermandois into the world—what can you expect of the rest of society? You must have youth and wealth and rank; nay, you must, if possible, have more than these, for the more incense you bring with you to burn at the shrine of the god, the more favorably will he regard the worshiper. Love is a religion, and his cult must in the nature of things be more costly than those of all other deities; love the spoiler stays for a moment, and then passes on; like the urchin of the streets, his course may be traced by the ravages that he has made. The wealth of feeling and imagination is the poetry of the garret; how should love exist there without that wealth?

If there are exceptions who do not subscribe to these Draconian laws of the Parisian code, they are solitary examples. Such souls live so far out of the main current that they are not borne away by the doctrines of society; they dwell beside some clear spring of ever-flowing water, without seeking to leave the green shade; happy to listen to the echoes of the infinite in everything around them and in their own souls, waiting in patience to take their flight for heaven, while they look with pity upon those of earth.

Rastignac, like most young men who have been early impressed by the circumstance of power and grandeur, meant to enter the lists fully armed; the burning ambition of conquest possessed him already; perhaps he was conscious of his powers, but as yet he knew neither the end to which his ambition was to be directed nor the means of attaining it. In default of the pure and sacred love that fills a life, ambition may become something very noble, subduing to itself every thought of personal interest, and setting as the end— the pre-eminent greatness, not of one man, but of a whole nation.

But the student had not yet reached the time of life when a man surveys the whole course of existence and judges it soberly. Hitherto he had scarcely so much as shaken off the spell of the fresh and gracious influences that envelop a childhood in the country, like green leaves and grass. He had hesitated on the brink of the Parisian Rubicon, and, in spite of the prickings of ambition, he still clung to a lingering tradition of an old ideal—the peaceful life of the noble in his château. But yesterday evening, at the sight of his rooms, those scruples had vanished. He had learned what it was to enjoy the material advantages of fortune, as he had already enjoyed the social advantages of birth; he ceased to be a provincial from that moment, and slipped naturally and easily into a position which opened up the prospect of a brilliant future.

So, as he waited for Delphine, in the pretty boudoir, where he felt that he had a certain right to be, he felt himself so far away from the Rastignac who came back to Paris a year ago, that, turning some power of inner vision upon this latter, he asked himself whether that past self bore any resemblance to the Rastignac of that moment.

"Madame is in her room," Thérèse came to tell him. The woman's voice made him start.

He found Delphine lying back in her low chair by the fireside, looking fresh and bright. The sight of her among the flowing draperies of muslin suggested some beautiful tropical flower, where the fruit is set amid the blossom.

"Well," she said, with a tremor in her voice, "here you are."

"Guess what I bring for you," said Eugène, sitting down beside her. He took possession of her arm to kiss her hand.

Mme. de Nucingen gave a joyful start as she saw the card. She turned to Eugène; there were tears in her eyes as she flung her arms about his neck, and drew him towards her in a frenzy of gratified vanity.

"And I owe this happiness to you—to *thee*" (she whispered the more intimate word in his ear); "but Thérèse is in my dressing-room, let us be prudent. This happiness—yes, for I may call it so, when it comes to me through *you*—is surely more than a triumph for self-love? No one has been willing to introduce me into that set. Perhaps just now I may seem to you to be frivolous, petty, shallow, like a Parisienne, but remember, my friend, that I am ready to give up all for you; and that if I long more than ever for an entrance into the Faubourg Saint-Germain, it is because I shall meet you there."

"Mme. de Beauséant's note seems to say very plainly that she does not expect to see the *Baron* de Nucingen at her ball; don't you think so?" said Eugène.

"Why, yes," said the Baroness as she returned the letter. "Those women have a talent for insolence. But it is of no consequence, I shall go. My sister is sure to be there, and sure to be very beautifully dressed. Eugène," she went on, lowering her voice, "she will go to dispel ugly suspicions. You do not know the things that people are saying about her! Only this morning Nucingen came to tell me that they had been discussing her at the club. Great heavens! on what does a woman's character and the honor of a whole family depend! I feel that I am nearly touched and wounded in my poor sister. According to some people, M. de Trailles must have put his name to bills for a hundred thousand francs, nearly all of them are overdue, and proceedings are threatened. In this predicament, it seems that my sister sold her diamonds to a Jew—the beatiful diamonds that belonged to her husband's mother, Mme. de Restaud the elder—you have seen her wearing them. In fact, nothing else has been talked about for the last two days. So I can see that Anastasie is sure to come to Mme. de Beauséant's ball in tissue of gold, and ablaze with diamonds, to draw all eyes upon her; and I will not be outshone. She has tried to eclipse me all her life; she has never been kind to me, and I have helped her so often, and always had money for her when she had none. But never mind other people now, to-day I mean to be perfectly happy."

At one o'clock that morning Eugène was still with Mme. de Nucingen. In the midst of their lovers' farewell, a farewell full of hope of bliss to come, she said in a troubled voice, "I am very fearful, superstitious. Give what name you like to my presentiments, but I am afraid that my happiness will be paid for by some horrible catastrophe."

"Child!" said Eugène.

"Ah! have we changed places, and am I the child to-night?" she asked laughingly.

Eugène went back to the Maison Vauquer, never doubting but that he should leave it for good on the morrow; and on the way he fell to dreaming the bright dreams of youth, when the cup of happiness has left its sweetness on the lips.

"Well?" cried Goriot, as Rastignac passed by his door.

"Yes," said Eugène; "I will tell you everything to-morrow."

"Everything, will you not?" cried the old man. "Go to bed. To-morrow our happy life will begin."

Next day, Goriot and Rastignac were ready to leave the lodging-house, and only awaited the good pleasure of a porter to move out of it; but towards noon there was a sound of wheels in the Rue Neuve-Sainte-Geneviève, and a carriage stopped before the door of the Maison Vauquer. Mme. de

Nucingen alighted, and asked if her father was still in the house, and, receiving an affirmative reply from Sylvie, ran lightly upstairs.

It so happened that Eugène was at home all unknown to his neighbor. At breakfast-time he had asked Goriot to superintend the removal of his goods, saying that he would meet him in the Rue d'Artois at four o'clock; but Rastignac's name had been called early on the list at the École de droit, and he had gone back at once to the Rue Neuve-Sainte-Geneviève. No one had seen him come in, for Goriot had gone to find a porter, and the mistress of the house was likewise out. Eugène had thought to pay her himself, for it struck him that if he left this, Goriot in his zeal would probably pay for him. As it was, Eugène went up to his room to see that nothing had been forgotten, and blessed his foresight when he saw the blank bill bearing Vautrin's signature lying in the drawer where he had carelessly thrown it on the day when he had repaid the amount. There was no fire in the grate, so he was about to tear it into little pieces, when he heard a voice speaking in Goriot's room, and the speaker was Delphine! He made no more noise, and stood still to listen, thinking that she should have no secrets from him; but after the first few words, the conversation between the father and daughter was so strange and interesting that it absorbed all his attention.

"Ah! thank heaven that you thought of asking him to give an account of the money settled on me before I was utterly ruined, father. Is it safe to talk?" she added.

"Yes, there is no one in the house," said her father faintly.

"What is the matter with you?" asked Mme. de Nucingen.

"God forgive you! you have just dealt me a staggering blow, child!" said the old man. "You cannot know how much I love you, or you would not have burst in upon me like this, with such news, especially if all is not lost. Has something so important happened that you must come here about it? In a few minutes we should have been in the Rue d'Artois."

"Eh! does one think what one is doing after a catastrophe? It has turned my head. Your attorney has found out the state of things now, but it was bound to come out sooner or later. We shall want your long business experience; and I came to you like a drowning man who catches at a branch. When M. Derville found that Nucingen was throwing all sorts of difficulties in his way, he threatened him with proceedings, and told him plainly that he would soon obtain an order from the president of the Tribunal. So Nucingen came to my room this morning, and asked if I meant to ruin us both. I told him that I knew nothing whatever about it, that I had a fortune, and ought to be put into possession of my fortune, and that my attorney was acting for me in the matter; I said again that I knew absolutely nothing about it, and could not possibly go into the subject with him. Wasn't that what you told me to tell him?"

"Yes, quite right," answered Goriot.

"Well, then," Delphine continued, "he told me all about his affairs. He had just invested all his capital and mine in business speculations; they have only just been started, and very large sums of money are locked up. If I were to compel him to refund my dowry now, he would be forced to file his petition; but if I will wait a year, he undertakes, on his honor, to double or treble my fortune, by investing it in building land, and I shall be mistress at last of the whole of my property. He was speaking the truth, father dear; he frightened me! He asked my pardon for his conduct; he has given me my liberty; I am free to act as I please on conditions that I leave him to carry on my business in my name. To prove his sincerity, he promised that M. Derville might inspect the accounts as often as I pleased, so that I might be assured that everything was being conducted properly. In short, he put himself into my power, bound hand and foot. He wishes the present arrangements as to the expenses of housekeeping to continue for two more years, and entreated me not to exceed my allowance. He showed me plainly that it was all that he could do to keep up appearances; he has broken with his opera dancer; he will be compelled to practice the most strict economy (in secret) if he is to bide his time with unshaken credit. I scolded, I did all I could to drive him to desperation, so as to find out more. He showed me his ledgers—he broke down and cried at last. I never saw a man in such a state. He lost his head completely, talked of killing himself, and raved till I felt quite sorry for him."

"Do you really believe that silly rubbish?"—— cried her father. "It was all got up for your benefit! I have had to do with Germans in the way of business; honest and straightforward they are prety sure to be, but when with their simplicity and frankness they are sharpers and humbugs as well, they are the worst rogues of all. Your husband is taking advantage of you. As soon as pressure is brought to bear on him he shams dead; he means to be more the master under your name than in his own. He will take advantage of the position to secure himself against the risks of business. He is as sharp as he is treacherous; he is a bad lot! No, no; I am not going to leave my girls behind me without a penny when I go to Père-Lachaise. I know something about business still. He has sunk his money in speculation, he says; very well, then there is something to show for it—bills, receipts, papers of some sort. Let him produce them, and come to an arrangement with you. We will choose the most promising of his speculations, take them over at our own risk, and have the securities transferred into your name; they shall represent the separate estate of Delphine Goriot, wife of the Baron de Nucingen. Does that fellow really take us for idiots? Does he imagine that I could stand the idea of your being without fortune, without bread, for forty-eight hours? I would not stand it a day—no, not a night, not a couple of hours! If there had been any foundation for the idea, I should never get over it. What! I have worked hard for forty years, carried sacks on my back, and sweated and pinched and saved all my life for you, my darlings, for you who made the toil and every burden borne for you seem light; and now, my fortune, my whole life, is to vanish in smoke! I should die raving mad if I believed a word of it. By all that's holiest in heaven and earth, we will have this cleared up at once; go through the books, have the whole business looked thoroughly into! I will not sleep, nor rest, nor eat until I have satisfied myself that all your fortune is in existence. Your money is settled upon you, God be thanked! and, luckily, your attorney, Maître Derville, is an honest man. Good Lord! you shall have your snug little million, your fifty thousand francs a year, as long as you live, or I will raise a racket in Paris, I will so! If the Tribunals put upon us, I will appeal to the Chambers. If I knew that you were well and comfortably off as far as money is concerned, that thought would keep me easy in spite of bad health and troubles. Money? why, it is life! Money does everything. That great dolt of an Alsatian shall sing to another tune! Look here, Delphine, don't give way, don't make a concession of half a quarter of a farthing to that fathead, who has ground you down and made you miserable. If he can't do without you, we will give him a good cudgeling, and keep him in order. Great heavens! my brain is on fire; it is as if there were something redhot inside my head. My Delphine lying on straw! You! my Fifine! Good gracious! Where are my gloves? Come, let us go at once; I mean to see everything with my own eyes—books, cash, and correspondence, the whole business. I shall have no peace until I know for certain that your fortune is secure!"

"Oh! father dear, be careful how you set about it! If there is the least hint of vengeance in the business, if you show yourself openly hostile, it will be all over with me. He knows whom he has to deal with; he thinks it quite natural that if you put the idea into my head, I should be uneasy about my money; but I swear to you that he has it in his own hands, and that he had meant to keep it. He is just the man to abscond with all the money and leave us in the lurch, the scoundrel! He knows quite well that I will not dishonor the name I bear by bringing him into a court of law. His position is strong and weak at the same time. If we drive him to despair, I am lost."

"Why, then, the man is a rogue?"

"Well, yes, father," she said, flinging herself into a chair. "I wanted to keep it from you to spare your feelings," and she burst into tears; "I did not want you to know that you had married me to such a man as he is. He is just the same in private life—body and soul and conscience—the same through and through—hideous! I hate him; I despise him! Yes, after all that that despicable Nucingen has told me, I cannot respect him any longer. A man capable of mixing himself up in such affairs, and of talking about them to me as he did, without the slightest scruple—it is because I have read him through and through that I am afraid of him. He, my husband, frankly proposed to give me my liberty, and do you know what that means? It means that if things turn out badly for him, I am to play into his hands, and be his stalking-horse."

"But there is law to be had! There is a Place de Grève for sons-in-law of that sort," cried her father; "why, I would guillotine him myself if there was no headsman to do it."

"No, father, the law cannot touch him. Listen, this is what he says, stripped of all his circumlocutions—'Take your choice, you and no one else can be my accomplice; either everything is lost, you are ruined and have not a farthing, or you will let me carry this business through myself.' Is that plain speaking? He *must* have my assistance. He is assured that his wife will deal fairly by him; he knows that I shall leave his money to him and be content with my own. It is an unholy and dishonest compact, and he holds out threats of ruin to compel me to consent to it. He is buying my conscience, and the price is liberty to be Eugène's wife in all but name. 'I connive at your errors, and you allow me to commit crimes and ruin poor families!' Is that sufficiently explicit? Do you know what he means by speculations? He buys up land in his own name, then he finds men of straw to run up houses upon it. These men make a bargain with a contractor to build the houses, paying them by bills at long dates; then in consideration of a small sum they leave my husband in possession of the houses, and finally slip through the fingers of the deluded contractors by going into bankruptcy. The name of the firm of Nucingen has been used to dazzle the poor contractors. I saw that. I noticed, too, that Nucingen had sent bills for large amounts to Amsterdam, London, Naples, and Vienna, in order to prove if necessary that large sums had been paid away by the firm. How could we get possession of those bills?"

Eugène heard a dull thud on the floor; Father Goriot must have fallen on his knees.

"Great heavens! what have I done to you? Bound my daughter to this scoundrel who does as he likes with her! Oh! my child, my child! forgive me!" eagerly cried the old man.

"Yes, if I am in the depths of despair, perhaps you are to blame," said Delphine. "We have so little sense when we marry! What do we know of the world, of business, or men, or life? Our fathers should think for us! Father dear, I am not blaming you in the least, forgive me for what I said. This is all my own fault. Nay, do not cry, papa," she said, kissing him.

"Do not you cry either, my little Delphine. Look up and

let me kiss away the tears. There! I shall find my wits and unravel this skein of your husband's winding."

"No, let me do that; I shall be able to manage him. He is fond of me, well and good; I shall use my influence to make him invest my money as soon as possible in landed property in my own name. Very likely I could get him to buy back Nucingen in Alsace in my name; that has always been a pet idea of his. Still, come to-morrow and go through the books, and look into the business. M. Derville knows little of mercantile matters. No, not to-morrow though. I do not want to be upset. Mme. de Beauséant's ball will be the day after to-morrow, and I must keep quiet, so as to look my best and freshest, and do honor to my dear Eugène!—— Come, let us see his room."

But as she spoke a carriage stopped in the Rue Neuve-Sainte-Geneviève, and the sound of Mme. de Restaud's voice came from the staircase. "Is my father in?" she asked of Sylvie.

This accident was luckily timed for Eugène, whose one idea had been to throw himself down on the bed and pretend to be asleep.

"Oh, father, have you heard about Anastasie?" said Delphine, when she heard her sister speak. "It looks as though some strange things had happened in that family."

"What sort of things?" asked Goriot. "This is like to be the death of me. My poor head will not stand a double misfortune."

"Good-morning, father," said the Countess from the threshold. "Oh! Delphine, are you here?"

Mme. de Restaud seemed taken aback by her sister's presence.

"Good-morning, Nasie," said the Baroness. "What is there so extraordinary in my being here? *I* see our father every day."

"Since when?"

"If you came yourself you would know."

"Don't tease, Delphine," said the Countess fretfully. "I am very miserable, I am lost. Oh! my poor father, it is hopeless this time!"

"What is it, Nasie?" cried Goriot. "Tell us all about it, child! How white she is! Quick, do something, Delphine; be kind to her, and I will love you even better, if that were possible."

"Poor Nasie!" said Mme. de Nucingen, drawing her sister to a chair. "We are the only two people in the world whose love is always sufficient to forgive you everything. Family affection is the surest, you see."

The Countess inhaled the salts and revived.

"This will kill me!" said their father. "There," he went on, stirring the smoldering fire, "come nearer, both of you. It is cold. What is it, Nasie? Be quick and tell me, this is enough to——"

"Well, then, my husband knows everything," said the Countess. "Just imagine it; do you remember, father, that bill of Maxime's some time ago? Well, that was not the first. I had paid ever so many before that. About the beginning of January M. de Trailles seemed very much troubled. He said nothing to me; but it is so easy to read the hearts of those you love, a mere trifle is enough; and then you feel things instinctively. Indeed, he was more tender and affectionate than ever, and I was happier than I had ever been before. Poor Maxime! in himself he was really saying good-by to me, so he has told me since; he meant to blow his brains out! At last I worried him so, and begged and implored so hard; for two hours I knelt at his knees and prayed and entreated, and at last he told me—that he owed a hundred thousand francs. Oh! papa! a hundred thousand francs! I was beside myself! You had not the money, I knew; I had eaten up all that you had——"

"No," said Goriot; "I could not have gotten it for you

unless I had stolen it. But I would have done that for you, Nasie! I will do it yet."

The words came from him like a sob, a hoarse sound like the death-rattle of a dying man; it seemed indeed like the agony of death when the father's love was powerless. There was a pause, and neither of the sisters spoke. It must have been selfishness indeed that could hear unmoved that cry of anguish that, like a pebble thrown over a precipice, revealed the depths of his despair.

"I found the money, father, by selling what was not mine to sell," and the Countess burst into tears.

Delphine was touched; she laid her head on her sister's shoulder, and cried too.

"Then it is all true," she said.

Anastasie bowed her head. Mme. de Nucingen flung her arms about her, kissed her tenderly, and held her sister to her heart.

"I shall always love you and never judge you, Nasie," she said.

"My angels!" murmured Goriot faintly. "Oh, why should it be trouble that draws you together?"

This warm and palpitating affection seemed to give the Countess courage.

"To save Maxime's life," she said, "to save all my own happiness, I went to the money-lender you know of, a man of iron forged in hell-fire; nothing can melt him; I took all the family diamonds that M. de Restaud is so proud of—his and mine too—and sold them to that M. Gobseck. *Sold them!* Do you understand? I saved Maxime, but I am lost. Restaud found it all out."

"How? Who told him? I will kill him," cried Goriot.

"Yesterday he sent to tell me to come to his room. I went—— 'Anastasie,' he said in a voice—oh! such a voice; that was enough, it told me everything—'where are your diamonds?' 'In my room——' 'No,' he said, looking straight at me, 'there they are on that chest of drawers——' and he lifted his handkerchief and showed me the casket. 'Do you know where they come from?' he said. I fell at his feet—— I cried; I besought him to tell me the death he wished to see me die."

"You said that!" cried Goriot. "By God in heaven, whoever lays a hand on either of you so long as I am alive may reckon on being roasted by slow fires! Yes, I will cut him in pieces like——"

Goriot stopped; the words died away in his throat.

"And then, dear, he asked something worse than death of me. Oh! heaven preserve all other women from hearing such words as I heard then!"

"I will murder that man," said Goriot quietly. "But he has only one life, and he deserves to die twice. And then, what next?" he added, looking at Anastasie.

"Then," the Countess resumed, "there was a pause, and he looked at me. 'Anastasie,' he said, 'I will bury this in silence; there shall be no separation; there are the children. I will not kill M. de Trailles. I might miss him if we fought, and as for other ways of getting rid of him, I should come into collision with the law. If I killed him in your arms, it would bring dishonor on *those* children. But if you do not want to see your children perish, nor their father nor me, you must first of all submit to two conditions. Answer me. Have I a child of my own?' I answered, 'Yes.' 'Which?' 'Ernest, our eldest boy.' 'Very well,' he said, 'and now swear to obey me in this particular from this time forward.' I swore. 'You will make over your property to me when I require you to do so.'"

"Do nothing of the kind!" cried Goriot. "Aha! M. de Restaud, you could not make your wife happy; she has looked for happiness and found it elsewhere, and you make her suffer for your own inaptitude? He will have to reckon with me. Make yourself easy, Nasie. Aha! he cares about his heir!

Good, very good. I will get hold of the boy; isn't he my grandson? What the blazes! I can surely go to see the brat! I will stow him away somewhere; I will take care of him, you may be quite easy. I will bring Restaud to terms, the monster! I shall say to him, 'A word or two with you! If you want your son back again, give my daughter her property, and leave her to do as she pleases.'"

"Father!"

"Yes. I am your father, Nasie, a father indeed! That rogue of a great lord had better not ill-treat my daughter. *Tonnerre!* What is it in my veins? There is the blood of a tiger in me; I could tear those two men to pieces! Oh! children, children! so this is what your lives are! Why, it is death!—— What will become of you when I shall be here no longer? Fathers ought to live as long as their children. Ah! Lord God in heaven! how ill Thy world is ordered! Thou hast a Son, if what they tell us is true, and yet Thou leavest us to suffer so through our children. My darlings, my darlings! to think that trouble only should bring you to me, that I should only see you with tears on your faces! Ah! yes, yes, you love me, I see that you love me. Come to me and pour out your griefs to me; my heart is large enough to hold them all. Oh! you might rend my heart in pieces, and every fragment would make a father's heart. If only I could bear all your sorrows for you!—— Ah! you were so happy when you were little and still with me——"

"We have never been happy since," said Delphine. "Where are the old days when we slid down the sacks in the great granary?"

"That is not all, father," said Anastasie in Goriot's ear. The old man gave a startled shudder. "The diamonds only sold for a hundred thousand francs. Maxime is hard pressed. There are twelve thousand francs still to pay. He has given me his word that he will be steady and give up play in future. His love is all that I have left in the world. I have paid such a fearful price for it that I shall die if I lose him now. I have sacrificed my fortune, my honor, my peace of mind, and my children for him. Oh! do something, so that at the least Maxime may be at large and live undisgraced in the world, where he will assuredly make a career for himself. Something more than my happiness is at stake; the children have nothing, and if he is sent to Sainte-Pélagie all his prospects will be ruined."

"I haven't the money, Nasie. I have *nothing*—nothing left. This is the end of everything. Yes, the world is crumbling into ruin, I am sure. Fly! Save yourselves! Ah! I have still my silver buckles left and half-a-dozen silver spoons and forks, the first I ever had in my life. But I have nothing else except my life annuity, twelve hundred francs——"

"Then what has become of your money in the funds?"

"I sold out, and only kept a trifle for my wants. I wanted twelve thousand francs to furnish some rooms for Delphine."

"In your own house?" asked Mme. de Restaud, looking at her sister.

"What does it matter where they were?" asked Goriot. "The money is spent now."

"I see how it is," said the Countess. "Rooms for M. de Rastignac. Poor Delphine, take warning by me!"

"M. de Rastignac is incapable of ruining the woman he loves, dear."

"Thanks! Delphine. I thought you would have been kinder to me in my troubles, but you never did love me."

"Yes, yes, she loves you, Nasie!" cried Goriot; "she was saying so only just now. We were talking about you, and she insisted that you were beautiful, and that she herself was only pretty!"

"Pretty!" said the Countess. "She is as hard as a marble statue."

"And if I am," cried Delphine, flushing up, "how have you treated me? You would not recognize me; you closed the doors of every house against me; you have never let an opportunity of mortifying me slip by. And when did I come, as you were always doing, to drain our poor father, a thousand francs at a time, till he is left as you see him now? That is all your doing, sister! I myself have seen my father as often as I could. I have not turned him out of the house, and then come and fawned upon him when I wanted money. I did not so much as know that he had spent those twelve thousand francs on me. I am economical, as you know; and when papa has made me presents, it has never been because I came and begged for them."

"You were better off than I. M. de Marsay was rich, as you have reason to know. You always were as slippery as gold. Good-by; I have neither sister nor——"

"Oh! hush, hush! Nasie!" cried her father.

"Nobody else would repeat what everybody has ceased to believe. You are an unnatural sister!" cried Delphine.

"Oh, children, children! hush! hush! or I will kill myself before your eyes."

"There, Nasie, I forgive you," said Mme. de Nucingen; "you are very unhappy. But I am kinder than you are. How could you say *that* just when I was ready to do anything in the world to help you, even to be reconciled with my husband, which for my own sake I—— Oh! it is just like you; you have behaved cruelly to me all through these nine years."

"Children, children, kiss each other!" cried the father. "You are angels, both of you."

"No. Let me alone," cried the Countess, shaking off the hand that her father had laid on her arm. "She is more merciless than my husband. Any one might think she was a model of all the virtues herself!"

"I would rather have people think that I owed money to M. de Marsay than own that M. de Trailles had cost me more than two hundred thousand francs," retorted Mme. de Nucingen.

"*Delphine!*" cried the Countess, stepping towards her sister.

"I shall tell you the truth about yourself if you begin to slander me," said the Baroness coldly.

"Delphine! you are a——"

Father Goriot sprang between them, grasped the Countess' hand, and laid his own over her mouth.

"Good heavens, father! What have you been handling this morning?" said Anastasie.

"Ah! well, yes, I ought not to have touched you," said the poor father, wiping his hands on his trousers, "but I have been packing up my things; I did not know that you were coming to see me."

He was glad that he had drawn down her wrath upon himself.

"Ah!" he sighed, as he sat down, "you children have broken my heart between you. This is killing me. My head feels as if it were on fire. Be good to each other and love each other! This will be the death of me! Delphine! Nasie! come, be sensible; you are both in the wrong. Come, Dedel," he added, looking through his tears at the Baroness, "she must have twelve thousand francs, you see; let us see if we can find them for her. Oh, my girls, do not look at each other like that!" and he sank on his knees beside Delphine.

"Ask her to forgive you—just to please me," he said in her ear. "She is more miserable than you are. Come now, Dedel."

"Poor Nasie!" said Delphine, alarmed at the wild extravagant grief in her father's face, "I was in the wrong, kiss me——"

"Ah! that is like balm to my heart," cried Father Goriot. "But how are we to find twelve thousand francs? I might offer myself as a substitute in the army——"

"Oh! father dear!" they both cried, flinging their arms about him. "No, no!"

"God reward you for the thought. We are not worth it, are we, Nasie?" asked Delphine.

"And besides, father dear, it would only be a drop in the bucket," observed the Countess.

"But is flesh and blood worth nothing?" cried the old man in his despair. "I would give body and soul to save you, Nasie. I would do a murder for the man who would rescue you. I would do, as Vautrin did, go to the hulks, go——" he stopped as if struck by a thunderbolt, and put both hands to his head. "Nothing left!" he cried, tearing his hair. "If I only knew of a way to steal money, but it is so hard to do it, and then you can't set to work by yourself, and it takes time to rob a bank. Yes, it is time I was dead; there is nothing left me to do but to die. I am no good in the world; I am no longer a father! No. She has come to me in her extremity, and, wretch that I am, I have nothing to give her. Ah! you put your money into a life annuity, old scoundrel; and had you not daughters? You did not love them. Die, die in a ditch, like the dog that you are! Yes, I am worse than a dog; a beast would not have done as I have done! Oh! my head—— it throbs as if it would burst."

"Papa!" cried both the young women at once, "do, pray, be reasonable!" and they clung to him to prevent him from dashing his head against the wall. There was a sound of sobbing.

Eugène, greatly alarmed, took the bill that bore Vautrin's signature, saw that the stamp would suffice for a larger sum, altered the figures, made it into a regular bill for twelve thousand francs, payable to Goriot's order, and went to his neighbor's room, determined to help him out of his present trouble by a great sacrifice on his own part.

"Here is the money, madame," he said, handing the piece of paper to her. "I was asleep; your conversation awoke me, and by this means I learned all that I owed to M. Goriot.

This bill can be discounted, and I shall meet it punctually at the due date."

The Countess stood motionless and speechless, but she held the bill in her fingers.

"Delphine," she said, with a white face, and her whole frame quivering with indignation, anger, and rage, " I forgave you everything; God is my witness that I forgave you, but I cannot forgive this! So this gentleman was there all the time, and you knew it! Your petty spite has led you to wreak your vengeance on me by betraying my secrets, my life, my children's lives, my shame, my honor! There, you are nothing to me any longer. I hate you. I will do all that I can to injure you. I will——"

Anger paralyzed her; the words died in her dry parched throat.

"Why, he is my son, my child; he is your brother, your preserver!" cried Goriot. "Kiss his hand, Nasie! Stay, I will embrace him myself," he said, straining Eugène to his breast in a frenzied clasp. "Oh my boy! I will be more than a father to you; I would be everything in the world to you; if I had God's power, I would fling worlds at your feet. Why don't you kiss him, Nasie? He is not a man, but an angel, an angel out of heaven."

"Never mind her, father; she is mad just now."

"Mad! am I? And what are you?" cried Mme. de Restaud.

"Children, children, I shall die if you go on like this," cried the old man, and he staggered and fell on the bed as if a bullet had struck him. "They are killing me between them," he said to himself.

The Countess fixed her eyes on Eugène, who stood stock-still; all his faculties were numbed by this violent scene.

"Sir?——" she said, doubt and inquiry in her face, tone, and bearing; she took no notice now of her father nor of Delphine, who was hastily unfastening his waistcoat.

"Madame," said Eugène, answering the question before it was asked, "I will meet the bill, and keep silence about it."

"You have killed our father, Nasie!" said Delphine, pointing to Goriot, who lay unconscious on the bed. The Countess fled.

"I freely forgive her," said the old man, opening his eyes; "her position is horrible; it would turn an older head than hers. Comfort Nasie, and be nice to her, Delphine; promise it to your poor father before he dies," he said, holding Delphine's hand in a convulsive clasp.

"Oh! what ails you, father?" she cried in real alarm.

"Nothing, nothing," said Goriot; "it will go off. There is something heavy pressing on my forehead, a little headache —— Ah! poor Nasie, what a life lies before her!"

Just as he spoke, the Countess came back again and flung herself on her knees before him. "Forgive me!" she cried.

"Come," said her father, "you are hurting me still more."

"Monsieur," the Countess said, turning to Rastignac, "misery made me unjust to you. You will be a brother to me, will you not?" and she held out her hand. Her eyes were full of tears as she spoke.

"Nasie," cried Delphine, flinging her arms round her sister, "my little Nasie, let us forget and forgive."

"No, no," cried Nasie; "I shall never forget!"

"Dear angels," cried Goriot, "it is as if a dark curtain over my eyes had been raised; your voices have called me back to life. Kiss each other once more. Well, now, Nasie, that bill will save you, won't it?"

"I hope so. I say, papa, will you write your name on it?"

"There! how stupid of me to forget that! But I am not feeling at all well, Nasie, so you must not remember it against me. Send and let me know as soon as you are out of your strait. No, I will go to you. No, after all, I will not go; I might meet your husband, and I should kill him on the spot. And as for signing away your property, I shall have a word to say about that. Quick, my child, and keep Maxime in order in future."

Eugène was too bewildered to speak.

"Poor Anastasie, she always had a violent temper," said Mme. de Nucingen, "but she has a good heart."

"She came back for the endorsement," said Eugène in Delphine's ear.

"Do you think so?"

"I only wish I could think otherwise. Do not trust her," he answered, raising his eyes as if he confided to heaven the thoughts that he did not venture to express.

"Yes, she is always acting a part to some extent."

"How do you feel now, dear Father Goriot?" asked Rastignac.

"I should like to go to sleep," he replied.

Eugène helped him to bed, and Delphine sat by the bedside, holding his hand until he fell asleep. Then she went.

"This evening at the Italiens," she said to Eugène, "and you can let me know how he is. To-morrow you will leave this place, monsieur. Let us go into your room. Oh! how frightful!" she cried on the threshold. "Why, you are even worse lodged than our father. Eugène, you have behaved well. I would love you more if that were possible; but, dear boy, if you are to succeed in life, you must not begin by flinging twelve thousand francs out of the windows like that. The Comte de Trailles is a confirmed gambler. My sister shuts her eyes to it. He would have made the twelve thousand francs in the same way that he wins and loses heaps of gold."

A groan from the next room brought them back to Goriot's bedside; to all appearance he was asleep, but the two lovers caught the words, "They are not happy!" Whether he was awake or sleeping, the tone in which they were spoken went to his daughter's heart. She stole up to the pallet-bed on which her father lay, and kissed his forehead. He opened his eyes.

"Ah! Delphine!" he said.

"How are you now?" she asked.

"Quite comfortable. Do not worry about me; I shall get up presently. Don't stay with me, children; go, go and be happy."

Eugène went back with Delphine as far as her door; but he was not easy about Goriot, and would not stay to dinner, as she proposed. He wanted to be back at the Maison Vauquer. Father Goriot had left his room, and was just sitting down to dinner as he came in. Bianchon had placed himself where he could watch the old man carefully; and when the old vermicelli-maker took up his square of bread and smelt it to find out the quality of the flour, the medical student, studying him closely, saw that the action was purely mechanical, and shook his head.

"Just come and sit over here, hospitaller of Cochin," said Eugène.

Bianchon went the more willingly because his change of place brought him next to the old lodger.

"What is wrong with him?" asked Rastignac.

"It is all up with him, or I am much mistaken! Something very extraordinary must have taken place; he looks to me as if he were in imminent danger of serous apoplexy. The lower part of his face is composed enough, but the upper part is drawn and distorted. Then there is that peculiar look about the eyes that indicates an effusion of serum in the brain; they look as if they were covered with a film of fine dust, do you notice? I shall know more about it by to-morrow morning."

"Is there any cure for it?"

"None. It may be possible to stave death off for a time

if a way could be found of setting up a reaction in the lower extremities; but if the symptoms do not abate by to-morrow evening, it will be all over with him, poor old fellow! Do you know what has happened to bring this on? There must have been some violent shock, and his mind has given way."

"Yes, there was," said Rastignac, remembering how the two daughters had struck blow on blow at their father's heart.

"But Delphine at any rate loves her father," he said to himself.

That evening at the opera Rastignac chose his words carefully, lest he should give Mme. de Nucingen needless alarm.

"Do not be anxious about him," she said, however, as soon as Eugène began, "our father has really a strong constitution, but this morning we gave him a shock. Our whole fortunes were in peril, so the thing was serious, you see. I could not live if your affection did not make me insensible to troubles that I should once have thought too hard to bear. At this moment I have but one fear left, but one misery to dread —to lose the love that has made me feel so glad to live. Everything else is as nothing to me compared with your love; I care for nothing else, for you are all the world to me. If I feel glad to be rich, it is for your sake. To my shame be it said, I think of my lover before my father. Do you ask why? I cannot tell you, but all my life is in you. My father gave me a heart, but you have taught it to beat. The whole world may condemn me; what does it matter if I stand acquitted in your eyes, for you have no right to think ill of me for the faults which a tyrannous love has forced me to commit for you! Do you think me an unnatural daughter? Oh! no, no one could help loving such a dear kind father as ours. But how could I hide the inevitable consequences of our miserable marriages from him? Why did he allow us to marry when we did? Was it not his duty to think for us and foresee for us? To-day I know he suffers as much as we do, but how can it be helped? And as for comforting him, we could not comfort him in the least. Our resignation would give him more pain and hurt him far more than complaints and upbraidings. There are times in life when everything turns to bitterness."

Eugène was silent, the artless and sincere outpouring made an impression on him.

Parisian women are often false, intoxicated with vanity, selfish and self-absorbed, frivolous and shallow; yet of all women, when they love, they sacrifice their personal feelings to their passion; they rise but so much the higher for all the pettiness overcome in their nature, and become sublime. Then Eugène was struck by the profound discernment and insight displayed by this woman in judging of natural affection, when a privileged affection had separated and set her at a distance apart. Mme. de Nucingen was piqued by the silence.

"What are you thinking about?" she asked.

"I am thinking about what you said just now. Hitherto I have always felt sure that I cared far more for you than you did for me."

She smiled, and would not give way to the happiness she felt, lest their talk should exceed the conventional limits of propriety. She had never heard the vibrating tones of a sincere and youthful love; a few more words, and she feared for her self-control.

"Eugène," she said, changing the conversation, "I wonder whether you know what has been happening? All Paris will go to Mme. de Beauséant's to-morrow. The Rochefides and the Marquis d'Ajuda have agreed to keep the matter a profound secret, but to-morrow the king will sign the marriage contract, and your poor cousin the Vicomtesse knows nothing of it as yet. She cannot put off her ball, and the Marquis will not be there. People are wondering what will happen?"

"The world laughs at baseness and connives at it. But this will kill Mme. de Beauséant."

"Oh, no," said Delphine, smiling, "you do not know

that kind of woman. Why, all Paris will be there, and so shall I; I ought to go there for your sake."

"Perhaps, after all, it is one of those absurd reports that people set in circulation here."

"We shall know the truth to-morrow."

Eugène did not return to the Maison Vauquer. He could not forego the pleasure of occupying his new rooms in the Rue d'Artois. Yesterday evening he had been obliged to leave Delphine soon after midnight, but that night it was Delphine who stayed with him until two o'clock in the morning. He rose late, and waited for Mme. de Nucingen, who came about noon to breakfast with him. Youth snatches eagerly at these rosy moments of happiness, and Eugène had almost forgotten Goriot's existence. The pretty things that surrounded him were growing familiar; this domestication in itself was one long festival for him, and Mme. de Nucingen was there to glorify it all by her presence. It was four o'clock before they thought of Goriot, and how he had looked forward to the new life in that house. Eugène said that the old man ought to be moved at once, lest he should grow too ill to move. He left Delphine, and hurried back to the lodging-house. Neither Father Goriot nor young Bianchon was in the dining-room with the others.

"Aha!" said the painter as Eugène came in, "Father Goriot has broken down at last. Bianchon is upstairs with him. One of his daughters—the Comtesse de Restaurama—came to see the old gentleman, and he would get up and go out, and made himself worse. Society is about to lose one of its brightest ornaments."

Rastignac sprang to the staircase.

"Hey! Monsieur Eugène!"

"Monsieur Eugène, the mistress is calling you," shouted Sylvie.

"It is this, sir," said the widow. "You and M. Goriot should by rights have moved out on the 15th of February.

That was three days ago; to-day is the 18th, I ought really to be paid a month in advance; but if you will engage to pay for both, I shall be quite satisfied."

"Why can't you trust him?"

"Trust him, indeed! If the old gentleman went off his head and died, those daughters of his would not pay me a farthing, and his things won't fetch ten francs. This morning he went out with all the spoons and forks he has left, I don't know why. He had got himself up to look quite young, and—Lord, forgive me—but I thought he had rouge on his cheeks; he looked quite young again."

"I will be responsible," said Eugène, shuddering with horror, for he foresaw the end.

He climbed the stairs and reached Father Goriot's room. The old man was tossing on his bed. Bianchon was with him.

"Good-evening, father," said Eugène.

The old man turned his glassy eyes on him, smiled gently, and said—

"How is *she*?"

"She is quite well. But how are you?"

"There is nothing much the matter."

"Don't tire him," said Bianchon, drawing Eugène into a corner of the room.

"Well?" asked Rastignac.

"Nothing but a miracle can save him now. Serous congestion has set in; I have put on mustard plasters, and luckily he can feel them, they are acting."

"Is it possible to move him?"

"Quite out of the question. He must stay where he is, and be kept as quiet as possible——"

"Dear Bianchon," said Eugène, "we will nurse him between us."

"I have had the head physician round from my hospital to see him."

"And what did he say?"

"He will give no opinion till to-morrow evening. He promised to look in again at the end of the day. Unluckily, the preposterous creature must needs go and do something foolish this morning; he will not say what it was. He is as obstinate as a mule. As soon as I begin to talk to him he pretends not to hear, and lies as if he were asleep instead of answering, or if he opens his eyes he begins to groan. Some time this morning he went out on foot in the streets, nobody knows where he went, and he took everything that he had of any value with him. He has been driving some confounded bargain, and it has been too much for his strength. One of his daughters has been here."

"Was it the Countess?" asked Eugène. "A tall, dark-haired woman, with large bright eyes, slender figure, and little feet?"

"Yes."

"Leave him to me for a bit," said Rastignac. "I will make him confess; he will tell me all about it."

"And meanwhile I will get my dinner. But try not to excite him; there is still some hope left."

"All right."

"How they will enjoy themselves to-morrow," said Father Goriot when they were alone. "They are going to a grand ball."

"What were you doing this morning, papa, to make yourself so poorly this evening that you have to stop in bed?"

"Nothing."

"Did not Anastasie come to see you?" demanded Rastignac.

"Yes," said Father Goriot.

"Well, then, don't keep anything from me. What more did she want of you?"

"Oh, she was very miserable," he answered, gathering up all his strength to speak. "It was this way, my boy. Since that affair of the diamonds, Nasie has not had a penny of her own. For this ball she had ordered a golden gown like a setting for a jewel. Her mantuamaker, a woman without a conscience, would not give her credit, so Nasie's waiting-woman advanced a thousand francs on account. Poor Nasie! reduced to such shifts! It cut me to the heart to think of it! But when Nasie's maid saw how things were between her master and mistress, she was afraid of losing her money, and came to an understanding with the dressmaker, and the woman refuses to send the ball-dress until the money is paid. The gown is ready, and the ball is to-morrow night; Nasie was in despair. She wanted to borrow my forks and spoons to pawn them. Her husband is determined that she shall go and wear the diamonds, so as to contradict the stories that are told all over Paris. How can she go to that heartless scoundrel and say, 'I owe a thousand francs to my dressmaker; pay her for me?' She cannot. I saw that myself. Delphine will be there too in a superb toilet, and Anastasie ought not to be outshone by her younger sister. And then—she was drowned in tears, poor girl! I felt so humbled yesterday when I had not the twelve thousand francs, that I would have given the rest of my miserable life to wipe out that wrong. You see, I could have borne anything once, but latterly this want of money has broken my heart. Oh! I did not do it by halves; I titivated myself up a bit, and went out and sold my spoons and forks and buckles for six hundred francs; then I went to old Daddy Gobseck and sold a year's interest in my annuity for four hundred francs down. Pshaw! I can live on dry bread, as I did when I was a young man; if I have done it before, I can do it again. My Nasie shall have one happy evening, at any rate. She shall be smart. The bank-note for a thousand francs is here under my pillow; it warms me to have it lying here under my head, for it is going to make my poor Nasie happy. She can turn that bad girl Victoire out of the house. A servant that cannot trust her mistress, did any one ever hear the like! I shall be quite well to-morrow. Nasie is coming at ten o'clock. They must not think that I am ill, or they will not go to the ball; they will stop and take care of me. To-morrow Nasie will come and hold me in her arms as if I were one of her children; her kisses will make me well again. After all, I might have spent the thousand francs on physic; I would far rather give them to my little Nasie, who can charm all the pain away. At any rate, I am some comfort to her in her misery; and that makes up for my unkindness in buying an annuity. She is in the depths, and I cannot draw her out of them now. Oh! I will go into business again, I will buy wheat in Odessa; out there, wheat fetches a quarter of the price it sells for here. There is a law against the importation of grain, but the good folk who made the law forgot to prohibit the introduction of wheat products and food stuffs made from corn. Hey! hey!—— That struck me this morning. There is a fine trade to be done in starch."

Eugene, watching the old man's face, thought that his friend was light-headed.

"Come," he said, "do not talk any more, you must rest ——." Just then Bianchon came up, and Eugène went down to dinner.

The two students sat up with him that night, relieving each other in turn. Bianchon brought up his medical books and studied; Eugène wrote letters home to his mother and sisters. Next morning Bianchon thought the symptoms more hopeful, but the patient's condition demanded continual attention, which the two students alone were willing to give—a task impossible to describe in the squeamish phraseology of the epoch. Leeches must be applied to the wasted body; the poultices, hot foot-baths, and other details of the treatment required the physical strength and devotion of the two young men. Mme. de Restaud did not come; but she sent a messenger for the money.

"I expected she would come herself; but it would have been a pity for her to come, she would have been anxious about me," said the father, and to all appearance he was well content.

At seven o'clock that evening Thérèse came with a letter from Delphine.

"What are you doing, dear friend? I have been loved for a very little while, and am I neglected already? In the confidences of heart and heart, I have learned to know your soul—you are too noble not to be faithful for ever, for you know that love with all its infinite subtle changes of feelings is never the same. Once you said, as we were listening to the prayer in 'Mosè in Egitto,' 'For some it is the monotony of a single note; for others, it is the infinite of sound.' Remember that I am expecting you this evening to take me to Mme. de Beauséant's ball. Every one knows now that the king signed M. d'Ajuda's marriage-contract this morning, and the poor Vicomtesse knew nothing of it until two o'clock this afternoon. All Paris will flock to her house, of course, just as a crowd fills the Place de Grève to see an execution. It is horrible, is it not, to go out of curiosity to see if she will hide her anguish, and whether she will die courageously? I certainly should not go, my friend, if I had been at her house before; but, of course, she will not receive society any more after this, and all my efforts would be in vain. My position is a very unusual one, and, besides, I am going there partly on your account. I am waiting for you. If you are not beside me in less than two hours, I do not know whether I could forgive such treason."

Rastignac took up a pen and wrote—

"I am waiting till the doctor comes to know if there is any hope of your father's life. He is lying dangerously ill.

I will come and bring you the news, but I am afraid it may be a sentence of death. When I come you can decide whether you can go to the ball. Yours a thousand times."

At half-past eight the doctor arrived. He did not take a very hopeful view of the case, but thought that there was no immediate danger. Improvements and relapses might be expected, and the good man's life and reason hung in the balance.

"It would be better for him to die at once," the doctor said as he took leave.

Eugène left Goriot to Bianchon's care, and went to carry the sad news to Mme. de Nucingen. Family feeling lingered in her, and this must put an end for the present to her plans of amusement.

"Tell her to enjoy her evening as if nothing had happened," cried Goriot. He had been lying in a sort of stupor, but he suddenly sat upright as Eugène went out.

Eugène, half-heartbroken, entered Delphine's room. Her hair had been dressed; she wore her dancing slippers; she had only to put on her ball-dress; but when the artist is giving the finishing stroke to his creation, the last touches require more time than the whole ground-work of the picture.

"Why! you are not dressed!" she cried.

"Madame, your father——"

"My father again!" she exclaimed, breaking in upon him. "You need not teach me what is due to my father, I have known my father this long while. Not a word, Eugène. I will hear what you have to say when you are dressed. My carriage is waiting, take it, go round to your rooms and dress, Thérèse has put out everything in readiness for you. Come back as soon as you can; we will talk about my father on the way to Mme. de Beauséant's. We must go early; if we have to wait our turn in a row of carriages, we shall be lucky if we get there by eleven o'clock."

"Madame——"

"Quick! not a word!" she cried, darting into her dressing-room for a necklace.

"Do go, Monsieur Eugène, or you will vex madame," said Thérèse, hurrying him away; and Eugène was too horror-stricken by this elegant parricide to resist.

He went to his rooms and dressed, sad, thoughtful, and dispirited. The world of Paris was like an ocean of mud for him just then; and it seemed that whoever set foot in that black mire must needs sink into it up to the chin.

"Their crimes are paltry," said Eugène to himself. "Vautrin was greater."

He had seen society in its three great phases—obedience, struggle, and revolt; the family, the world, and Vautrin; and he hesitated in his choice. Obedience was dull, revolt impossible, struggle hazardous. His thoughts wandered back to the home circle. He thought of the quiet uneventful life, the pure happiness of the days spent among those who loved him there. Those loving and beloved beings passed their lives in obedience to the natural laws of the hearth, and in that obedience found a deep and constant serenity, unvexed by torments such as these. Yet, for all his good impulses, he could not bring himself to make profession of the religion of pure souls to Delphine, nor to prescribe the duties of piety to her in the name of love. His education had begun to bear its fruits; he loved selfishly already. Besides, his tact had discovered to him the real nature of Delphine; he divined instinctively that she was capable of stepping over her father's corpse to go to the ball; and within himself he felt that he had neither the strength of mind to play the part of mentor, nor the strength of character to vex her, nor the courage to leave her to go alone.

"She would never forgive me for putting her in the wrong over it," he said to himself. Then he turned the doctor's dictum over in his mind; he tried to believe that Goriot was not so dangerously ill as he had imagined, and ended by collecting together a sufficient quantity of traitorous excuses for Delphine's conduct. She did not know how ill her father was; the kind old man himself would have made her go to the ball if she had gone to see him. So often it happens that this one or that stands condemned by the social laws that govern family relations; and yet there are peculiar circumstances in the case, differences of temperament, divergent interests, innumerable complications of family life that excuse the apparent offense.

Eugène did not wish to see too clearly; he was ready to sacrifice his conscience to his mistress. Within the last few days his whole life had undergone a change. Woman had entered into his world and thrown it into chaos, family claims dwindled away before her; she had appropriated all his being to her uses. Rastignac and Delphine found each other at a crisis in their lives when their union gave them the most poignant bliss. Their passion, so long proved, had only gained in strength by the gratified desire that often extinguishes passion. This woman was his, and Eugène recognized that not until then had he loved her; perhaps love is only gratitude for pleasure. This woman, vile or sublime, he adored for the pleasures she had brought as her dower; and Delphine loved Rastignac as Tantalus would have loved some angel who had satisfied his hunger and quenched the burning thirst in his parched throat.

"Well," said Mme. de Nucingen when he came back in evening dress, "how is my father?"

"Very dangerously ill," he answered; "if you will grant me a proof of your affection, we will just go in to see him on the way."

"Very well," she said. "Yes, but afterwards. Dear Eugène, do be nice, and don't preach to me. Come."

They set out for the ball. Eugène said nothing for a while, apparently absorbed in deep meditation.

"What is it now?" she asked.

"I can hear the death-rattle in your father's throat," he said, almost angrily. And with the hot indignation of youth, he told the story of Mme. de Restaud's vanity and cruelty, of her father's final act of self-sacrifice, that had brought about this struggle between life and death, of the price that had been paid for Anastasie's golden embroideries. Delphine cried.

"I shall look frightful," she thought. She dried her tears.

"I will nurse my father; I will not leave his bedside," she said aloud.

"Ah! now you are as I would have you," exclaimed Rastignac.

The lamps of five hundred carriages lit up the darkness about the Hôtel de Beauséant. A gendarme in all the glory of his uniform stood on either side of the brightly lighted gateway. The great world was flocking thither that night in its eager curiosity to see the great lady at the moment of her fall, and the rooms on the ground floor were already full to overflowing, when Mme. de Nucingen and Rastignac appeared. Never since Louis XIV. tore her lover away from La Grande Mademoiselle, and the whole court hastened to visit that unfortunate princess, had a disastrous love affair made such a sensation in Paris. But the youngest daughter of the almost royal house of Burgundy had risen proudly above her pain, and moved till the last moment like a queen in this world— its vanities had always been valueless for her, save in so far as they contributed to the triumph of her passion. The salons were filled with the most beautiful women in Paris, resplendent in their toilets, and radiant with smiles. Ministers and ambassadors, the most distinguished men at court, men bedizened with decorations, stars, and ribbons, men who bore the most illustrious names in France, had gathered about the Vicomtesse.

The music of the orchestra vibrated in wave after wave of

sound from the golden ceiling of the palace, now made desolate for its queen.

Madame de Beauséant stood at the door of the first salon to receive the guests who were styled her friends. She was dressed in white, and wore no ornament in the plaits of hair braided about her head; her face was calm; there was no sign there of pride, nor of pain, nor of joy that she did not feel. No one could read her soul; she stood there like some Niobe carved in marble. For a few intimate friends there was a tinge of satire in her smile; but no scrutiny saw any change in her, nor had she looked otherwise in the days of the glory of her happiness. The most callous of her guests admired her as young Rome applauded some gladiator who could die smiling. It seemed as if society had adorned itself for a last audience of one of its sovereigns.

"I was afraid that you would not come," she said to Rastignac.

"Madame," he said, in an unsteady voice, taking her speech as a reproach, "I shall be the last to go, that is why I am here."

"Good," she said, and she took his hand. "You are perhaps the only one that I can trust here among all these. Oh, my friend, when you love, love a woman whom you are sure that you can love always. Never forsake a woman."

She took Rastignac's arm, and went towards a sofa in the card-room.

"I want you to go to the Marquis," she said. "Jacques, my footman, will go with you; he has a letter that you will take. I am asking the Marquis to give my letters back to me. He will give them all up, I like to think that. When you have my letters, go up to my room with them. Some one shall bring me word."

She rose to go to meet the Duchesse de Langeais, her most intimate friend, who had come like the rest of the world.

Rastignac went. He asked for the Marquis d'Ajuda at the

Hôtel Rochefide, feeling certain that the latter would be spending his evening there, and so it proved. The Marquis went to his own house with Rastignac, and gave a casket to the student, saying as he did so, "They are all there."

He seemed as if he was about to say something to Eugène, to ask about the ball, or the Vicomtesse; perhaps he was on the brink of the confession that, even then, he was in despair, and knew that his marriage would be a fatal mistake; but a proud gleam shone in his eyes, and with deplorable courage he kept his noblest feelings a secret.

"Do not even mention my name to her, my dear Eugène." He grasped Rastignac's hand sadly and affectionately, and turned away from him. Eugène went back to the Hôtel Beauséant, the servant took him to the Vicomtesse's room. There were signs there of preparations for a journey. He sat down by the fire, fixed his eyes on the cedar-wood casket, and fell into deep mournful musings. Mme. de Beauséant loomed up largely in these imaginings, like a goddess in the Iliad.

"Ah! my friend!——" said the Vicomtesse; she crossed the room and laid her hand on Rastignac's shoulder. He saw the tears in his cousin's uplifted eyes, saw that one hand was raised to take the casket, and that the fingers of the other trembled. Suddenly she took the casket, put it in the fire, and watched it burn.

"They are dancing," she said. "They all came very early; but death will be long in coming. Hush! my friend," and she laid a finger on Rastignac's lips, seeing that he was about to speak. "I shall never see Paris again. I am taking my leave of this world. At five o'clock this morning I shall set out on my journey; I mean to bury myself in the remotest part of Normandy. I have had very little time to make my arrangements; since three o'clock this afternoon I have been busy signing documents, setting my affairs in order; there was no one whom I could send to——"

She broke off.

"He was sure to be——"

Again she broke off; the weight of her sorrow was more than she could bear. In such moments as these everything is agony, and some words are impossible to utter.

"And so I counted upon you to do me this last piece of service this evening," she said. "I should like to give you some pledge of friendship. I shall often think of you. You have seemed to me to be kind and noble, fresh-hearted and true, in this world where such qualities are seldom found. I should like you to think sometimes of me. Stay," she said, glancing about her, "there is this box that has held my gloves. Every time I opened it before going to a ball or to the theatre, I used to feel that I must be beautiful, because I was so happy; and I never touched it except to lay some gracious memory in it: there is so much of my old self in it, of a Madame de Beauséant who now lives no longer. Will you take it? I will leave directions that it is to be sent to you in the Rue d'Artois. Mme. de Nucingen looked very charming this evening. Eugène, you must love her. Perhaps we may never see each other again, my friend; but be sure of this, that I shall pray for you who have been kind to me. Now let us go downstairs. People shall not think that I am weeping. I have all time and eternity before me, and where I am going I shall be alone, and no one will ask me the reason of my tears. One last look round first."

She stood for a moment. Then she covered her eyes with her hands for an instant, dashed away the tears, bathed her face with cold water, and took the student's arm.

"Let us go!" she said.

This suffering, endured with such noble fortitude, shook Eugène with a more violent emotion than he had felt before. They went back to the ballroom, and Mme. de Beauséant went through the rooms on Eugène's arm—the last delicately gracious act of a gracious woman. In another moment he saw the sisters, Mme. de Restaud and Mme. de Nucingen.

The Countess shone in all the glory of her magnificent diamonds; every stone must have scorched like fire, she was never to wear them again. Strong as love and pride might be in her, she found it difficult to meet her husband's eyes. The sight of her was scarcely calculated to lighten Rastignac's sad thoughts; through the blaze of those diamonds he seemed to see the wretched pallet-bed on which Father Goriot was lying. The Vicomtesse misread his melancholy; she withdrew her hand from his arm.

"Come," she said to him, "I must not deprive you of a pleasure."

Eugène was soon claimed by Delphine. She was delighted with the impression that she had made, and eager to lay at her lover's feet the homage she had received in this new world in which she hoped to live and move, henceforth, a conspicuous figure.

"What do you think of Nasie?" she asked him.

"She has discounted everything, even her own father's death," said Rastignac.

Towards four o'clock in the morning the rooms began to empty. A little later the music ceased, and the Duchesse de Langeais and Rastignac were left in the great ballroom. The Vicomtesse, who thought to find the student there alone, came back there at the last. She had taken leave of M. de Beauséant, who had gone off to bed, saying again as he went, "It is a great pity, my dear, to shut yourself up at your age! Pray stay among us."

Mme. de Beauséant saw the Duchess, and, in spite of herself, an exclamation broke from her.

"I saw how it was, Clara," said Mme. de Langeais. "You are going from among us, and you will never come back. But you must not go until you have heard me, until we have understood each other."

She took her friend's arm, and they went together into the next room. There the Duchess looked at her with tears in her eyes; she held her friend in a close embrace, and kissed her cheek.

"I could not let you go without a word, dearest; the remorse would have been too hard to bear. You can count upon me as surely as upon yourself. You have shown yourself great this evening; I feel that I am worthy of your friendship, and I mean to prove myself worthy of it. I have not always been kind; I was in the wrong; forgive me, dearest; I wish I could unsay anything that may have hurt you; I take back those words. One common sorrow has brought us together again, for I do not know which of us is the more miserable. M. de Montreveau was not here to-night; do you understand what that means? None of those who saw you to-night, Clara, will ever forget you. I mean to make one last effort. If I fail, I shall go into a convent. Clara, where are you going?"

"Into Normandy, to Courcelles. I shall love and pray there until the day when God shall take me from this world. M. de Rastignac!" called the Vicomtesse, in a tremulous voice, remembering that the young man was waiting there.

The student knelt to kiss his cousin's hand.

"Good-by, Antoinette!" said Mme. de Beauséant. "May you be happy." She turned to the student. "You are young," she said; you have some beliefs still left. I have been privileged, like some dying people, to find sincere and reverent feeling in those about me as I take my leave of this world."

It was nearly five o'clock that morning when Rastignac came away. He had put Mme. de Beauséant into her traveling carriage, and received her last farewells, spoken amid fast-falling tears; for no greatness is so great that it can rise above the laws of human affection, or live beyond the jurisdiction of pain, as certain demagogues would have the people believe. Eugène returned on foot to the Maison Vauquer through the cold and darkness. His education was nearly complete.

"There is no hope for poor Father Goriot," said Bianchon, as Rastignac came into the room. Eugène looked for a while at the sleeping man, then he turned to his friend. "Dear fellow, you are content with the modest career you have marked out for yourself; keep to it. I am in hell, and I must stay there. Believe everything that you hear said of the world, nothing is too impossibly bad. No Juvenal could paint the horrors hidden away under the covering of gems and gold."

At two o'clock in the afternoon Bianchon came to wake Rastignac, and begged him to take charge of Goriot, who had grown worse as the day wore on. The medical student was obliged to go out.

"Poor old man, he has not two days to live, maybe not many hours," he said; "but we must do our utmost, all the same, to fight the disease. It will be a very troublesome case, and we shall want money. We can nurse him between us, of course, but, for my own part, I have not a penny. I have turned out his pockets, and rummaged through his drawers— result, *nix*. I asked him about it while his mind was clear, and he told me he had not a farthing of his own. What have you?"

"I have twenty francs left," said Rastignac; "but I will take them to the roulette table, I shall be sure to win."

"And if you lose?"

"Then I shall go to his sons-in-law and his daughters and ask them for money."

"And suppose they refuse?" Bianchon retorted. "The most pressing thing just now is not really money; we must put mustard poultices, as hot as they can be made, on his feet and legs. If he calls out, there is still some hope for him. You know how to set about doing it, and, besides, Christophe will help you. I am going round to the dispensary to persuade them to let us have the things we want on credit. It is a pity that we could not move him to the hospital; poor fellow, he would be better there. Well, come along, I leave you in charge; you must stay with him till I come back."

The two young men went back to the room where the old man was lying. Eugène was startled at the change in Goriot's face, so livid, distorted, and feeble.

"How are you, papa?" he said, bending over the pallet-bed. Goriot turned his dull eyes upon Eugène, looked at him attentively, and did not recognize him. It was more than the student could bear; the tears came into his eyes.

"Bianchon, ought we to have curtains put up in the windows?"

"No, the temperature and the light do not affect him now. It would be a good thing for him if he felt heat or cold; but we must have a fire in any case to make tisanes and heat the other things. I will send round a few sticks; they will last till we can have in some firewood. I burned all the bark fuel you had left, as well as his, poor man, yesterday and during the night. The place was so damp that the water stood in drops on the walls; I could hardly get the room dry. Christophe came in and swept the floor, but the place is like a stable; I had to burn juniper, the smell was something horrible."

"*Mon Dieu!*" said Rastignac. "To think of those daughters of his."

"One moment, if he asks for something to drink, give him this," said the house student, pointing to a large white jar. "If he begins to groan, and the belly feels hot and hard to the touch, you know what to do; get Christophe to help you. If he should happen to grow much excited, and begin to talk a good deal, and even to ramble in his talk, do not be alarmed. It would not be a bad symptom. But send Christophe to the Hospice Cochin. Our doctor, my chum, or I will come and apply moxas. We had a great consultation this morning while you were asleep. A surgeon, a pupil of Gall's, came, and our house surgeon, and the head physician from the Hôtel-Dieu. Those gentlemen considered that the symptoms were very unusual and interesting; the case must be carefully watched, for it throws a light on several obscure and rather important scientific problems. One of the authorities says that if there is more pressure of serum on one or other portion of the brain, it should affect his mental capacities in such and such directions. So if he should talk, notice very carefully what kind of ideas his mind seems to run on; whether memory, or penetration, or the reasoning faculties are exercised; whether sentiments or practical questions fill his thoughts; whether he makes forecasts or dwells on the past; in fact, you must be prepared to give an accurate report of him. It is quite likely that the extravasation fills the whole brain, in which case he will die in the imbecile state in which he is lying now. You cannot tell anything about these mysterious nervous diseases. Suppose the crash came here," said Bianchon, touching the back of the head, "very strange things have been known to happen; the brain sometimes partially recovers, and death is delayed. Or the congested matter may pass out of the brain altogether through channels which can only be determined by a post-mortem examination. There is an old man at the Hospital for Incurables, an imbecile patient, in his case the effusion has followed the direction of the spinal cord; he suffers the most horrible agonies, but still he lives."

"Did they enjoy themselves?" It was Father Goriot who spoke. He had recognized Eugène.

"Oh! he thinks of nothing but his daughters," said Bianchon. "Scores of times last night he said to me, 'They are dancing now! She has her dress.' He called them by their names. He made me cry, the devil take it, calling with that tone in his voice, for 'Delphine! my little Delphine!

and Nasie!' Upon my word," said the medical student, "it was enough to make any one burst out crying."

"Delphine," said the old man, "she is there, isn't she? I knew she was there," and his eyes sought the door.

"I am going down now to tell Sylvie to get the poultices ready," said Bianchon. "They ought to go on at once."

Rastignac was left alone with the old man. He sat at the foot of the bed, and gazed at the face before him, so horribly changed that it was shocking to see.

"Noble natures cannot dwell in this world," he said; "Mme. de Beauséant has fled from it, and there he lies dying. What place indeed is there in the shallow, petty, frivolous thing called society, for noble thoughts and feelings?"

Pictures of yesterday's ball rose up in his memory, in strange contrast to the death-bed scene before him. Bianchon suddenly appeared.

"I say, Eugène, I have just seen our head surgeon at the hospital, and I ran all the way back here. If the old man shows any signs of reason, if he begins to talk, cover him with a mustard poultice from the neck to the base of the spine, and send round for us."

"Dear Bianchon," exclaimed Eugène.

"Oh! it is an interesting case from a scientific point of view," said the medical student, with all the enthusiasm of a neophyte.

"So!" said Eugène. "Am I really the only one who cares for the poor old man for his own sake?"

"You would not have said so if you had seen me this morning," returned Bianchon, who did not take offense at this speech. "Doctors who have seen a good deal of practice never see anything but the disease, but, my dear fellow, I can see the patient still."

He went. Eugène was left alone with the old man, and with an apprehension of a crisis that set in, in fact, before very long.

"Ah! dear boy, is that you?" said Father Goriot, recognizing Eugène.

"Did you feel better?" asked the law student, taking his hand.

"Yes. My head felt as if it were being screwed in a vise, but now it is set free again. Did you see my girls? They will be here directly; as soon as they know that I am ill they will hurry here at once; they used to take such care of me in the Rue de la Jussienne! Great heavens! if only my room was fit for them to come into! There has been a young man here, who has burned up all my bark fuel."

"I can hear Christophe coming upstairs," Eugène answered. "He is bringing up some firewood that that young man has sent you."

"Good, but how am I to pay for the wood? I have not a penny left, dear boy. I have given everything, everything. I am a pauper now. Well, at least the golden gown was grand, was it not? (Ah! what pain this is!) Thanks, Christophe! God will reward you, my boy; I have nothing left now."

Eugène went over to Christophe and whispered in the man's ear, "I will pay you well, and Sylvie too, for your trouble."

"My daughters told you that they were coming, didn't they, Christophe? Go again to them, and I will give you five francs. Tell them that I am not feeling well, that I should like to kiss them both and see them once again before I die. Tell them that, but don't alarm them more than you can help."

Rastignac signed to Christophe to go, and the man hurriedly departed.

"They will come before long," the old man went on. "I know them so well. My tender-hearted Delphine! If I am going to die, she will feel it so much! And so will Nasie. I do not want to die; they will cry if I die; and if I die, dear Eugène, I shall not see them any more. It will be very dreary there where I am going. For a father it is hell to be without your children; I have served my apprenticeship already since they married. My heaven was in the Rue de la Jussienne. Eugène, do you think that if I go to heaven I could come back to earth, and be near them in spirit? I have heard some such things said. Is it true? It is as if I could see them at this moment as they used to be when we all lived in the Rue de la Jussienne. They used to come downstairs of a morning. 'Good-morning, papa!' they used to say; and I would take them on my knees; we had all sorts of little games of play together, and they had such pretty coaxing ways. We always had breakfast together, too, every morning, and they had dinner with me—in fact, I was a father then. I enjoyed my children. They did not think for themselves so long as they lived in the Rue de la Jussienne; they knew nothing of the world; they loved me with all their hearts. *Mon Dieu!* why could they not always be little girls? (Oh! my head! this racking pain in my head!) Ah! ah! forgive me, children; this pain is fearful; it must be agony indeed, for you have used me to endure pain. *Mon Dieu!* if only I held their hands in mine, I should not feel it at all. Do you think that they are on the way? Christophe is so stupid; I ought to have gone myself. *He* will see them. But you went to the ball yesterday; just tell me how they looked. They did not know that I was ill, did they, or they would not have been dancing, poor little things? Oh! I must not be ill any longer. They stand too much in need of me; their fortunes are in danger. And such husbands as they are bound to! I must get well! (Oh! what pain this is! what pain this is!—— ah! ah!) I must get well, you see; for they *must* have money, and I know how to set about making some. I will go to Odessa and manufacture starch there. I am an old hand, I will make millions. (Oh! this is agony!)"

Goriot was silent for a moment; it seemed to require his whole strength to endure the pain.

"If they were here, I should not complain," he said. "So why should I complain now?"

He seemed to grow drowsy with exhaustion, and lay quietly for a long time. Christophe came back; and Rastignac, thinking that Goriot was asleep, allowed the man to give his story aloud.

"First of all, sir, I went to Madame la Comtesse," he said; "but she and her husband were so busy that I couldn't get to speak to her. When I insisted that I must see her, M. de Restaud came out to me himself, and went on like this —'M. Goriot is dying, is he? Very well, it is the best thing he can do. I want Mme. de Restaud to transact some important business, when it is all finished she can go.' The gentleman looked angry, I thought. I was just going away when Mme. de Restaud came out into an ante-chamber through a door that I did not notice, and said, 'Christophe, tell my father that my husband wants me to discuss some matters with him, and I cannot leave the house, the life or death of my children is at stake; but as soon as it is over, I will come.' As for Madame la Baronne, that is another story! I could not speak to her either, and I did not even see her. Her waiting-woman said, 'Ah, yes, but madame only came back from a ball at a quarter to five this morning; she is asleep now, and if I wake her before mid-day she will be cross. As soon as she rings, I will go and tell her that her father is worse. It will be time enough then to tell her bad news!' I begged and I prayed, but, there! it was no good. Then I asked for M. le Baron, but he was out."

"To think that neither of his daughters should come!" exclaimed Rastignac. "I will write to them both."

"Neither of them!" cried the old man, sitting upright in bed. "They are busy, they are asleep, they will not come! I knew that they would not. Not until you are dying do you know your children——— Oh! my friend, do not marry; do not have children! You give them life; they give you your death-blow. You bring them into the world, and they send you out of it. No, they will not come. I have known that these ten years. Sometimes I have told myself so, but I did not dare to believe it."

The tears gathered and stood without overflowing the red sockets.

"Ah! if I were rich still, if I had kept my money, if I had not given all to them, they would be with me now; they would fawn on me and cover my cheeks with their kisses! I should be living in a great mansion; I should have grand apartments and servants and a fire in my room; and *they* would be about me all in tears, and their husbands and their children. I should have had all that; now, I have nothing. Money brings everything to you; even your daughters. My money. Oh! where is my money? If I had plenty of money to leave behind me, they would nurse me and tend me; I should hear their voices, I should see their faces. Ah, God! who knows? They both of them have hearts of stone. I loved them too much; it was not likely that they should love me. A father ought always to be rich; he ought to keep his children well in hand, like unruly horses. I have gone down on my knees to them. Wretches! this is the crowning act that brings the last ten years to a proper close. If you but knew how much they made of me just after they were married. (Oh! this is cruel torture!) I had just given them each eight hundred thousand francs; they were bound to be civil to me after that, and their husbands too were civil. I used to go to their houses; it was, 'My kind father' here, 'My dear father' there. There was always a place for me at their tables. I used to dine with their husbands now and then, and they were very respectful to me. I was still worth something, they thought. How should they know? I have not said anything about my affairs. It is worth while to be civil to a man who has given his daughters eight hundred thousand francs apiece; and they showed me every attention then—but it was all for my money. Grand people are not great. I found that out by experience! I went to the theatre with them in their carriage; I might stay as long as I cared to stay at their evening parties. In fact, they acknowledged me as their father; publicly they owned that they were my daughters. But I was always a shrewd one, you see, and nothing was lost upon me. Everything went straight to the mark and pierced my heart. I saw quite well that it was all sham and pretense, but there is no help for such things as these. I felt less at my ease at their dinner table than I did downstairs here. I had nothing to say for myself. So these grand folks would ask in my son-in-law's ear, 'Who may that gentleman be?' 'The father-in-law with the dollars; he is very rich.' 'The devil he is!' they would say, and look again at me with the respect due to my money. Well, if I was in the way sometimes, I paid dearly for my mistakes. And, besides, who is perfect? (My head is one sore!) Dear Monsieur Eugène, I am suffering so now, that a man might die of the pain; but it is nothing, nothing to be compared with the pain I endured when Anastasie made me feel, for the first time, that I had said something stupid. She looked at me, and that glance of hers opened all my veins. I used to want to know everything, to be learned; and one thing I did learn thoroughly —I knew that I was not wanted here on earth.

"The next day I went to Delphine for comfort, and what should I do there but make some stupid blunder that made her angry with me. I was like one driven out of his senses. For a week I did not know what to do; I did not dare to go to see them for fear they should reproach me. And that was how they both turned me out of the house.

"Oh, God! Thou knowest all the misery and anguish that I have endured; Thou hast counted all the wounds that have been dealt to me in these years that have aged and changed me and whitened my hair and drained my life; why dost Thou make me to suffer so to-day? Have I not more than expiated the sin of loving them too much? They themselves have been the instruments of vengeance; they have tortured me for my sin of affection.

"Ah, well! fathers know no better; I loved them so; I went back to them as a gambler goes to the gaming-table. This love was my vice, you see, my mistress—they were everything in the world to me. They were always wanting something or other, dresses and ornaments, and whatnot; their maids used to tell me what they wanted, and I used to give them the things for the sake of the welcome that they bought for me. But, at the same time, they used to give me little lectures on my behavior in society; they began about it at once. Then they began to feel ashamed of me. That is what comes of having your children well brought up. I could not go to school again at my time of life. (This pain is fearful! *Mon Dieu!* These doctors! these doctors! If they would open my head, it would give me some relief!) Oh, my daughters, my daughters! Anastasie! Delphine! If I could only see them! Send for the police, and make them come to me! Justice is on my side, the whole world is on my side, I have natural rights, and the law with me. I protest! The country will go to ruin if a father's rights are trampled underfoot. That is easy to see. The whole world turns on fatherly love; fatherly love is the foundation of society; it will crumble into ruin when children do not love their fathers. Oh! if I could only see them, and hear them, no matter what they said; if I could simply hear their voices, it would soothe the pain. Delphine! Delphine most of all. But tell them when they come not to look so coldly at me as they do. Oh! my friend, my good Monsieur Eugène, you do not know what it is when all the golden light in a glance suddenly turns to a leaden gray. It has been one long winter here since the light in their eyes shone no more for me. I have had nothing but disappointments to devour. Disappointment has been my daily bread; I have lived on humiliation and insults. I have swallowed down all the affronts for which they sold me my poor stealthy little moments of joy; for I love them so! Think of it! a father hiding himself to get a glimpse of his children! I have given all my life to them, and to-day they will not give me an hour! I am hungering and thirsting for them, my heart is burning in me, but they will not come to bring relief in the agony, for I am dying now, I feel that this is death. Do they not know what it means to trample on a father's corpse? There is a God in heaven who avenges us fathers whether we will or no.

"Oh! they will come! Come to me, darlings, and give me one more kiss; one last kiss, the Viaticum for your father, who will pray God for you in heaven. I will tell Him that you have been good children to your father, and plead your cause with God! After all, it is not their fault. I tell you they are innocent, my friend. Tell every one that it is not their fault, and no one need be distressed on my account. It is all my own fault, I taught them to trample upon me. I loved to have it so. It is no one's affair but mine; man's justice and God's justice have nothing to do in it. God would be unjust if He condemned them for anything they may have done to me. I did not behave to them properly; I was stupid enough to resign my rights. I would have humbled myself in the dust for them. What could you expect? The most beautiful nature, the noblest soul, would have been spoiled by such indulgence. I am a wretch, I am justly punished. I, and I only, am to blame for all their sins; I spoiled them. To-day they are as eager for pleasure as they used to be for sugar-plums. When they were little girls I indulged them in every whim. They had a carriage of their own when they were fifteen. They have never been crossed. I am guilty, and not they—but I sinned through love.

"My heart would open at the sound of their voices. I can

hear them; they are coming. Yes! yes! they are coming. The law demands that they should be present at their father's death-bed; the law is on my side. It would only cost them the hire of a cab. I would pay that. Write to them, tell them that I have millions to leave to them! On my word of honor, yes. I am going to manufacture Italian paste foods at Odessa. I understand the trade. There are millions to be made in it. Nobody has thought of the scheme as yet. You see, there will be no waste, no damage in transit, as there always is with wheat and flour. Hey! hey! and starch too; there are millions to be made in the starch trade! You will not be telling a lie. Millions, tell them; and even if they really come because they covet the money, I would rather let them deceive me; and I shall see them in any case. I want my children! I gave them life; they are mine, mine!" and he sat upright. The head thus raised, with its scanty white hair, seemed to Eugène like a threat; every line that could still speak spoke of menace.

"There, there, dear father," said Eugène, "lie down again; I will write to them at once. As soon as Bianchon comes back I will go for them myself, if they do not come before."

"If they do not come?" repeated the old man, sobbing. "Why, I shall be dead before then; I shall die in a fit of rage, of rage! Anger is getting the better of me. I can see my whole life at this minute. I have been cheated! They do not love me—they have never loved me all their lives! It is all clear to me. They have not come, and they will not come. The longer they put off their coming, the less they are likely to give me this joy. I know them. They have never cared to guess my disappointments, my sorrows, my wants; they never cared to know my life; they will have no presentiment of my death; they do not even know the secret of my tenderness for them. Yes, I see it all now. I have laid my heart open so often that they take everything I do for them as a matter of course. They might have asked me for the very eyes out of my head, and I would have bidden them to pluck them out. They think that all fathers are like theirs. You should always make your value felt. Their own children will avenge me. Why, for their own sakes they should come to me! Make them understand that they are laying up retribution for their own death-beds. All crimes are summed up in this one—— Go to them; just tell them that if they stay away it will be parricide! There is enough laid to their charge already without adding that to the list. Cry aloud as I do now, 'Nasie! Delphine! here! Come to your father; the father who has been so kind to you is lying ill!' Not a sound; no one comes! Then am I to die like a dog? This is to be my reward—I am forsaken at the last. They are wicked, heartless women; curses on them, I loathe them. I shall rise at night from my grave to curse them again; for, after all, my friends, have I done wrong! They are behaving very badly to me, eh?—— What am I saying? Did you not tell me just now that Delphine was in the room? She is more tender-hearted than her sister—— Eugène, you are my son, you know. You will love her; be a father to her! Her sister is very unhappy. And there are their fortunes! Ah, God! I am dying, this anguish is almost more than I can bear! Cut off my head; leave me nothing but my heart."

"Christophe!" shouted Eugène, alarmed by the way in which the old man moaned, and by his cries, "go for M. Bianchon, and send a cab here for me. I am going to fetch them, dear father; I will bring them back to you."

"Make them come! Compel them to come! Call out the Guard, the military, anything and everything, but make them come!" He looked at Eugène, and a last gleam of intelligence shone in his eyes. "Go to the authorities, to the public prosecutor, let them bring them here; come they shall!"

"But you have cursed them."

"Who said that!" said the old man in dull amazement. "You know quite well that I love them, I adore them! I shall be quite well again if I can see them—— Go for them, my good neighbor, my dear boy, you are kind-hearted; I wish I could repay you for your kindness, but I have nothing to give you now, save the blessing of a dying man. Ah! if I could only see Delphine, to tell her to pay my debt to you. If the other cannot come, bring Delphine to me at any rate. Tell her that unless she comes, you will not love her any more. She is so fond of you that she will come to me then. Give me something to drink! There is a fire in my bowels. Press something against my forehead! If my daughters would lay their hands there, I think I should get better—— *Mon Dieu!* who will recover their money for them when I am gone?—— I will manufacture vermicelli out in Odessa; I will go to Odessa for their sakes."

"Here is something to drink," said Eugène, supporting the dying man on his left arm, while he held a cup of tisane to Goriot's lips.

"How you must love your own father and mother!" said the old man, and grasped the student's hands in both of his. It was a feeble, trembling grasp. "I am going to die; I shall die without seeing my daughters; do you understand? To be always thirsting, and never to drink; that has been my life for the last ten years—— I have no daughters, my sons-in-law killed them. No, since their marriages they have been dead to me. Fathers should petition the Chambers to pass a law against marriage. If you love your daughters, do not let them marry. A son-in-law is a rascal who poisons a girl's mind and contaminates her whole nature. Let us have no more marriages! It robs us of our daughters; we are left alone upon our death-beds, and they are not with us then. They ought to pass a law for dying fathers. This is awful! It cries for vengeance! They cannot come, because my sons-in-law forbid them!—— Kill them!—— Restaud and the Alsatian, kill them both! They have murdered me between them —— Death or my daughters!—— Ah! it is too late, I am dying, and they are not here!—— Dying without them! —— Nasie! Fifine! Why do you not come to me? Your papa is going——"

"Dear Father Goriot, calm yourself. There, there, lie quietly and rest; don't worry yourself, don't think."

"I shall not see them. Oh! the agony of it!"

"You *shall* see them."

"Really?" cried the old man, still wandering. "Oh! shall I see them; I shall see them and hear their voices. I shall die happy. Ah! well, after all, I do not wish to live; I cannot stand this much longer; this pain that grows worse and worse. But, oh! to see them, to touch their dresses—ah! nothing but their dresses, that is very little; still, to feel something that belongs to them. Let me touch their hair with my fingers—— their hair——"

His head fell back on the pillow, as if a sudden heavy blow had struck him down, but his hands groped feebly over the quilt, as if to find his daughters' hair.

"My blessing on them——" he said, making an effort, "my blessing——"

His voice died away. Just at that moment Bianchon came into the room.

"I met Christophe," he said; "he is gone for your cab."

Then he looked at the patient, and raised the closed eyelids with his fingers. The two students saw how dead and lustreless the eyes beneath had grown.

"He will not get over this, I am sure," said Biancon. He felt the old man's pulse, and laid a hand over his heart.

"The machinery works still; more is the pity, in his state it would be better for him to die."

"Ah! my word, it would!"

"What is the matter with you? You are as pale as death."

"Dear fellow, the moans and cries that I have just heard—— There is a God! Ah! yes, yes, there is a God, and He has made a better world for us, or this world of ours would be a nightmare. I could have cried like a child; but this is too tragical, and I am sick at heart."

"We want a lot of things, you know; and where is the money to come from?"

Rastignac took out his watch.

"There, be quick and pawn it. I do not want to stop on the way to the Rue du Helder; there is not a moment to lose, I am afraid, and I must wait here till Christophe comes back. I have not a farthing; I shall have to pay the cabman when I get home again."

Rastignac rushed down the stairs, and drove off to the Rue du Helder. The awful scene through which he had just passed quickened his imagination, and he grew fiercely indignant. He reached Mme. de Restaud's house only to be told by the servant that his mistress could see no one.

"But I have brought a message from her father, who is dying," Rastignac told the man.

"The Count has given us the strictest orders, sir——"

"If it is M. de Restaud who has given the orders, tell him that his father-in-law is dying, and that I am here and must speak with him at once."

The men went.

Eugène waited for a long while. "Perhaps her father is dying at this moment," he thought.

Then the man came back, and Eugène followed him to the little drawing-room. M. de Restaud was standing before the fireless grate, and did not ask his visitor to seat himself.

"Monsieur le Comte," said Rastignac, "M. Goriot, your father-in-law, is lying at the point of death in a squalid den in the Latin Quarter. He has not a penny to pay for firewood; he is expected to die at any moment, and keeps calling for his daughter——"

"I feel very little affection for M. Goriot, sir, as you probably are aware," the Count answered coolly. "His character has been compromised in connection with Mme. de Restaud; he is the author of the misfortunes that have embittered my life and troubled my peace of mind. It is a matter of perfect indifference to me if he lives or dies. Now you know my feelings with regard to him. Public opinion may blame me, but I care nothing for public opinion. Just now I have other and much more important matters to think about than the things that fools and chatterers may say about me. As for Mme. de Restaud, she cannot leave the house; she is in no condition to do so. And, besides, I shall not allow her to leave it. Tell her father that as soon as she has done her duty by her husband and child she shall go to see him. If she has any love for her father, she can be free to go to him, if she chooses, in a few seconds; it lies entirely with her——"

"Monsieur le Comte, it is no business of mine to criticise your conduct; you can do as you please with your wife, but may I count upon you keeping your word with me? Well, then, promise me to tell her that her father has not twenty-four hours to live; that he looks in vain for her, and has cursed her already as he lies on his death-bed—that is all I ask."

"You can tell her yourself," the Count answered, impressed by the thrill of indignation in Eugène's voice.

The Count led the way to the room where his wife usually sat. She was drowned in tears, and lay crouching in the depths of an armchair, as if she were tired of life and longed to die. It was piteous to see her. Before venturing to look at Rastignac, she glanced at her husband in evident and abject terror that spoke of complete prostration of body and mind; she seemed crushed by a tyranny both mental and physical. The Count jerked his head towards her; she construed this as a permission to speak.

"I heard all that you said, monsieur. Tell my father that

if he knew all he would forgive me—— I did not think there was such torture in the world as this; it is more than I can endure, monsieur! But I will not give way as long as I live," she said, turning to her husband. "I am a mother. Tell my father that I have never sinned against him in spite of appearances!" she cried aloud in her despair.

Eugène bowed to the husband and wife; he guessed the meaning of the scene, and that this was a terrible crisis in the Countess' life. M. de Restaud's manner had told him that his errand was a fruitless one; he saw that Anastasie had no longer any liberty of action. He came away amazed and bewildered, and hurried to Mme. de Nucingen. Delphine was in bed.

"Poor dear Eugène, I am ill," she said. "I caught cold after the ball, and I am afraid of pneumonia. I am waiting for the doctor to come."

"If you were at death's door," Eugène broke in, "you must be carried somehow to your father. He is calling for you. If you could hear the faintest of those cries, you would not feel ill any longer."

"Eugène, I dare say my father is not quite so ill as you say; but I cannot bear to do anything that you do not approve, so I will do just as you wish. As for *him*, he would die of grief I know if I went out to see him and brought on a dangerous illness. Well, I will go as soon as I have seen the doctor. Ah!" she cried out, "you are not wearing your watch, how is that?"

Eugène reddened.

"Eugène, Eugène! if you have sold it already or lost it —— Oh! it would be very wrong of you!"

The student bent over Delphine and said in her ear, "Do you want to know? Very well, then, you shall know. Your father has nothing left to pay for the shroud that they will lay him in this evening. Your watch has been pawned, for I had nothing either."

Delphine sprang out of bed, ran to her desk, and took out her purse. She gave it to Eugène, and rang the bell, crying—

"I will go, I will go at once, Eugène. Leave me, I will dress. Why, I should be an unnatural daughter! Go back; I will be there before you. Thérèse," she called to the waiting-woman, "ask M. de Nucingen to come upstairs at once and speak to me."

Eugène was almost happy when he reached the Rue Neuve-Sainte-Geneviève; he was so glad to bring the news to the dying man that one of his daughters was coming. He fumbled in Delphine's purse for money, so as to dismiss the cab at once; and discovered that the young, beautiful, and wealthy woman of fashion had only seventy francs in her private purse. He climbed the stairs and found Bianchon supporting Goriot, while the house surgeon from the hospital was applying moxas to the patient's back—under the direction of the physician, it was the last expedient of science, and it was tried in vain.

"Can you feel them?" asked the physician. But Goriot had caught sight of Rastignac, and answered, "They are coming, are they not?"

"There is hope yet," said the surgeon; "he can speak."

"Yes," said Eugène, "Delphine is coming, and will be here shortly."

"Oh! that is nothing!" said Bianchon; "he has been talking about his daughters all the time. He calls for them as a man impaled calls for water, they say——"

"We may as well give up," said the physician, addressing the surgeon. "Nothing more can be done now; the case is hopeless."

Bianchon and the house surgeon stretched the dying man out again on his loathsome bed.

"But the sheets ought to be changed," added the physician. "Even if there is no hope left, something is due to human nature. I shall come back again, Bianchon," he said, turning to the medical student. "If he complains again, rub some laudanum over the diaphragm."

He went, and the house surgeon went with him.

"Come, Eugène, pluck up heart, my boy," said Bianchon, as soon as they were alone; "we must set about changing his sheets, and put him into a clean shirt. Go and tell Sylvie to bring up some sheets and come and help us to make the bed."

Eugène went downstairs, and found Mme. Vauquer engaged in setting the table; Sylvie was helping her. Eugène had scarcely opened his mouth before the widow walked up to him with the acidulous sweet smile of a cautious shopkeeper who is anxious neither to lose money nor to offend a customer.

"My dear Monsieur Eugène," she said, when he had spoken, "you know quite as well as I do that Father Goriot has not a brass farthing left. If you give out clean linen for a man who is going to just turn up his eyes, you are not likely to see your sheets again, for one is sure to be wanted to wrap him in. Now, you owe me a hundred and forty-four francs as it is, add forty francs to that for the pair of sheets, and then there are several little things, besides the candle that Sylvie will give you; altogether, it will all mount up to at least two hundred francs, which is more than a poor widow like me can afford to lose. Lord! now, Monsieur Eugène, look at it fairly. I have lost quite enough in these five days since this run of ill-luck set in for me. I would rather than ten crowns that the old gentleman had moved out as you said. It sets the other lodgers against the house. It would not take much to make me send him to the workhouse. In short, just put yourself in my place. I have to think of my establishment first, for I have my own living to make."

Eugène hurried up to Goriot's room.

"Bianchon," he cried, "the money or the watch?"

"There it is on the table, or the three hundred and sixty-odd francs that are left of it. I paid up all the old scores out of it before they let me have the things. The pawn ticket lies there under the money."

Rastignac hurried downstairs.

"Here, madame," he said in disgust, "let us square accounts. M. Goriot will not stay much longer in your house, nor shall I——"

"Yes, he will go out feet foremost, poor old gentleman," she said, counting the francs with a half-facetious, half-lugubrious expression.

"Let us get this over," said Rastignac.

"Sylvie, look out some sheets, and go upstairs to help the gentlemen."

"You won't forget Sylvie," said Mme. Vauquer speaking in Eugène's ear; "she has been sitting up these two nights."

As soon as Eugène's back was turned, the old woman hurried after her handmaid.

"Take the sheets that have had the sides turned into the middle, number 7. Lord! they are plenty good enough for a corpse," she said in Sylvie's ear.

Eugène, by this time, was part of the way upstairs, and did not overhear the elderly economist.

"Quick," said Bianchon, "let us change his shirt. Hold him upright."

Eugène went to the head of the bed and supported the dying man, while Bianchon drew off his shirt; and then Goriot made a movement as if he tried to clutch something to his breast, uttering a low inarticulate moaning the while, like some dumb animal in mortal pain.

"Ah yes!" cried Bianchon. "It is the little locket and the chain made of hair that he wants; we took it off a while ago when we put the blisters on him! Poor fellow! he must have it again. There it lies on the chimney-piece."

Eugène went to the chimney-piece and found a little plait of faded golden hair—Mme. Goriot's hair, no doubt. He read the name on the little round locket, ANASTASIE on the one side, DELPHINE on the other. It was the symbol of his own heart that the father always wore on his breast. The curls of hair inside the locket were so fine and soft that it was plain they had been taken from two childish heads. When the old man felt the locket once more, his chest heaved with a long deep sigh of satisfaction, like a groan. It was something terrible to see, for it seemed as if the last quiver of the nerves were laid bare to their eyes, the last communication of sense to the mysterious point within whence our sympathies come and whither they go. A delirious joy lighted up the distorted face. The terrific and vivid force of the feeling that had survived the power of thought made such an impression on the students that the dying man felt their hot tears falling on him, and gave a shrill cry of delight.

"Nasie! Fifine!"

"There is life in him yet," said Bianchon.

"What does he go on living for?" said Sylvie.

"To suffer," answered Rastignac.

Bianchon made a sign to his friend to follow his example, knelt down and passed his arms under the sick man, and Rastignac on the other side did the same, so that Sylvie, standing in readiness, might draw the sheet from beneath and replace it with the one that she had brought. Those tears, no doubt, had misled Goriot; for he gathered up all his remaining strength in a last effort, stretched out his hands, groped for the students' heads, and as his fingers caught convulsively at their hair, they heard a faint whisper—

"Ah! my angels!"

Two words, two inarticulate murmurs, shaped into words by the soul which fled forth with them as they left his lips.

"Poor dear!" cried Sylvie, melted by that exclamation; the expression of the great love raised for the last time to a sublime height by that most ghastly and involuntary of lies.

The father's last breath must have been a sigh of joy, and in that sigh his whole life was summed up; he was cheated even at the last. They laid Father Goriot upon his wretched bed with reverent hands. Thenceforward there was no expression on his face, only the painful traces of the struggle between life and death that was going on in the machine; for that kind of cerebral consciousness that distinguishes between pleasure and pain in a human being was extinguished; it was only a question of time—and the mechanism itself would be destroyed.

"He will lie like this for several hours, and die so quietly at last that we shall not know when he goes; there will be no rattle in the throat. The brain must be completely suffused."

As he spoke there was a footstep on the staircase, and a young woman hastened up, panting for breath.

"She has come too late," said Rastignac.

But it was not Delphine; it was Thérèse, her waiting-woman, who stood in the doorway.

"Monsieur Eugène," she said, "Monsieur and Madame have had a terrible scene about some money that Madame (poor thing!) wanted for her father. She fainted, and the doctor came, and she had to be bled, calling out all the while, 'My father is dying; I want to see papa!' It was heartbreaking to hear her——"

"That will do, Thérèse. If she came now, it would be trouble thrown away. M. Goriot cannot recognize any one now."

"Poor, dear gentleman, is he as bad as all that?" said Thérèse.

"You don't want me now, I must go and look after my dinner; it is half-past four," remarked Sylvie. The next instant she all but collided with Mme. de Restaud on the landing outside.

There was something awful and appalling in the sudden apparition of the Countess. She saw the bed of death by the dim light of the single candle, and her tears flowed at the sight of her father's passive features, from which the life had almost ebbed. Bianchon with thoughtful tact then left the room.

"I could not escape soon enough," she said to Rastignac.

The student bowed sadly in reply. Mme. de Restaud took her father's hand and kissed it.

"Forgive me, father! You used to say that my voice would call you back from the grave; ah! come back for one moment to bless your penitent daughter. Do you hear me? Oh! this is fearful! No one on earth will ever bless me henceforth; every one hates me; no one loves me but you in all the world. My own children will hate me. Take me with you, father; I will love you, I will take care of you. He does not hear me—— I am mad——"

She fell on her knees, and gazed wildly at the human wreck before her.

"My cup of misery is full," she said, turning her eyes upon Eugène. "M. de Trailles has fled, leaving enormous debts behind him, and I have found out that he was deceiving me. My husband will never forgive me, and I have left my fortune in his hands. I have lost all my illusions. Alas! I have forsaken the one heart that loved me (she pointed to her father as she spoke), and for whom? I have held his kindness cheap, and slighted his affection; many and many a time I have given him pain, ungrateful wretch that I am!"

"He knew it," said Rastignac.

Just then Goriot's eyelids unclosed; it was only a muscular contraction, but the Countess' sudden start of reviving hope was no less dreadful than the dying eyes.

"Is it possible that he can hear me?" cried the Countess. "No," she answered herself, and sat down beside the bed. As Mme. de Restaud seemed to wish to sit by her father, Eugène went down to take a little food. The boarders were already assembled.

"Well," remarked the painter, as he joined them, "it seems that there is to be a death-orama upstairs."

"Charles, I think you might find something less painful to joke about," said Eugène.

"So we may not laugh here," returned the painter. "What harm does it do? Bianchon said that the old man was quite insensible."

"Well, then, said the employé from the Muséum, "he will die as he has lived."

"My father is dead!" shrieked the Countess.

The terrible cry brought Sylvie, Rastignac, and Bianchon; Mme. de Restaud had fainted away. When she recovered they carried her downstairs, and put her into the cab that stood waiting at the door. Eugène sent Thérèse with her, and bade the maid take the Countess to Mme. de Nucingen.

Bianchon came down to them.

"Yes, he is dead," he said.

"Come, sit down to dinner, gentlemen," said Mme. Vauquer, "or the soup will be cold."

The two students sat down together.

"What is the next thing to be done?" Eugène asked of Bianchon.

"I have closed his eyes and composed his limbs," said Bianchon. "When the certificate has been officially registered at the mayor's office, we will sew him in his winding-sheet and bury him somewhere. What do you think we ought to do?"

"He will not smell at his bread like this any more," said the painter, mimicking the old man's little trick.

"Oh, hang it all!" cried the tutor, "let Father Goriot drop, and let us have something else for a change. He is a standing dish, and we have had him with every sauce this hour or more. It is one of the privileges of the good city of Paris that anybody may be born, or live, or die there without attracting any attention whatsoever. Let us profit by the advantages of civilization. There are fifty or sixty deaths every day; if you have a mind to do it, you can sit down at any time and wail over whole hecatombs of dead in Paris. Father Goriot has gone off the hooks, has he? So much the better for him. If you venerate his memory, keep it to yourselves, and let the rest of us feed in peace."

"Oh, to be sure," said the widow, "it is all the better for him that he is dead. It looks as though he had had trouble enough, poor soul, while he was alive."

And this was all the funeral oration delivered over him who had been for Eugène the type and embodiment of fatherhood.

The fifteen lodgers began to talk as usual. When Bianchon and Eugène had satisfied their hunger, the rattle of spoons and forks, the boisterous conversation, the expressions on the faces that bespoke various degrees of want of feeling, gluttony, or indifference, everything about them made them shiver with loathing. They went out to find a priest to watch that night with the dead. It was necessary to measure their last pious cares by the scanty sum of money that remained. Before nine o'clock that evening the body was laid out on the bare sacking of the bedstead in the desolate room; a lighted candle stood on either side, and the priest watched at the foot. Rastignac made inquiries of this latter as to the expenses of the funeral, and wrote to the Baron de Nucingen and the Comte de Restaud, entreating both gentlemen to authorize their man of business to defray the charges of laying their father-in-law in the grave. He sent Christophe with the letters; then he went to bed, tired out, and slept.

Next day Bianchon and Rastignac were obliged to take the certificate to the registrar themselves, and by twelve o'clock the formalities were completed. Two hours went by; no word came from the Count nor from the Baron; nobody appeared to act for them, and Rastignac had already been obliged to pay the priest. Sylvie asked ten francs for sewing the old man in his winding-sheet and making him ready for the grave, and Eugène and Bianchon calculated that they had scarcely sufficient to pay for the funeral, if nothing was forthcoming from the dead man's family. So it was the medical student who laid him in a pauper's coffin, despatched from Bianchon's hospital, whence he obtained it at a cheaper rate.

"Let us play those wretches a trick," said he. "Go to the cemetery, buy a grave for five years at Père-Lachaise, and arrange with the church and the undertaker to have a third-class funeral. If the daughters and their husbands decline to repay you, you can carve this on the headstone—'*Here lies M. Goriot, father of the Comtesse de Restaud and the Baronne de Nucingen, interred at the expense of two students.*'"

Eugène took part of his friend's advice, but only after he had gone in person first to M. and Mme. de Nucingen and then to M. and Mme. de Restaud—a fruitless errand. He went no farther than the doorstep in either house. The servants had received strict orders to admit no one.

"Monsieur and madame can see no visitors. They have just lost their father, and are in deep grief over their loss."

Eugène's Parisian experience told him that it was idle to press the point. Something clutched strangely at his heart when he saw that it was impossible to reach Delphine.

"Sell some of your ornaments," he wrote hastily in the porter's room, "so that your father may be decently laid in his last resting-place."

He sealed the note, and begged the porter to give it to Thérèse for her mistress; but the man took it to the Baron de Nucingen, who flung the note into the fire. Eugène, having finished his errands, returned to the lodging-house about three o'clock. In spite of himself, the tears came into his eyes. The coffin, in its scanty covering of black cloth, was standing there on the pavement before the gate, on two chairs. A withered sprig of hyssop was soaking in the holy water bowl of silver-plated copper; there was not a soul in the street, not a passer-by had stopped to sprinkle the coffin; there was not even an attempt at a black drapery over the wicket. It was a pauper who lay there; no one made a pretense of mourning for him; he had neither friends nor kindred—there was no one to follow him to the grave.

Bianchon's duties compelled him to be at the hospital, but he had left a few lines for Eugène, telling his friend about the arrangements he had made for the burial service. The house student's note told Rastignac that a mass was beyond their means, that the ordinary office for the dead was cheaper and must suffice, and that he had sent word to the undertaker by Christophe. Eugène had scarcely finished reading Bianchon's scrawl, when he looked up and saw the little circular gold locket that contained the hair of Goriot's two daughters in Mme. Vauquer's hands.

"How dared you take it?" he asked.

"Good Lord! is that to be buried along with him?" retorted Sylvie, "It is gold."

"Of course it shall!" Eugène answered indignantly; "he shall at any rate take one thing that may represent his daughters into the grave with him."

When the hearse came, Eugène had the coffin carried into the house again, unscrewed the lid, and reverently laid on the old man's breast the token that recalled the days when Delphine and Anastasie were innocent little maidens, before they began "to think for themselves," as he had moaned out in his agony.

Rastignac and Christophe and the two undertaker's men were the only followers of the funeral. The Church of Saint-Étienne du Mont was only a little distance from the Rue Neuve-Sainte-Geneviève. When the coffin had been deposited in a low, dark, little chapel, the law student looked round in vain for Goriot's two daughters or their husbands. Christophe was his only fellow-mourner; Christophe, who appeared to think it was his duty to attend the funeral of the man who had put him in the way of such handsome tips. As they waited there in the chapel for the two priests, the chorister, and the beadle, Rastignac grasped Christophe's hand. He could not utter a word just then.

"Yes, Monsieur Eugène," said Christophe, "he was a good and worthy man, who never said one word louder than another; he never did any one any harm, and gave nobody any trouble."

The two priests, the chorister, and the beadle came, and said and did as much as could be expected for seventy francs in an age when religion cannot afford to say prayers for nothing.

The ecclesiastics chanted a psalm, the *Libera nos* and the *De profundis*. The whole service lasted about twenty minutes. There was but one mourning coach, which the priest and chorister agreed to share with Eugène and Christophe.

"There is no one else to follow us," remarked the priest, "so we may as well go quickly, and so save time; it is half-past five."

But just as the coffin was put in the hearse, two empty carriages, with the armorial bearings of the Comte de Restaud and the Baron de Nucingen, arrived and followed in the procession to Père-Lachaise. At six o'clock Goriot's coffin was lowered into the grave, his daughters' servants standing round the while. The ecclesiastic recited the short prayer that the students could afford to pay for, and then both priests and lackeys disappeared at once. The two grave-diggers flung in several spadefuls of earth, and then stopped and asked Rastignac for their fee. Eugène felt in vain in his pocket, and was obliged to borrow five francs of Christophe. This thing, so trifling in itself, gave Rastignac a terrible pang of distress. It was growing dusk, the damp twilight fretted his nerves; he gazed down into the grave, and the tears he shed were drawn from him by the sacred emotion, a single-hearted sorrow.

When such tears fall on earth, their radiance reaches heaven. And with those tears that fell on Father Goriot's grave, Eugène Rastignac's youth ended. He folded his arms and gazed at the clouded sky; and Christophe, after a glance at him, turned and went—Rastignac was left alone.

He went a few paces farther, to the highest point of the cemetery, and looked out over Paris and the windings of the Seine; the lamps were beginning to shine on either side of the river. His eyes turned almost eagerly to the space between the column of the Place Vendôme and the cupola of the Invalides; there lay the shining world that he had wished to reach. He glanced over that humming hive, seeming to draw a foretaste of its honey, and said magniloquently—

"Henceforth there is war between us."

And by way of throwing down the glove to society, Rastignac went to dine with Mme. de Nucingen.

M. GOBSECK.

To M. le Baron Barchou de Penhoen.

Among all the pupils of the Oratorian school at Vendôme, we are, I think, the only two who have afterwards met in mid-career of a life of letters—we who once were cultivating Philosophy when by rights we should have been minding our De viris. When we met, you were engaged upon your noble works on German philosophy, and I upon this study. So neither of us has missed his vocation; and you, when you see your name here, will feel, no doubt, as much pleasure as he who inscribes his work to you. Your old schoolfellow,

1840. DE BALZAC.

IT was one o'clock in the morning, during the winter of 1829–30, but in the Vicomtesse de Grandlieu's salon two persons stayed on who did not belong to her family circle. A young and good-looking man heard the clock strike, and took his leave. When the courtyard echoed with the sound of a departing carriage, the Vicomtesse looked up, saw that no one was present save her brother and a friend of the family finishing their game of piquet, and went across to her daughter. The girl, standing by the chimney-piece, apparently examining a transparent fire-screen, was listening to the sounds from the courtyard in a way that justified certain maternal fears.

"Camille," said the Vicomtesse, "if you continue to behave to young Comte de Restaud as you have done this evening, you will oblige me to see no more of him here. Listen, child, and if you have any confidence in my love, let me guide you in life. At seventeen one cannot judge of past or future, nor of certain social considerations. I have only one thing to say to you. M. de Restaud has a mother, a mother who would waste millions of francs; a woman of no birth, a Mlle. Goriot; people talked a good deal about her at one time. She behaved so badly to her own father, that she certainly does not deserve to have so good a son. The young Count adores her, and maintains her in her position with dutifulness worthy of all praise, and he is extremely good to his brother and sister. But however admirable *his* behavior may be," the Vicomtesse added with a shrewd expression, "so long as his mother lives, any family would take alarm at the idea of intrusting a daughter's fortune and future to young Restaud."

"I overheard a word now and again in your talk with Mlle. de Grandlieu," cried the friend of the family, "and it made me anxious to put in a word of my own. I have won, M. le Comte," he added, turning to his opponent. "I shall throw you over and go to your niece's assistance."

"See what it is to have an attorney's ears!" exclaimed the Vicomtesse. "My dear Derville, how could you know what I was saying to Camille in a whisper?"

"I knew it from your looks," answered Derville, seating himself in a low chair by the fire.

Camille's uncle went to her side, and Mme. de Grandlieu took up her position on a hearth stool between her daughter and Derville.

"The time has come for telling a story, which should modify your judgment as to Ernest de Restaud's prospects."

"A story!" cried Camille. "Do begin at once, monsieur."

The glance that Derville gave the Vicomtesse told her that this tale was meant for her. The Vicomtesse de Grandlieu, be it said, was one of the greatest ladies in the Faubourg Saint-Germain, by reason of her fortune and her ancient name; and though it may seem improbable that a Paris attorney should speak so familiarly to her, or be so much at home in her house, the fact is nevertheless easily explained.

When Mme. de Grandlieu returned to France with the royal family, she came to Paris, and at first lived entirely on the pension allowed her out of the civil list by Louis XVIII.—an intolerable position. The Hôtel de Grandlieu had been sold by the Republic. It came to Derville's knowledge that there were flaws in the title, and he thought that it ought to return to the Vicomtesse. He instituted proceedings for nullity of contract, and gained the day. Encouraged by this success, he used legal quibbles to such purpose that he compelled some institution or other to disgorge the forest of Liceney. Then he won certain lawsuits against the Canal d'Orléans, and recovered a tolerably large amount of property, with which the Emperor had endowed various public institutions. So it fell out that, thanks to the young attorney's skillful management, Mme. de Grandlieu's income reached the sum of some sixty thousand francs, to say nothing of the vast sums returned to her by the law of indemnity. And Derville, a man of high character, well-informed, modest, and pleasant in company, became the house-friend of the family.

By his conduct of Mme. de Grandlieu's affairs he had fairly earned the esteem of the Faubourg Saint-Germain, and numbered the best families among his clients; but he did not take advantage of his popularity, as an ambitious man might have done. The Vicomtesse would have had him sell his practice and enter the magistracy, in which career advancement would have been swift and certain with such influence at his disposal; but he persistently refused all offers. He only went into society to keep up his connections, but he occasionally spent an evening at the Hôtel de Grandlieu. It was a very lucky thing for him that his talents had been brought into the light by his devotion to Mme. de Grandlieu, for his practice otherwise might have gone to pieces. Derville had not an attorney's soul. Since Ernest de Restaud had appeared at the Hôtel de Grandlieu, and he had noticed that Camille felt attracted to the young man, Derville had been as assiduous in his visits as any dandy of the Chaussée-d'Antin newly admitted to the noble Faubourg. At a ball only a few days before, when he happened to stand near Camille, and said, indicating the Count—

"It is a pity that yonder youngster has not two or three million francs, is it not?"

"Is it a pity? I do not think so," the girl answered. "M. de Restaud has plenty of ability; he is well educated, and the minister, his chief, thinks well of him. He will be a remarkable man, I have no doubt. 'Yonder youngster' will have as much money as he wishes when he comes into power."

"Yes, but suppose that he were rich already?"

"Rich already?" repeated Camille, flushing red. "Why, all the girls in the room would be quarreling for him," she added, glancing at the quadrilles.

"And then," retorted the attorney, "Mlle. de Grandlieu might not be the one towards whom his eyes are always turned? That is what that red color means! You like him, do you not? Come, speak out."

Camille suddenly rose to go.

"She loves him," Derville thought.

Since that evening, Camille had been unwontedly attentive to the attorney, who approved of her liking for Ernest de Restaud. Hitherto, although she knew well that her family lay under great obligations to Derville, she had felt respect rather than real friendship for him, their relation was more a matter of politeness than of warmth of feeling; and by her manner, and by the tones of her voice, she had always made him sensible of the distance which socially lay between them. Gratitude is a charge upon the inheritance which the second generation is apt to repudiate.

"This adventure," Derville began after a pause, "brings

the one romantic event in my life to my mind. You are laughing already," he went on; "it seems so ridiculous, doesn't it, that an attorney should speak of a romance in his life? But once I was five-and-twenty, like everybody else, and even then I had seen some queer things. I ought to begin at the beginning by telling you about some one whom it is impossible that you should have known. The man in question was a usurer.

"Can you grasp a clear notion of that sallow, wan face of his? I wish the Académie would give me leave to dub such faces the *lunar* type. It was like silver-gilt, with the gilt rubbed off. His hair was iron-gray, sleek, and carefully combed; his features might have been cast in bronze; Talleyrand himself was not more impassive than this moneylender. A pair of little eyes, yellow as a ferret's, and with scarce an eyelash to them, peered out from under the sheltering peak of a shabby old cap, as if they feared the light. He had the thin lips that you see in Rembrandt's or Metsu's portraits of alchemists and shrunken old men, and a nose so sharp at the tip that it put you in mind of a gimlet. His voice was low; he always spoke suavely; he never flew into a passion. His age was a problem; it was hard to say whether he had grown old before his time, or whether by economy of youth he had saved enough to last him his life.

"This room, and everything in it, from the green baize of his bureau to the strip of carpet by the bed, was as clean and threadbare as the chilly sanctuary of some elderly spinster who spends her days in rubbing her furniture. In winter-time, the live brands of the fire smoldered all day in a bank of ashes; there was never any flame in his grate. He went through his day, from his uprising to his evening coughing-fit, with the regularity of a pendulum, and in some sort was a clockwork man, wound up by a night's slumber. Touch a wood-louse on an excursion across your sheet of paper, and the creature shams death; and in something the same way my acquaintance would stop short in the middle of a sentence, while a cart went by, to save the strain to his voice. Following the example of Fontanelle, he was thrifty of pulse-strokes, and concentrated all human sensibility in the innermost sanctuary of self.

"His life flowed soundless as the sands of an hour-glass. His victims sometimes flew into a rage and made a great deal of noise, followed by a great silence; so is it in a kitchen after a fowl's neck has been wrung.

"Towards evening this bill of exchange incarnate would assume ordinary human shape, and his metals were metamorphosed into a human heart. When he was satisfied with his day's business, he would rub his hands; his inward glee would escape like smoke through every rift and wrinkle of his face. In no other way is it possible to give an idea of the mute play of muscle which expressed sensations similar to the soundless laughter of 'Leather-Stocking.' Indeed, even in transports of joy, his conversation was confined to monosyllables; he wore the same non-committal countenance.

"This was the neighbor chance found for me in the house in the Rue des Grès, where I used to live when as yet I was only a second clerk finishing my third year's studies. The house is damp and dark, and boasts no courtyard. All the windows look on the street; the whole dwelling, in claustral fashion, is divided into rooms or cells of equal size, all opening upon a long corridor dimly lit with borrowed lights. The place must have been part of an old convent once. So gloomy was it, that the gaiety of eldest sons forsook them on the stairs before they reached my neighbor's door. He and his house were much alike; even so does the oyster resemble his native rock.

"I was the one creature with whom he had any communication, socially speaking; he would come in to ask for a light, to borrow a book or a newspaper, and of an evening he would allow me to go into his cell, and when he was in the humor we would chat together. These marks of confidence were the results of four years of neighborhood and my own sober conduct. From sheer lack of pence, I was bound to live pretty much as he did. Had he any relations or friends? Was he rich or poor? Nobody could give an answer to these questions. I myself never saw money in his room. Doubtless his capital was safely stowed in the strong rooms of the bank. He used to collect his bills himself as they fell due, running all over Paris on a pair of shanks as skinny as a stag's. On occasion he could be a martyr to prudence. One day, when he happened to have gold in his pockets, a double napoleon worked its way somehow or other out of his fob and fell, and another lodger following him up the stairs picked up the coin and returned it to its owner.

"'That isn't mine!' said he with a start of surprise. 'Mine, indeed! If I were rich, should I live as I do!'

"He made his cup of coffee himself every morning on the cast-iron chafing dish which stood all day in the black angle of the grate; his dinner came in from a cookshop; and our old porter's wife went up at the prescribed hour to set his room in order. Finally, a whimsical chance, in which Sterne would have seen predestination, had named the man Gobseck. When I did business for him later, I came to know that he was about seventy-six years old at the time when we became acquainted. He was born about 1740, in some outlying suburb of Antwerp, of a Dutch father and a Jewish mother, and his name was Jean-Esther Van Gobseck. You remember how all Paris took an interest in that murder case, a woman named "The Holland Belle?" I happened to mention it to my old neighbor, and he answered without the slightest symptom of interest or surprise, 'She is my grandniece.'

"That was the only remark drawn from him by the death of his sole surviving next of kin, his sister's grand-daughter. From reports of the case I found that "The Holland Belle" was in fact named Sara Van Gobseck. When I asked by what curious chance his grandniece came to bear his surname, he smiled—

"'The women never marry in our family.'

"Singular creature, he had never cared to find out a single relative among four generations counted on the female side. The thought of his heirs was abhorrent to him; and the idea that his wealth could pass into other hands after his death simply inconceivable.

"He was a child, ten years old, when his mother shipped him off as cabin-boy on a voyage to the Dutch Straits settlements, and there he knocked about for twenty years. The inscrutable lines on that sallow forehead kept the secret of horrible adventures, sudden panic, unhoped-for luck, romantic cross events, joys that knew no limit, hunger endured and love trampled underfoot, fortunes risked, lost, and recovered, life endangered time and time again, and saved, it may be, by one of the rapid, ruthless decisions absolved by necessity. He had known Admiral Simeuse, M. de Lally, M. de Kergarouët, M. d'Estaing, Le Bailli de Suffren, M. de Portenduère, Lord Cornwallis, Lord Hastings, Tippoo Sahib's father, Tippoo Sahib himself. The bully who served Mahadaji Sindhia, King of Delhi, and did so much to found the power of the Mahrattas, had had dealings with M. Gobseck. Long residence at St. Thomas brought him in contact with Victor Hughes and other notorious pirates. In his quest of fortune he had left no stone unturned; witness an attempt to discover the treasure of that tribe of savages so famous in Buenos Ayres and its neighborhood. He had a personal knowledge of the events of the American War of Independence. But if he spoke of the Indies or of America, as he did very rarely with me, and never with any one else, he seemed to regard it as an indiscretion and to repent of it afterwards. If humanity and sociability are in some sort a religion, M. Gobseck might be ranked as an infidel; but though I set myself to study him, I must confess, to my shame, that his real nature was impenetrable up to the very last. I even felt doubts at times as to his sex. If all usurers are like this one, I maintain that they belong to the neuter gender.

"Did he adhere to his mother's religion? Did he look on Gentiles as his legitimate prey? Had he turned Roman Catholic, Lutheran, Mahometan, Brahmin, or whatnot? I never knew anything whatsoever about his religious opinions, and so far as I could see, he was indifferent rather than incredulous.

"One evening I went in to see this man who had turned himself to gold; the usurer, whom his victims (his clients, as he styled them) were wont to call Daddy Gobseck, perhaps ironically, perhaps by way of antiphrasis. He was sitting in his armchair, motionless as a statue, staring fixedly at the mantle-shelf, where he seemed to read the figures of his statements. A lamp, with a pedestal that had once been green, was burning in the room; but so far from taking color from its smoky light, his face seemed to stand out positively paler against the background. He pointed to a chair set for me, but not a word did he say.

"'What thoughts can this being have in his mind?' said I to myself. 'Does he know that a God exists; does he know there are such things as feeling, woman, happiness?' I pitied him as I might have pitied a diseased creature. But, at the same time, I knew quite well that while he had millions of francs at his command, he possessed the world no less in idea—that world which he had explored, ransacked, weighed, appraised, and exploited.

"'Good-day, Daddy Gobseck,' I began, as I quietly took the seat pointed out to me.

"He turned his face towards me, with a slight contraction of his bushy, black eyebrows; this characteristic shade of expression in him meant as much as the most jubilant smile on a southern face.

"'You look just as gloomy as you did that day when the

news came of the failure of that bookseller whose sharpness you admired so much, though you were one of his victims.'

"'One of his victims?' he repeated, with a look of astonishment.

"'Yes. Did you not refuse to accept composition at the meeting of creditors until he undertook privately to pay you your debt in full; and did he not give you bills accepted by the insolvent firm; and then, when he set up in business again, did he not pay you the dividend upon those bills of yours, signed as they were by the bankrupt firm?'

"'He was a sharp one, but I had it out of him.'

"'Then have you some bills to protest? To-day is the 30th, I believe.'

"It was the first time that I had spoken to him of money. He looked ironically up at me; then in those bland accents, not unlike the husky tones which the tiro draws from a flute, he answered, 'I am amusing myself.'

"'So you amuse yourself now and again?'

"'Do you imagine that the only poets in the world are those who print their verses?' he asked, with a pitying look and shrug of the shoulders.

"'Poetry in that head!' thought I, for as yet I knew nothing of his life.

"'What life could be as glorious as mine?' he continued, and his eyes lighted up. 'You are young, your mental visions are colored by youthful blood, you see women's faces in the fire, while I see nothing but coals in mine. You have all sorts of beliefs, while I have no beliefs at all. Keep your illusions—if you can. Now I will show you life with the discount taken off. Go wherever you like, or stay at home by the fireside with your wife, there always comes a time when you settle down in a certain groove, the groove of your preference; and then happiness consists in the exercise of your faculties by applying them to realities. Anything more in the way of precept is false. My principles have been various, among various men; I had to change them with every change of latitude. Things that we admire in Europe are punishable in Asia, and a vice in Paris becomes a necessity when you have passed the Azores. There are no such things as hard-and-fast rules; there are only conventions adapted to the climate. Fling a man headlong into one social melting-pot after another, and convictions and forms and moral systems become so many meaningless words to him. The one thing that always remains, the one sure instinct that nature has implanted in us, is the instinct of self-preservation. In European society you call this instinct self-interest. If you had lived as long as I have, you would know that there is but one concrete reality invariable enough to be worth caring about, and that is—GOLD. Gold represents every form of human power. I have traveled. I found out that there were either hills or plains everywhere: the plains are monotonous, the hills a weariness; consequently, place may be left out of the question. As to manners; man is man all the world over. The same battle between the poor and the rich is going on everywhere; it is inevitable everywhere; consequently, it is better to exploit than to be exploited. Everywhere you find the man of thews and sinews who toils, and the lymphatic man who torments himself; and pleasures are everywhere the same, for when all sensations are exhausted, all that survives is vanity —vanity is the abiding substance of us, the *I* in us. Vanity is only to be satisfied by gold in floods. Our dreams need time and physical means and painstaking thought before they can be realized. Well, gold contains all things in embryo; gold realizes all things for us.

"'None but fools and invalids can find pleasure in shuffling cards all evening long to find out whether they shall win a few pence at the end. None but driveling idiots could spend time in inquiring into all that is happening around them, whether Madame Such-an-One slept single on her couch or in company, whether she has more blood than lymph, more temperament than virtue. None but the dupes, who fondly imagine that they are useful to their like, can interest themselves in laying down rules for political guidance amid events which neither they nor any one else foresee, nor ever will foresee. None but simpletons can delight in talking about stage players and repeating their sayings; making the daily promenade of a caged animal over a rather larger area; dressing for others, eating for others, priding themselves on a horse or a carriage such as no neighbor can have until three days later. What is all this but Parisian life summed up in a few phrases? Let us find a higher outlook on life than theirs. Happiness consists either in strong emotions which drain our vitality, or in methodical occupation which makes existence like a bit of English machinery, working with the regularity of clockwork. A higher happiness than either consists in a curiosity, styled noble, a wish to learn nature's secrets, or to attempt by artificial means to imitate nature to some extent. What is this in two words but science and art, or passion or calm? Ah! well, every human passion wrought up to its highest pitch in the struggle for existence comes to parade itself here before me—as I live in calm. As for your scientific curiosity, a kind of wrestling bout in which man is never uppermost, I replace it by an insight into all the springs of action in man and woman. To sum up, the world is mine without effort of mine, and the world has not the slightest hold on me. Listen to this,' he went on, ' I will tell you the history of my morning, and you will divine my pleasures.'

"He got up, pushed the bolt of the door, drew a tapestry curtain across it with a sharp grating sound of the rings on the rod, then he sat down again.

"'This morning,' he said, 'I had only two amounts to collect; the rest of the bills that were due I gave away instead of cash to my customers yesterday. So much saved, you see, for when I discount a bill I always deduct two francs for a hired brougham—expenses of collection. A pretty thing it would be, would it not, if my clients were to set *me* trudging all over Paris for a half-a-dozen francs of discount, when no man is my master, and I only pay seven francs in the shape of taxes?

"'The first bill for a thousand francs was presented by a young fellow, a smart buck with a spangled waistcoat, and an eyeglass, and a tilbury and an English horse, and all the rest of it. The bill bore the signature of one of the prettiest women in Paris, married to a count, a great landowner. Now, how came that countess to put her name to a bill of exchange, legally not worth the paper it was written upon, but practically very good business; for these women, poor things, are afraid of the scandal that a protested bill makes in a family, and would give themselves away in payment sooner than fail? I wanted to find out what that bill of exchange really represented. Was it stupidity, imprudence, love, or charity?

"'The second bill, bearing the signature "Fanny Malvaut," came to me from a linen-draper on the high way to bankruptcy. Now, no creature who has any credit with a bank comes to *me*. The first step to my door means that a man is desperately hard up; that the news of his failure will soon come out; and, most of all, it means that he has been everywhere else first. The stag is always at bay when I see him, and a pack of creditors are hard upon his track. The Countess lived in the Rue du Helder, and my Fanny in the Rue Montmartre. How many conjectures I made as I set out this morning! If these two women were not able to pay, they would show me more respect than they would show their own fathers. What tricks and grimaces would not the Countess try for a thousand francs! She would be so nice to me, she would talk to me in that ingratiating tone peculiar to endorsers of bills, she would pour out a torrent of coaxing words, perhaps she would beg and pray, and I———' (here the old man turned his pale eyes upon me)—'and I not to be moved, inexorable!' he continued. 'I am there as the avenger, the apparition of remorse. So much for hypotheses. I reached the house.

"'"Madame la Comtesse is asleep," says the maid.

"'"When can I see her?"

"'"At twelve o'clock."

"'"Is Madame la Comtesse ill?"

"'"No, sir, but she only came home at three o'clock this morning from a ball."

"'"My name is Gobseck, tell her that I shall call again at twelve o'clock," and out I went, leaving traces of my muddy boots on the carpet which covered the paved staircase. I like to leave mud on a rich man's carpet; it is not petty spite; I like to make them feel a touch of the claws of necessity. In the Rue Montmartre I thrust open the old gateway of a poor-looking house, and looked into a dark courtyard where the sunlight never shines. The porter's lodge was grimy, the window looked like the sleeve of some shabby wadded gown —greasy, dirty, and full of holes.

"'"Mlle. Fanny Malvaut?"

"'"She has gone out; but if you have come about a bill, the money is waiting for you."

"'"I will look in again," said I.

"'As soon as I knew that the porter had the money for me, I wanted to know what the girl was like; I pictured her as pretty. The rest of the morning I spent in looking at the prints in the shop windows along the boulevard; then, just as it struck twelve, I went through the Countess' ante-chamber.

"'"Madame has just this minute rung for me," said the maid; "I don't think she can see you yet."

"'"I will wait," said I, and sat down in an easy-chair.

"'Venetian shutters were opened, and presently the maid came hurrying back.

"'"Come in, sir."

"'From the sweet tone of the girl's voice, I knew that

the mistress could not be ready to pay. What a handsome woman it was that I saw in another moment! She had flung an India shawl hastily over her bare shoulders, covering herself with it completely, while it revealed the bare outlines of the form beneath. She wore a loose gown trimmed with snowy ruffles, which told plainly that her laundress' bills amounted to something like two thousand francs in the course of a year. Her dark curls escaped from beneath a bright India handkerchief, knotted carelessly about her head after the fashion of Creole women. The bed lay in disorder that told of broken slumber. A painter would have paid money to stay a while to see the scene that I saw. Under the luxurious hanging draperies, the pillow, crushed into the depths of an eider-down quilt, its lace border standing out in contrast against the background of blue silk, bore a vague impress that kindled the imagination. A pair of satin slippers gleamed from the great bearskin rug spread by the carved mahogany lions at the bedfoot, where she had flung them off in her weariness after the ball. A crumpled gown hung over a chair, the sleeves touching the floor; stockings which a breath would have blown away were twisted about the leg of an easy-chair; white ribbon garters straggled over a settee. A fan of price, half unfolded, glittered on the chimney-piece. Drawers stood open; flowers, diamonds, gloves, a bouquet, a girdle, were littered about. The room was full of vague sweet perfume. And—beneath all the luxury and disorder, beauty and incongruity—I saw misery crouching in wait for her or for her adorer, misery rearing its head, for the countess had begun to feel the edge of those fangs. Her tired face was an epitome of the room strewn with relics of past festival. The scattered gew-gaws, pitiable this morning, when gathered together and coherent, had turned heads the night before.

"'What efforts to drink of the Tantalus cup of bliss I could read in these traces of love stricken by the thunderbolt remorse—in this visible presentment of a life of luxury, extravagance, and riot. There were faint red marks on her young face, signs of the fineness of the skin; but her features were coarsened, as it were, and the circles about her eyes were unwontedly dark. Nature nevertheless was so vigorous in her, that these traces of past folly did not spoil her beauty. Her eyes glittered. She looked like some Herodias of da Vinci's (I have dealt in pictures), so magnificently full of life and energy was she; there was nothing starved nor stinted in feature or outline; she awakened desire; it seemed to me that there was some passion in her yet stronger than love. I was taken with her. It was a long while since my heart had throbbed; so I was paid then and there—for I would give a thousand francs for a sensation that should bring me back memories of youth.

"'"Monsieur," she said, finding a chair for me, "will you be so good as to wait?"

"'"Until this time to-morrow, madame," I said, folding up the bill again. "I cannot legally protest this bill any sooner." And within myself I said—" Pay the price of your luxury, pay for your name, pay for your ease, pay for the monopoly which you enjoy! The rich have invented judges and courts of law to secure their goods, and the guillotine— that candle in which so many an ignorant moth burns his wings. But for you who lay in silk, under silken coverlets, there is remorse, and grinding of teeth beneath a smile, and those fantastical lions' jaws are gaping to set their fangs in your heart."

"'"Protest the bill! Can you mean it?" she cried, with her eyes upon me; "could you have so little consideration for me?"

"'"If the King himself owed money to me, madame, and did not pay it, I should summons him even sooner than any other debtor."

"'While we were speaking, somebody tapped gently at the door.

"'"I cannot see any one," she cried imperiously.

"'"But, Anastasie, I particularly wish to speak to you."

"'"Not just now, dear," she answered in a milder tone, but with no sign of relenting.

"'"What nonsense! You are talking to some one," said the voice, and in came a man who could only be the Count.

"'The countess gave me a glance. I saw how it was. She was thoroughly in my power. There was a time, when I was young, and might perhaps have been stupid enough not to protest the bill. At Pondicherry, in 1763, I let a woman off, and nicely she paid me out afterwards. I deserved it; what call was there for me to trust her?'

"'"What does this gentleman want?" asked the Count.

"'I could see that the Countess was trembling from head to foot; the white satin skin of her throat was rough, "turned to goose-flesh," to use the familiar expression. As for me, I laughed in myself without moving a muscle.

"'"This gentleman is one of my tradesmen," she said.

"'The Count turned his back on me; I drew the bill half out of my pocket. After that inexorable movement, she came over to me and put a diamond into my hands. "Take it," she said, "and be gone."

"'We exchanged values, and I made my bow and went. The diamond was quite worth twelve hundred francs to me. Out in the courtyard I saw a swarm of flunkeys, brushing their liveries, waxing their boots, and cleaning sumptuous equipages.

"'"This is what brings these people to me!" said I to myself. "It is to keep up this kind of thing that they steal millions with all due formalities, and betray their country. The great lord, and the little man who apes the great lord, bathes in mud once for all to save himself a splash or two when he goes afoot through the streets."

"' Just then the great gates were opened to admit a cabriolet. It was the same young fellow who had brought the bill to me.

21

"'"Sir," I said, as he alighted, "here are two hundred francs, which I beg you to return to Mme. la Comtesse, and have the goodness to tell her that I hold the pledge which she deposited with me this morning at her disposition for a week."

"'He took the two hundred francs, and an ironical smile stole over his face; it was as if he had said, "Aha! so she has paid it, has she?—— Faith, so much the better!" I read the Countess' future in his face. That good-looking, fair-haired young gentleman is a heartless gambler; he will ruin himself, ruin her, ruin her husband, ruin the children, eat up their portions, and work more havoc in Parisian salons than a whole battery of howitzers in a regiment.

"'I went back to see Mlle. Fanny in the Rue Montmartre, climbed a very steep, narrow staircase, and reached a two-room apartment on the fifth floor. Everything was as neat as a new ducat. I did not see a speck of dust on the furniture in the first room, where Mlle. Fanny was sitting. Mlle. Fanny herself was a young Parisian girl, quietly dressed, with a delicate fresh face and a winning look. The arrangement of her neatly brushed chestnut hair in a double curve on her forehead lent a refined expression to blue eyes, clear as crystal. The broad daylight streaming in through the short curtains against the window-pane fell with softened light on her girlish face. A pile of shaped pieces of linen told me that she was a sempstress. She looked like the spirit of solitude. When I held out the bill, I remarked that she had not been at home when I called in the morning.

"'"But the money was left with the porter's wife," said she.

"'I pretended not to understand.

"'"You go out early, mademoiselle, it seems."

"'"I very seldom leave my room; but when you work all night, you are obliged to take a bath sometimes."

"'I looked at her. A glance told me all about her life. Here was a girl condemned by misfortune to toil, a girl who came of honest farmer folk, for she had still a freckle or two that told of country birth. There was an indefinable atmosphere of goodness about her; I felt as if I were breathing sincerity and frank innocence. It was refreshing to my lungs. Poor innocent child, she had faith in something; there was a crucifix and a sprig or two of green box above her poor little painted wooden bedstead; I felt touched, or somewhat inclined that way. I felt ready to offer to charge no more than twelve per cent., and so give something towards establishing her in a good way of business.

" ' "But may be she has a little youngster of a cousin," I said to myself, "who would raise money on her signature and sponge on the poor girl."

" ' So I went away, keeping my generous impulses well under control; for I have frequently had occasion to observe that when benevolence does no harm to him who gives, it is the ruin of him who takes. When you came in I was thinking that Fanny Malvaut would make a nice little wife; I was thinking of the contrast between her pure, lonely life and the life of the Countess—she has sunk as low as a bill of exchange already, she will sink to the lowest depths of degradation before she has done!' I scrutinized him during the deep silence that followed, but in a moment he spoke again. 'Well,' he said, ' do you think that it is nothing to have this power of insight into the deepest recesses of the human heart, to embrace so many lives, to see the naked truth underlying it all? There are no two dramas alike: there are hideous sores, deadly chagrins, love scenes, misery that soon will lay under the ripples of the Seine, young men's joys that lead to the scaffold, the laughter of despair, and sumptuous banquets. Yesterday it was a tragedy. A worthy soul of a father drowned himself because he could not support his family. To-morrow it is a comedy; some youngster will try to rehearse the scene of M. Dimanche, brought up to date. You have heard people extol the eloquence of our latter-day preachers; now and again I have wasted my time by going to hear them;

they produced a change in my opinions, but in my conduct (as somebody said, I can't recollect his name), in my conduct—never! Well, well; these good priests and your Mirabeaus and Vergniauds and the rest of them are mere stammering beginners compared with these orators of mine.

"'Often it is some girl in love, some gray-headed merchant on the verge of bankruptcy, some mother with a son's wrong-doing to conceal, some starving artist, some great man whose influence is on the wane, and, for lack of money, is likely to lose the fruit of all his labors—the power of their pleading has made me shudder. Sublime actors such as these play for me, for an audience of one, and they cannot deceive me. I can look into their inmost thoughts, and read them as God reads them. Nothing is hidden from me. Nothing is refused to the holder of the purse-strings to loose and to bind. I am rich enough to buy the consciences of those who control the action of ministers, from their office boys to their mistresses. Is not that power? I can possess the fairest women, receive their softest caresses; is not that pleasure? And is not your whole social economy summed up in terms of power and pleasure?

"'There are ten of us in Paris, silent, unknown kings, the arbiters of your destinies. What is life but a machine set in motion by money? Know this for certain—methods are always confounded with results; you will never succeed in separating the soul from the senses, spirit from matter. Gold is the spiritual basis of existing society. The ten of us are bound by the ties of common interest; we meet on certain days of the week at the Café Thémis near the Pont Neuf, and there, in conclave, we reveal the mysteries of finance. No fortune can deceive us; we are in possession of family secrets in all directions. We keep a kind of "Black Book," in which we note the most important bills issued, drafts on public credit, or on banks, or given and taken in the course of business. We are the Casuists of the Paris Bourse, a kind of Inquisition weighing and analyzing the most insignificant actions of every man of any fortune, and our forecasts are infallible. One of us looks out over the judicial world, one over the financial, another surveys the administrative, and yet another the business world. I myself keep an eye on eldest sons, artists, people in the great world, and gamblers—on the most sensational side of Paris. Every one who comes to us lets us into his neighbor's secrets. Thwarted passion and mortified vanity are great babblers. Vice and disappointment and vindictiveness are the best of all detectives. My colleagues, like myself, have enjoyed all things, are sated with all things, and have reached the point when power and money are loved for their own sake.

"'Here,' he said, indicating his bare, chilly room, 'here the most high-mettled gallant, who chafes at a word and draws sword for a syllable elsewhere, will entreat with clasped hands. There is no city merchant so proud, no woman so vain of her beauty, no soldier of so bold a spirit, but that they entreat me here, one and all, with tears of rage or anguish in their eyes. Here they kneel—the famous artist, and the man of letters, whose name will go down to posterity. Here, in short' (he lifted his hand to his forehead), 'all the inheritances and all the concerns of all Paris are weighed in the balance. Are you still of the opinion that there are no delights behind the blank mask which so often has amazed you by its impassiveness?' he asked, stretching out that livid face which reeked of money.

"I went back to my room, feeling stupefied. The little, wizened, old man had grown great. He had been metamorphosed under my eyes into a strange visionary symbol; he had come to be the power of gold personified. I shrank, shuddering, from life and my kind.

"'Is it really so?' I thought; 'must everything be resolved into gold?'

"I remember that it was long before I slept that night. I

saw heaps of gold all about me. My thoughts were full of the lovely Countess; I confess, to my shame, that the vision completely eclipsed another quiet, innocent figure, the figure of the woman who had entered upon a life of toil and obscurity; but on the morrow, through the clouds of slumber, Fanny's sweet face rose before me in all its beauty, and I thought of nothing else."

"Will you take a glass of *eau sucrée?*" asked the Vicomtesse, interrupting Derville.

"I should be glad of it."

"But I can see nothing in this that can touch our concerns," said Mme. de Grandlieu, as she rang the bell.

"Sardanapalus!" cried Derville, flinging out his favorite invocation. "Mademoiselle Camille will be wide awake in a moment if I say that her happiness depended not so long ago upon Daddy Gobseck; but as the old gentleman died at the age of ninety, M. de Restaud will soon be in possession of a handsome fortune. This requires some explanation. As for Fanny Malvaut, you know her; she is my wife."

"Poor fellow, he would admit that, with his usual frankness, with a score of people to hear him!" said the Vicomtesse.

"I would proclaim it to the universe," said the attorney.

"Go on, drink your glass, my poor Derville. You will never be anything but the happiest and the best of men."

"I left you in the Rue du Helder," remarked the uncle, raising his face after a gentle doze. "You had gone to see a countess; what have you done with her?"

"A few days after my conversation with the old Dutchman," Derville continued, "I sent in my thesis, and became first a licentiate in law, and afterwards an advocate. The old miser's opinion of me went up considerably. He consulted me (gratuitously) on all the ticklish bits of business which he undertook when he had made quite sure how he stood, business which would have seemed unsafe to any ordinary practitioner. This man, over whom no one appeared to have the slightest influence, listened to my advice with something like respect. It is true that he always found that it turned out very well.

"At length I became head-clerk in the office where I had worked for three years, and then I left the Rue des Grès for rooms in my employer's house. I had my board and lodging and a hundred and fifty francs per month. It was a great day for me!

"When I went to bid the usurer good-by, he showed no sign of feeling, he was neither cordial nor sorry to lose me, he did not ask me to come to see him, and only gave me one of those glances which seemed in some way to reveal a power of second-sight.

"By the end of the week my old neighbor came to see me with a tolerably thorny bit of business, an expropriation, and he continued to ask my advice with as much freedom as if he paid for it.

"My principal was a man of pleasure and expensive tastes; before the second year (1818–1819) was out he had gotten himself into difficulties, and was obliged to sell his practice. A professional connection in those days did not fetch the present exorbitant prices, and my principal asked a hundred and fifty thousand francs. Now an active man, of competent knowledge and intelligence, might hope to pay off the capital in ten years, paying interest and living respectably in the meantime—if he could command confidence. But I was the seventh child of a small tradesman at Noyon, I had not a sou to my name, nor personal knowledge of any capitalist but Daddy Gobseck. An ambitious idea, and an indefinable glimmer of hope, put heart into me. To Gobseck I betook myself, and slowly one evening I made my way to the Rue des Grès. My heart thumped heavily as I knocked at his door in the gloomy house. I recollected all the things that he used to tell me, at a time when I myself was very far from suspecting the violence of the anguish awaiting those who crossed his threshold. Now it was I who was about to beg and pray like so many others.

"'Well, no, not *that*,' I said to myself; 'an honest man must keep his self-respect wherever he goes. Success is not worth cringing for; let us show him a front as decided as his own.'

"Daddy Gobseck had taken my room since I left the house, so as to have no neighbor; he had made a little grated window too in his door since then, and did not open until he had taken a look at me and saw who I was.

"'Well,' said he, in his thin, flute notes, 'so your principal is selling his practice.'

"'How did you know that?' said I; 'he has not spoken of it as yet except to me.'

"The old man's lips were drawn in puckers, like a curtain, to either corner of his mouth, as a soundless smile bore a hard glance company.

"'Nothing else would have brought you here,' he said drily, after a pause, which I spent in confusion.

"'Listen to me, M. Gobseck,' I began, with such serenity as I could assume before the old man, who gazed at me with steady eyes. There was a clear light burning in them that disconcerted me.

"He made a gesture as if to bid me 'Go on.' 'I know that it is not easy to work on your feelings, so I will not waste my eloquence on the attempt to put my position before you— I am a penniless clerk, with no one to look to but you, and no heart in the world but yours can form a clear idea of my probable future. Let us leave hearts out of the question. Business is business, and business is not carried on with sentimentality like romances. Now to the facts. My principal's practice is worth in his hands about twenty thousand francs per annum; in my hands, I think it would bring in forty thousand. He is willing to sell it for a hundred and fifty thousand francs. And *here*,' I said, striking my forehead, 'I feel that if you would lend me the purchase-money, I could clear it off in ten years' time.'

"' Come, that is plain speaking,' said Daddy Gobseck, and he held out his hand and grasped mine. ' Nobody since I have been in business has stated the motives of his visit more clearly. Guarantees?' asked he, scanning me from head to foot. ' None to give,' he added after a pause. ' How old are you?'

"' Twenty-five in ten days' time,' said I, ' or I could not open the matter.'

"' Precisely.'

"' Well?'

"' It is possible.'

"' My word, we must be quick about it, or I shall have some one buying over my head.'

"' Bring your certificate of birth round to-morrow morning, and we will talk. I will think it over in the meantime,' he replied.

" Next morning, at eight o'clock, I stood in the old man's room. He took the document, put on his spectacles, coughed, spat, wrapped himself up in his black greatcoat, and read the whole certificate through from beginning to end. Then he turned it over and over, looked at me, coughed again, fidgeted about in his chair, and said, ' We will try to arrange this bit of business.'

" I trembled.

"' I make fifty per cent. on my capital,' he continued, ' sometimes I make a hundred, two hundred, five hundred per cent.'

" I turned pale at the words.

"' But as we are acquaintances, I shall be satisfied to take twelve and a half per cent. per '—(he hesitated)—' well, yes, from you I would be content to take thirteen per cent. per annum. Will that suit you?'

"'Yes,' I answered.

"'But if it is too much, stick up for yourself, Grotius!' (a name he jokingly gave me). 'When I ask you for thirteen per cent., it is all in the way of business; look into it, see if you can pay it; I don't like a man to agree too easily. Is it too much?'

"'No,' said I, 'I will make up for it by working a little harder.'

"'Gad! your clients will pay for it!' said he, looking at me wickedly out of the corner of his eyes.

"'No, by all the devils in hell!' cried I, 'it shall be I who will pay. I would sooner cut my hand off than flay people.'

"'Good-night,' said Daddy Gobseck.

"'Why, fees are all according to scale,' I added.

"'Not for compromises and settlements out of court, and cases where litigants come to terms,' said he. 'You can send in a bill for thousands of francs, six thousand even at a swoop (it depends on the importance of the case), for conferences with So-and-so, and expenses, and drafts, and memorials, and your jargon. A man must learn to look out for business of this kind. I will recommend you as a most competent, clever attorney. I will send you such a lot of work of this sort that your colleagues will be fit to burst with envy. Werbrust, Palma, and Gigonnet, my cronies, shall hand over their expropriations to you; they have plenty of them, the Lord knows! So you will have two practices—the one you are buying, and the other I will build up for you. You ought almost to pay me fifteen per cent. on my loan.'

"'So be it, but no more,' said I, with the firmness which means that a man is determined not to concede another point.

"Daddy Gobseck's face relaxed; he looked pleased with me.

"'I shall pay the money over to your principal myself,' said he, 'so as to establish a lien on the purchase and caution-money.'

"'Oh, anything you like in the way of guarantees.'

"'And besides that, you will give me bills for the amount made payable to a third party (name left blank), fifteen bills of ten thousand francs each.'

"'Well, so long as it is acknowledged in writing that this is a double——'

"'No!' Gobseck broke in upon me. 'No! Why should I trust you any more than you trust me?'

"I kept silence.

"'And furthermore,' he continued, with a sort of good-humor, 'you will give me your advice without charging fees so long as I live, will you not?'

"'So be it; so long as there is no outlay.'

"'Precisely,' said he. 'Ah, by-the-by, you will allow me to go to see you?' (Plainly the old man found it not so easy to assume the air of good-humor.)

"'I shall always be glad.'

"'Ah! yes, but it would be very difficult to arrange of a morning. You will have your affairs to attend to, and I have mine.'

"'Then come in the evening.'

"'Oh, no!' he answered briskly, 'you ought to go into society and see your clients, and I myself have my friends at my café.'

"'His friends!' thought I to myself. 'Very well,' said I, 'why not come at dinner-time?'

"'That is the time,' said Gobseck, 'after 'Change, at five o'clock. Good, you will see me Wednesdays and Saturdays. We will talk over business like a pair of friends. Aha! I am gay, sometimes. Just give me the wing of a partridge and a glass of champagne, and we will have our chat together. I know a great many things that can be told now at this distance of time; I will teach you to know men, and what is more, women?'

"'Oh! a partridge and a glass of champagne if you like.'

"'Don't do anything foolish, or I shall lose my faith in you. And don't set up housekeeping in a grand way. Just one old general servant. I will come and see that you keep your health. I have capital invested in your head, he! he! so I am bound to look after you. There, come round in the evening, and bring your principal with you!'

"'Would you mind telling me, if there is no harm in asking, what was the good of my birth certificate in this business?' I asked, when the little old man and I stood on the doorstep.

"Jean-Esther Van Gobseck shrugged his shoulders, smiled maliciously, and said, 'What blockheads youngsters are! Learn, master attorney (for learn you must, if you don't mean to be taken in), that integrity and brains in a man under thirty are commodities which can be mortgaged. After that age there is no counting on a man.'

"And with that he shut the door.

"Three months later I was an attorney. Before very long, madame, it was my good-fortune to undertake the suit for the recovery of your estates. I won the day, and my name became known. In spite of the exorbitant rate of interest, I paid off Gobseck in less than five years. I married Fanny Malvaut, whom I loved with all my heart. There was a parallel between her life and mine, between our hard work and our luck, which increased the strength of feeling on either side. One of her uncles, a well-to-do farmer, died and left her seventy thousand francs, which helped to clear off the loan. From that day my life has been nothing but happiness and prosperity. Nothing is more utterly uninteresting than a happy man, so let us say no more on that head, and return to the rest of the characters.

"About a year after the purchase of the practice, I was

dragged into a bachelor breakfast-party given by one of our number who had lost a bet to a young man greatly in vogue in the fashionable world. M. de Trailles, the flower of the dandyism of that day, enjoyed a prodigious reputation."

"But he is still enjoying it," put in the Comte de Born. "No one wears his clothes with a finer air, nor drives a tandem with a better grace. It is Maxime's gift; he can gamble, eat, and drink more gracefully than any man in the world. He is a judge of horses, hats, and pictures. All the women lose their heads over him. He always spends something like a hundred thousand francs a year, and no creature can discover that he has an acre of land or a single dividend warrant. The typical knight-errant of our salons, our boudoirs, our boulevards, an amphibian half-way between a man and a woman— Maxime de Trailles is a singular being, fit for anything, and good for nothing, quite as capable of perpetrating a benefit as of planning a crime; sometimes base, sometimes noble, more often bespattered with mire than besprinkled with blood, knowing more of anxiety than of remorse, more concerned with his digestion than with any mental process, shamming passion, feeling nothing. Maxime de Trailles is a brilliant link between the hulks and the best society; he belongs to the eminently intelligent class from which a Mirabeau, or a Pitt, or a Richelieu springs at times, though it is more wont to produce Counts of Horn, Fouquier-Tinvilles, and Coignards."

"Well," pursued Derville, when he had heard the Vicomtesse's brother to the end, "I had heard a good deal about this individual from poor Father Goriot, a client of mine; and I had already been at some pains to avoid the dangerous honor of his acquaintance, for I came across him sometimes in society. Still, my chum was so pressing about this breakfast party of his that I could not well get out of it, unless I wished to earn a name for squeamishness. Madame, you could hardly imagine what a bachelor's breakfast-party is like. It means superb display and a studied refinement seldom seen;

the luxury of a miser when vanity leads him to be sumptuous for a day.

"You are surprised as you enter the room at the neatness of the table, dazzling by reason of its silver and crystal and linen damask. Life is here in full bloom; the young fellows are graceful to behold; they smile and talk in low, demure voices like so many brides; everything about them looks girlish. Two hours later you might take the room for a battlefield after the fight. Broken glasses, serviettes crumpled and torn to rags lie strewn about among the nauseous-looking remnants of food on the dishes. There is an uproar that stuns you, jesting toasts, a fire of witticisms and bad jokes; faces are empurpled, eyes inflamed and expressionless; unintentional confidences tell you the whole truth. Bottles are smashed, and songs trolled out in the height of a diabolical racket; men call each other out, hang on each other's necks, or fall to fisticuffs; the room is full of a horrid, close scent made up of a hundred odors, and noise enough for a hundred voices. No one has any notion of what he is eating or drinking or saying. Some are depressed, others babble; one will turn monomaniac, repeating the same word over and over again like a bell set jangling; another tries to keep the tumult within bounds; the steadiest will propose an orgie. If any one in possession of his faculties should come in, he would think that he had interrupted a Bacchanalian rite.

"It was in the thick of such a chaos that M. de Trailles tried to insinuate himself into my good graces. My head was fairly clear, I was upon my guard. As for him, though he pretended to be decently drunk, he was perfectly cool, and knew very well what he was about. How it was done I do not know, but the upshot of it was that when we left Grignon's rooms about nine o'clock in the evening, M. de Trailles had thoroughly bewitched me. I had given him my promise that I would introduce him the next day to our Papa Gobseck. The words 'honor,' 'virtue,' 'countess,' 'honest woman,' and 'ill-luck' were mingled in his discourse with magical potency, thanks to that golden tongue of his.

"When I awoke next morning, and tried to recollect what I had done the day before, it was with great difficulty that I could make a connected tale from my impressions. At last, it seemed to me that the daughter of one of my clients was in danger of losing her reputation, together with her husband's love and esteem, if she could not get fifty thousand francs together in the course of the morning. There had been gaming debts, and carriage-builders' accounts, money lost to heaven knows whom. My magician of a boon companion had impressed it upon me that she was rich enough to make good these reverses by a few years of economy. But only now did I begin to guess the reasons of his urgency. I confess, to my shame, that I had not the shadow of a doubt but that it was a matter of importance that Daddy Gobseck should make it up with this dandy. I was dressing when the young gentleman appeared.

"'M. le Comte,' said I, after the usual greetings, 'I fail to see why you should need me to effect an introduction to Van Gobseck, the most civil and smooth-spoken of capitalists. Money will be forthcoming if he has any, or rather, if you can give him adequate security.'

"'Monsieur,' said he, 'it does not enter into my thoughts to force you to do me a service, even though you have passed your word.'

"'Sardanapalus!' said I to myself, 'am I going to let that fellow imagine for one moment that I will not keep my word with him?'

"'I had the honor of telling you yesterday,' said he, 'that I had fallen out with Daddy Gobseck most inopportunely; and as there is scarcely another man in Paris who can come down on the nail with a hundred thousand francs, at the end of the month, I begged of you to make my peace with him. But let us say no more about it——'

"M. de Trailles looked at me with civil insult in his expression, and made as if he would take his leave.

"'I am ready to go with you,' said I.

"When we reached the Rue des Grès, my dandy looked about him with a circumspection and uneasiness that set me wondering. His face grew livid, flushed, and yellow, turn and turn about, and by the time that Gobseck's door came in sight the perspiration stood in drops on his forehead. We were just getting out of the cabriolet, when a hackney cab turned into the street. My companion's hawk's-eye detected a woman in the depths of the vehicle. His face lighted up with a gleam of almost savage joy; he called to a little boy who was passing, and gave him his horse to hold. Then we went up to the old bill-discounter.

"'M. Gobseck,' said I, 'I have brought one of my most intimate friends to see you (whom I trust as I would trust the devil,' I added for the old man's private ear). 'To oblige me you will do your best for him (at the ordinary rate), and pull him out of his difficulty (if it suits your convenience).'

"M. de Trailles made his bow to M. Gobseck, took a seat, and listened to us with a courtier-like attitude; its charming humility would have touched your heart to see, but my M. Gobseck sits in his chair by the fireside without moving a muscle or changing a feature. He looked very much like the statue of Voltaire under the peristyle of the Théâtre-Français, as you see it of an evening; he had partly risen as if to bow, and the skull cap that covered the top of his head, and the narrow strip of sallow forehead exhibited, completed his likeness to the man of marble.

"'I have no money to spare except for my own clients,' said he.

"'So you are cross because I may have tried in other quarters to ruin myself?' said the Count, laughing.

"'Ruin yourself!' repeated M. Gobseck ironically.

"'Were you about to remark that it is impossible to ruin a

man who has nothing?' inquired the dandy. 'Why I defy you to find a better *stock* in Paris!' he cried, swinging round on his heels.

"This half-earnest buffoonery produced not the slightest effect upon M. Gobseck.

"'Am I not on intimate terms with the Ronquerolles, the Marsays, the Franchessinis, the two Vandenesses, the Ajuda-Pintos—all the most fashionable young men in Paris, in short? A prince and an ambassador (you know them both) are my partners at play. I draw my revenues from London and Carlsbad and Baden and Bath. Is not this the most brilliant of all industries!'

"'True.'

"'You make a sponge of me, begad! so you do. You encourage me to go and swell myself out in society, so that you can squeeze me when I am hard up; but you yourselves are sponges, just as I am, and death will give you a squeeze some day.'

"'That is possible.'

"'If there were no spendthrifts, what would become of you? The pair of us are like soul and body.'

"'Precisely so.'

"'Come, now, give us your hand, Grandaddy Gobseck, and be magnanimous if this is "true" and "possible" and "precisely so."'

"'You come to me,' the usurer answered coldly, 'because Girard, Palma, Werbrust, and Gigonnet are full up of your paper; they are offering it at a loss of fifty per cent.; and as it is likely they only gave you half the figure on the face of the bills, they are not worth five-and-twenty per cent. of their supposed value. I am your most obedient! Can I in common decency lend a stiver to a man who owes thirty thousand francs, and has not one farthing?' M. Gobseck continued. 'The day before yesterday you lost ten thousand francs at a ball at the Baron de Nucingen's.'

"'Sir,' said the Count, with rare impudence, 'my affairs are no concern of yours,' and he looked the old man up and down. 'A man has no debts till payment is due.'

"'True.'

"'My bills will be duly met.'

"'That is possible.'

"'And at this moment the question between you and me is simply whether the security I am going to offer is sufficient for the sum I have come to borrow.'

"'Precisely.'

"A cab stopped at the door, and the sound of wheels filled the room.

"'I will bring something directly which perhaps will satisfy you,' cried the young man, and he left the room.

"'Oh! my son,' exclaimed M. Gobseck, rising to his feet, and stretching out his arms to me, 'if he has good security, you have saved my life. It would be the death of me. Werbrust and Gigonnet imagined that they were going to play off a trick on me; and now, thanks to you, I shall have a good laugh at their expense to-night.'

"There was something frightful about the old man's ecstasy. It was the one occasion when he opened his heart to me; and that flash of joy, swift though it was, will never be effaced from my memory.

"'Favor me so far as to stay here,' he added. 'I am armed, and a sure shot. I have gone tiger-hunting, and fought on the deck when there was nothing for it but to win or die; but I don't care to trust myself to yonder elegant scoundrel.'

"He sat down again in his armchair before his bureau, and his face grew pale and impassive as before.

"'Ah!' he continued, turning to me, 'you will see that lovely creature I once told you about; I can hear a fine lady's step in the corridor; it is she, no doubt;' and, as a matter of fact, the young man came in with a woman on his arm. I recognized the Countess, whose levée M. Gobseck had described for me, one of Father Goriot's two daughters.

"The Countess did not see me at first; I stayed where I was in the bay window, with my face against the pane; but I saw her give Maxime a suspicious glance as she came into the money-lender's damp, dark room. So beautiful was she, that in spite of her faults I felt sorry for her. There was a terrible storm of anguish in her heart; the haughty, proud features were drawn and distorted with pain which she strove in vain to disguise. The young man had come to be her evil genius. I admired M. Gobseck, whose perspicacity had foreseen their future four years ago at the first bill which she endorsed.

"'Probably,' said I to myself, 'this monster with the angel's face controls every possible spring of action in her: rules her through vanity, jealousy, pleasure, and the current of life in the world.'"

The Vicomtesse de Grandlieu broke in on the story.

"Why, the woman's very virtues have been turned against her," she exclaimed. "He has made her shed tears of devotion, he has brought out the utmost natural generosity of woman, and then abused her kindness and made her pay very dearly for unhallowed bliss."

Derville did not understand the signs which Mme. de Grandlieu made to him.

"I confess," he said, "that I had no inclination to shed tears over the lot of this unhappy creature, so brilliant in society, so repulsive to eyes that could read her heart; I shuddered rather at the sight of her murderer, a young angel with such a clear brow, such red lips and white teeth, such a winning smile. There they stood before their judge, he scrutinizing them much as some old fifteenth-century Dominican inquisitor might have peered into the dungeons of the Holy Office while the torture was administered to two Moors.

"The Countess spoke tremulously. 'Sir,' she said, 'is

there any way of obtaining the value of these diamonds, and of keeping the right of repurchase?' She held out a jewel-case.

"'Yes, madame,' I put in, and came forwards.

"She looked at me, and a shudder ran through her as she recognized me, and gave me the glance which means, 'Say nothing of this,' all the world over.

"'This,' said I, 'constitutes a sale with faculty of redemption, as it is called, a formal agreement to transfer and deliver over a piece of property, either real estate or personalty, for a given time, on the expiration of which the previous owner recovers his title to the property in question, upon payment of a stipulated sum.'

"She breathed more freely. The Count looked black; he had grave doubts whether Gobseck would lend very much on the diamonds after such a fall in their value. Gobseck, impassive as ever, had taken up his magnifying glass, and was quietly scrutinizing the jewels. If I were to live for a hundred years, I should never forget the sight of his face at that moment. There was a flush in his pale cheeks; his eyes seemed to have caught the sparkle of the stones, for there was an unnatural glitter in them. He rose and went to the light, holding the diamonds close to his toothless mouth, as if he meant to devour them; mumbling vague words over them, holding up bracelets, sprays, necklaces, and tiaras one after another, to judge of their water, whiteness, and cutting; taking them out of the jewel-case and putting them in again, letting the play of the light bring out all their fires. He was more like a child than an old man; or, rather, childhood and dotage seemed to meet in him.

"'Fine stones! The set would have fetched three hundred thousand francs before the Revolution. What water. Genuine Asiatic diamonds from Golconda or Visapur. Do you know what they are worth? No, no; no one in Paris but Gobseck can appreciate them. In the time of the empire such a set would have cost another two hundred thousand francs!'

"He gave a disgusted shrug, and added—

"'But now diamonds are going down in value every day. The Brazilians have swamped the market with them since the peace; but the India stones are a better color. Others wear them now besides court ladies. Does madame go to court?'

"While he flung out these terrible words, he examined one stone after another with delight which no words can describe.

"'Flawless!' he said. 'Here is a speck!—— here is a flaw!—— A fine stone that!'

"His haggard face was so lighted up by the sparkling jewels, that it put me in mind of a dingy old mirror, such as you see in country inns. The glass receives every luminous image without reflecting the light, and a traveler bold enough to look for his face in it beholds a man in an apoplectic fit.

"'Well?' asked the Count, clapping Gobseck on the shoulder.

"The old boy trembled. He put down his playthings on his bureau, took his seat, and was a money-lender once more —hard, cold, and polished as a marble column.

"'How much do you want?'

"'One hundred thousand francs for three years,' said the Count.

"'That is possible,' said Gobseck, and from a mahogany box (Gobseck's jewel-case) he drew out a faultlessly adjusted pair of scales!

"He weighed the diamonds, calculating the value of stones and setting at sight (heaven knows how!), delight and severity struggling in the expression of his face the meanwhile. The Countess was plunged in a kind of a stupor; to me, watching her, it seemed that she was fathoming the depths of the abyss into which she had fallen. There was remorse still left in that woman's soul. Perhaps a hand held out in human charity might save her. I would try.

"'Are the diamonds your personal property, madame?' I asked in a clear voice.

"'Yes, monsieur,' she said, looking at me with proud eyes.

"'Make out the deed of purchase with power of redemption, chatterbox,' said Gobseck to me, resigning his chair at the bureau in my favor.

"'Madame is without doubt a married woman?' I tried again.

"She nodded abruptly.

"'Then I will not draw up the deed,' said I.

"'And why not?' asked M. Gobseck.

"'Why not?' echoed I, as I drew the old man into the bay window so as to speak aside with him. 'Why not? This woman is under her husband's control; the agreement would be void in law; you could not possibly assert your ignorance of a fact recorded on the very face of the document itself. You would be compelled at once to produce the diamonds deposited with you, according to the weight, value, and cutting therein described.'

"M. Gobseck cut me short with a nod, and turned towards the guilty couple.

"'He is right!' he said. 'That puts the whole thing in a different light. Eighty thousand francs down, and you leave the diamonds with me,' he added, in a husky, flute-like voice. 'In the way of property, possession is as good as a title.'

"'But——' objected the young man.

"'You can take it or leave it,' continued M. Gobseck, returning the jewel-case to the lady as he spoke.

"'I have too many risks to run.'

"'It would be better to throw yourself at your husband's feet,' I bent to whisper in her ear.

"The usurer doubtless knew what I was saying from the movement of my lips. He gave me a cool glance. The Count's face grew livid. The Countess was visibly wavering.

Maxime stepped up to her, and, low as he spoke, I could catch the words—

"'Adieu, dear Anastasie, may you be happy! As for me, by to-morrow my troubles will be over.'

"'Sir!' cried the lady, turning to M. Gobseck, 'I accept your offer.'

"'Come, now,' returned M. Gobseck. 'You have been a long time in coming to it, my fair lady.'

"He wrote out a cheque for fifty thousand francs on the Bank of France, and handed it to the Countess.

"'Now,' continued he with a smile, such a smile as you will see in portraits of M. Voltaire, 'now I will give you the rest of the amount in bills, thirty thousand francs' worth of paper as good as bullion. This gentleman here has just said, "My bills will be met when they are due,"' added he, producing certain drafts bearing the Count's signature, all protested the day before at the request of some of the confraternity, who had probably made them over to him (M. Gobseck) at a considerably reduced figure.

"The young man growled out something, in which the words 'Old scoundrel!' were audible. Daddy Gobseck did not move an eyebrow. He drew a pair of pistols out of a pigeon-hole, remarking cooly—

"'As the insulted man, I fire first.'

"'Maxime, you owe this gentleman an explanation,' cried the trembling Countess in a low voice.

"'I had no intention of giving offense,' stammered Maxime.

"'I am quite sure of that,' M. Gobseck answered calmly; 'you had no intention of meeting your bills, that was all.'

"The Countess rose, bowed, and vanished, with a great dread gnawing her, I doubt not. M. de Trailles was bound to follow, but before he went he managed to say—

"'If either of you gentlemen should forget himself, I will have his blood, or he will have mine.'

"'Amen!' called Daddy Gobseck as he put his pistols back in their place; 'but a man must have blood in his veins though before he can risk it, my son, and you have nothing but mud in yours.'

"When the door was closed, and the two vehicles had gone, M. Gobseck rose to his feet and began to prance about.

"'I have the diamonds! I have the diamonds!' he cried again and again, 'the beautiful diamonds! such diamonds! and tolerably cheap, too. Aha! aha! Werbrust and Gigonnet, you thought you had old Papa Gobseck! *Ego sum papa!* I am master of the lot of you! Paid! paid, principal and interest! How silly they will look to-night when I shall come out with this story between two games of dominoes!'

"The dark glee, the savage ferocity aroused by the possession of a few water-white pebbles, set me shuddering. I was dumb with amazement.

"'Aha! There you are, my boy!' said he. 'We will dine together. We will have some fun at your place, for I haven't a home of my own, and these restaurants, with their broths, and sauces, and wines, would poison the devil himself.'

"Something in my face suddenly brought back the usual cold, impassive expression to his.

"'You don't understand it,' he said, and, sitting down by the hearth, he put a tin saucepan full of milk on the brasier. 'Will you breakfast with me?' continued he. 'Perhaps there will be enough here for two.'

"'Thanks,' said I, 'I do not breakfast till noon.'

"I had scarcely spoken before hurried footsteps sounded from the passage. The stranger stopped at M. Gobseck's door and rapped; there was that in the knock which suggested a man transported with rage. M. Gobseck reconnoitred him through the grating; then he opened the door, and in came a man of thirty-five or so, judged harmless apparently in spite of his anger. The new-comer, who was quite plainly dressed, bore a strong resemblance to the late Duc de Richelieu. You must often have met him, he was the Countess' husband, a man with the aristocratic figure (permit the expression to pass) peculiar to statesmen of your Faubourg.

"'Sir,' said this person, addressing himself to M. Gobseck, who had quite recovered his tranquillity, 'did my wife go out of this house just now?'

"'That is possible.'

"'Well, sir, do you not take my meaning?'

"'I have not the honor of the acquaintance of my lady your wife,' returned Gobseck. 'I have had a good many visitors this morning, women and men, and mannish young ladies, and young gentlemen who look like young ladies. I should find it very hard to say——'

"'A truce to jesting, sir! I mean the woman who has this moment gone out from you.'

"'How can I know whether she is your wife or not? I never had the pleasure of seeing you before.'

"'You are mistaken, M. Gobseck,' said the Count, with profound irony in his voice. 'We have met before, one morning in my wife's bedroom. You had come to demand payment for a bill—no bill of hers.'

"'It was no business of mine to inquire what value she had received for it,' said M. Gobseck, with a malignant look at the Count. 'I had come by the bill in the way of business. At the same time, monsieur,' continued M. Gobseck, quietly pouring coffee into his bowl of milk, without a trace of excitement or hurry in his voice, ' you will permit me to observe that your right to enter my house and expostulate with me is far from proven to my mind. I came of age in the sixty-first year of the preceding century.'

"'Sir,' said the Count, 'you have just bought family diamonds, which do not belong to my wife, for a mere trifle.'

"'Without feeling it incumbent upon me to tell you my private affairs, I will tell you this much, M. le Comte—if

Mme. la Comtesse has taken your diamonds, you should have sent a circular round to all the jewelers, giving them notice not to buy them; she might have sold them separately.'

"'You know my wife, sir!' roared the Count.

"'True.'

"'She is in her husband's power.'

"'That is possible.'

"'She had no right to dispose of those diamonds——'

"'Precisely.'

"'Very well, sir?'

"'Very well, sir. I knew your wife, and she is in her husband's power; I am quite willing, she is in the power of a good many people; but—I—do—*not*—know—your diamonds. If Mme. la Comtesse can put her name to a bill, she can go into business of course, and buy and sell diamonds on her own account. The thing is plain on the face of it!'

"'Good-day, sir!' cried the Count, now white with rage. 'There are courts of justice.'

"'Quite so.'

"'This gentleman here,' he added, indicating me, 'was a witness of the sale.'

"That is possible.'

"The Count turned to go. Feeling the gravity of the affair, I suddenly put in between the two belligerents.

"'M. le Comte,' said I, 'you are right, and M. Gobseck is by no means in the wrong. You could not prosecute the purchaser without bringing your wife into court, and the whole of the odium would not fall on her. I am an attorney, and I owe it to myself, and still more to my professional position, to declare that the diamonds of which you speak were purchased by M. Gobseck in my presence; but, in my opinion, it would be unwise to dispute the legality of the sale, especially as the goods are not readily recognizable. In equity your contention would lie, in law it would collapse. M. Gobseck is too honest a man to deny that the sale was a profitable transaction, more especially as my conscience, no less than my duty, compels me to make the admission. But once bring the case into a court of law, M. le Comte, the issue would be doubtful. My advice to you is to come to terms with M. Gobseck, who can plead that he bought the diamonds in all good faith; you would be bound in any case to return the purchase money. Consent to an arrangement, with power to redeem at the end of seven or eight months, or a year even, or any convenient lapse of time, for the repayment of the sum borrowed by Mme. la Comtesse, unless you would prefer to repurchase them outright and give security for repayment.'

"Gobseck dipped his bread into the bowl of coffee, and ate with perfect indifference; but at the words 'come to terms,' he looked at me as much as to say, 'A fine fellow that! he has learned something from my lessons!' And I, for my part, riposted with a glance, which he understood uncommonly well. The business was dubious and shady; there was pressing need of coming to terms. Gobseck could not deny all knowledge of it, for I should appear as a witness. The Count thanked me with a smile of good-will.

"In the debate which followed, Gobseck showed greed enough and skill enough to baffle a whole congress of diplomatists; but in the end I drew up an instrument, in which the Count acknowledged the receipt of eighty-five thousand francs, interest included, in consideration of which Gobseck undertook to return the diamonds to the Count.

"'What waste!' exclaimed he as he put his signature to the agreement. 'How is it possible to bridge such a gulf?'

"'Have you many children, sir?' Gobseck asked gravely.

"The Count winced at the question; it was as if the old money-lender, like an experienced physician, had put his finger at once on the sore spot. The Comtesse's husband did not reply.

"'Well,' said Gobseck, taking the pained silence for answer, 'I know your story by heart. The woman is a fiend, but perhaps you love her still; I can well believe it; she made an impression on me. Perhaps, too, you would rather save your fortune, and keep it for one or two of your children? Well, fling yourself into the whirlpool of society, lose that fortune at play, come to Gobseck pretty often. The world will say that I am a Jew, a Tartar, a usurer, a pirate, will say that I have ruined you! I snap my fingers at them! If anybody insults me, I lay my man out; nobody is a surer shot nor handles a rapier better than your servant. And every one knows it. Then, have a friend—if you can find one—and make over your property to him by a fictitious sale. You call that a *fidei commissum*, don't you?' he asked, turning to me.

"The Count seemed to be entirely absorbed in his own thoughts.

"'You shall have your money to-morrow,' he said, 'have the diamonds in readiness,' and he went.

"'There goes one who looks to me to be as stupid as an honest man,' M. Gobseck said coolly when the Count had gone.

"'Say rather stupid as a man of passionate nature.'

"'The Count owes you your fee for drawing up the agreement!' M. Gobseck called after me as I took my leave.

"One morning, a few days after the scene which initiated me into the terrible depths beneath the surface of the life of a woman of fashion, the Count came into my private office.

"'I have come to consult you on a matter of grave moment,' he said, 'and I begin by telling you that I have perfect confidence in you, as I hope to prove to you. Your behavior to Mme. de Grandlieu is above all praise,' the Count went on. (You see, madame, that you have paid me a thousand times over for a very simple matter.)

"I bowed respectfully, and replied that I had done nothing but the duty of an honest man.

"'Well,' the Count went on, 'I have made a great many inquiries about the singular personage to whom you owe your position. And from all that I can learn, M. Gobseck is a philosopher of the Cynic school. What do you think of his probity?'

"'M. le Comte,' said I, 'M. Gobseck is my benefactor—at fifteen per cent.,' I added, laughing. 'But his avarice does not authorize me to paint him to the life for a stranger's benefit.'

"'Speak out, sir. Your frankness cannot injure M. Gobseck or yourself. I do not expect to find an angel in a pawnbroker.'

"'Daddy Gobseck,' I began, 'is intimately convinced of the truth of the principle which he takes for a rule of life. In his opinion, money is a commodity which you may sell cheap or dear, according to circumstances, with a clear conscience. A capitalist, by charging a high rate of interest, becomes in his eyes a secured partner by anticipation in the profits of a paying concern or speculation. Apart from the peculiar philosophical views of human nature and financial principles, which enable him to behave like a usurer, I am fully persuaded that, out of his business, he is the most loyal and upright soul in Paris. There are two men in him; he is petty and great—a miser and a philosopher. If I were to die and leave a family behind me, he would be the guardian whom I should appoint. This was how I came to see M. Gobseck in this light, monsieur. I know nothing of his past life. He may have been a pirate, may, for anything I know, have been all over the world, trafficking in diamonds, or men, or women, or state secrets; but this I affirm of him—never has human soul been more thoroughly tempered and tried. When I paid off my loan, I asked him, with a little circumlocution of course, how it was that he had made me pay such an exorbitant rate of interest; and why, seeing that I was a friend, and he meant to do me a kindness, he should not have yielded to the wish and made it complete. " My son," he said, "I released you from all need to feel any gratitude by giving you ground for the belief that you owed me nothing." So we are the best friends in the world. That answer, monsieur, gives you the man better than any amount of description.'

"'I have made up my mind once and for all,' said the Count. 'Draw up the necessary papers; I am going to transfer my property to Gobseck. I have no one but you to trust to in the draft of the counter-deed, which will declare that this transfer is a simulated sale, and that Gobseck as trustee will administer my estate (as he knows how to administer), and undertakes to make over my fortune to my eldest son when he comes of age. Now, sir, this I must tell you: I should be afraid to have that precious document in my own keeping. My boy is so fond of his mother, that I cannot trust him with it. So dare I beg of you to keep it for me? In case of death, Gobseck would make you legatee of my property. Every contingency is provided for.'

"The Count paused for a moment. He seemed greatly agitated.

"'A thousand pardons,' he said at length; 'I am in great pain, and have very grave misgivings as to my health. Recent troubles have disturbed me very painfully, and forced me to take this great step.'

"'Allow me first to thank you, monsieur,' said I, 'for the trust you place in me. But I am bound to deserve it by pointing out to you that you are disinheriting your—other children. They bear your name. Merely as the children of a once-loved wife, now fallen from her position, they have a claim to an assured existence. I tell you plainly that I cannot accept the trust with which you propose to honor me unless their future is secured.'

"The Count trembled violently at the words, and tears came into his eyes as he grasped my hand, saying, 'I did not know my man thoroughly. You have made me both glad and sorry. We will make provision for the children in the counter-deed.'

"I went with him to the door; it seemed to me that there was a glow of satisfaction in his face at the thought of this act of justice.

"Now, Camille, this is how a young wife takes the first step to the brink of a precipice. A quadrille, a ballad, a picnic party is sometimes cause sufficient of frightful evils. You are hurried on by the presumptuous voice of vanity and pride, on the faith of a smile or through giddiness and folly! Shame and misery and remorse are three furies awaiting every woman the moment she oversteps the limits——"

"Poor Camille can hardly keep awake," the Vicomtesse hastily broke in. "Go to bed, child; you have no need of appalling pictures to keep you pure in heart and conduct."

Camille de Grandlieu took the hint and went.

"You were going rather too far, dear M. Derville," said the Vicomtesse, "an attorney is not a mother of daughters nor yet a preacher."

"But any newspaper is a thousand times——"

"Poor Derville!" exclaimed the Vicomtesse, "what has come over you? Do you really imagine that I allow a daughter of mine to read the newspapers? Go on," she added after a pause.

"Three months after everything was signed and sealed between the Count and Gobseck——"

"You can call him the Comte de Restaud, now that Camille is not here," said the Vicomtesse.

"So be it! Well, time went by, and I saw nothing of the counter-deed, which by rights should have been in my hands. An attorney in Paris lives in such a whirl of business that with certain exceptions which we make for ourselves, we have not the time to give each individual client the amount of interest which he himself takes in his affairs. Still, one day when Gobseck came to dine with me, I asked him as we left the table if he knew how it was that I had heard no more of M. de Restaud.

"'There are excellent reasons for that,' he said; 'the noble Count is at death's door. He is one of the soft stamp that cannot learn how to put an end to chagrin, and allow it to wear them out instead. Life is a craft, a profession; every man must take the trouble to learn that business. When he has learned what life is by dint of painful experiences, the fibre of him is toughened, and acquires a certain elasticity, so that he has his sensibilities under his own control; he disciplines himself till his nerves are like steel springs, which always bend, but never break; given a sound digestion, and a man in such training ought to live as long as the cedars of Lebanon, and famous trees they are.'

"'Then is the Count actually dying?' I asked.

"'That is possible,' said Gobseck; 'the winding up of his estate will be a juicy bit of business for you.'

"I looked at my man, and said, by way of sounding him—

"'Just explain to me how it is that we, the Count and I, are the only men in whom you take an interest?'

"'Because you are the only two who have trusted me without finessing,' he said.

"Although this answer warranted my belief that Gobseck would act fairly even if the counter-deed were lost, I resolved to go to see the Count. I pleaded a business engagement, and we separated.

"I went straight to the Rue du Helder, and was shown into a room where the Countess sat playing with her children. When she heard my name, she sprang up and came to meet me, then she sat down and pointed without a word to a chair by the fire. Her face wore the inscrutable mask beneath which women of the world conceal their most vehement emotions. Trouble had withered that face already. Nothing of its beauty now remained, save the marvelous outlines in which its principal charm had lain.

"'It is essential, madame, that I should speak to M. le Comte——'

"'If so, you would be more favored than I am,' she said, interrupting me. 'M. de Restaud will see no one. He will hardly allow his doctor to come, and will not be nursed even by me. When people are ill, they have such strange fancies! They are like children, they do not know what they want.'

"'Perhaps, like children, they know very well what they want.'

"The Countess reddened. I almost repented a thrust worthy of Gobseck. So, by way of changing the conversation, I added, 'But M. de Restaud cannot possibly lie there alone all day, madame.'

"'His oldest boy is with him,' she said.

"It was useless to gaze at the Countess; she did not blush this time, and it looked to me as if she were resolved more firmly than ever that I should not penetrate into her secrets.

"'You must understand, madame, that my proceeding is no way indiscreet. It is strongly to his interest——' I bit my lips, feeling that I had gone the wrong way to work. The Countess immediately took advantage of my slip.

"'My interests are in no way separate from my husband's, sir,' said she. 'There is nothing to prevent you addressing yourself to me——'

"'The business which brings me here concerns no one but M. le Comte,' I said firmly.

"'I will let him know of your wish to see him.'

"The civil tone and expression assumed for the occasion did not impose upon me; I divined that she would never allow me to see her husband. I chatted on about indifferent matters for a little while, so as to study her; but, like all women who have once begun to plot for themselves, she could dissimulate with the rare perfection which, in your sex, means the last degree of perfidy. If I may dare to say it, I looked for anything from her, even a crime. She produced this feeling in me, because it was so evident from her manner and in all that she did or said, down to the very inflections of her voice, that she had an eye to the future. I went.

"Now I will pass on to the final scenes of this adventure, throwing in a few circumstances brought to light by time, and some details guessed by Gobseck's perspicacity or by my own.

"When the Comte de Restaud apparently plunged into the vortex of dissipation, something passed between the husband and wife, something which remains an impenetrable secret, but the wife sank even lower in the husband's eyes. As soon as he became so ill that he was obliged to take to his bed, he manifested his aversion for the Countess and the two youngest children. He forbade them to enter his room, and any attempt to disobey his wishes brought on such dangerous attacks that the doctor implored the Countess to submit to her husband's wish.

"Mme. de Restaud had seen the family estates and property, nay, the very mansion in which she lived, pass into the hands of Gobseck, who appeared to play the fantastic part of ogre so far as their wealth was concerned. She partially understood what her husband was doing, no doubt. M. de Trailles was traveling in England (his creditors had been a little too pressing of late), and no one else was in a position to enlighten the lady, and explain that her husband was taking precautions against her at Gobseck's suggestion. It is said that she held out for a long while before she gave the signature required by French law for the sale of the property; nevertheless the Count gained his point. The Countess was convinced that her husband was realizing his fortune, and that somewhere or other there would be a little bunch of notes representing the amount; they had been deposited with a notary, or perhaps at the bank, or in some safe hiding-place. Following out her train of thought, it was evident that M. de Restaud must of necessity have some kind of document in his possession by which any remaining property could be recovered and handed over to his son.

"So she made up her mind to keep the strictest possible watch over the sick-room. She ruled despotically in the house, and everything in it was submitted to this feminine espionage. All day she sat in the salon adjoining her husband's room, so that she could hear every syllable that he uttered, every least movement that he made. She had a bed put there for her of a night, but she did not sleep very much. The doctor was entirely in her interests. Such wifely devotion seemed praiseworthy enough. With the natural subtlety of perfidy, she took care to disguise M. de Restaud's repugnance for her, and feigned distress so perfectly that she gained a sort of celebrity. Straight-laced women were even found to say that she had expiated her sins. Always before her eyes she beheld a vision of the destitution to follow on the Count's death if her presence of mind should fail her; and in these ways the wife, repulsed from the bed of pain on which her husband lay and groaned, had drawn a charmed circle round about it. So near, yet kept at a distance; all-powerful, but in disgrace, the apparently devoted wife was lying in wait for death and opportunity; crouching like the ant-lion at the bottom of his spiral pit, ever on the watch for the prey that cannot escape, listening to the fall of every grain of sand.

"The strictest censor could not but recognize that the Countess pushed maternal sentiment to the last degree. Her father's death had been a lesson to her, people said. She worshiped her children. They were so young that she could hide the disorders of her life from their eyes, and could win their love; she had given them the best and most brilliant education. I confess that I cannot help admiring her and feeling sorry for her. Gobseck used to joke me about it. Just about that time she had discovered Maxime's baseness, and was expiating the sins of the past in tears of blood. I am sure of it. Hateful as were the measures which she took for regaining control of her husband's money, were they not the result of a mother's love, and a desire to repair the wrongs she had done her children? And again, it may be, like many a woman who has experienced the storms of lawless love, she felt a longing to lead a virtuous life again. Perhaps she only learned the worth of that life when she came to reap the woful harvest sown by her errors.

"Every time that little Ernest came out of his father's room, she put him through a searching examination as to all that his father had done or said. The boy willingly complied with his mother's wishes, and told her even more than she asked in her anxious affection, as he thought.

"My visit was a ray of light for the Countess. She was determined to see in me the instrument of the Count's vengeance, and resolved that I should not be allowed to go near the dying man. I augured ill of all this, and earnestly wished for an interview, for I was not easy in my mind about the fate of the counter-deed. If it should fall into the Countess' hands, she might turn it to her own account, and that would be the beginning of a series of interminable lawsuits between her and Gobseck. I knew the usurer well enough to feel convinced that he would never give up the property to her; there was room for plenty of legal quibbling over a series of transfers, and I alone knew all the ins and outs of the matter. I was minded to prevent such a tissue of misfortune, so I went to the Countess a second time.

"I have noticed, madame," said Derville, turning to the Vicomtesse, and speaking in a confidential tone, "certain moral phenomena to which we do not pay enough attention. I am naturally an observer of human nature, and instinctively I bring a spirit of analysis to the business that I transact in the interest of others, when human passions are called into lively play. Now, I have often noticed, and always with new wonder, that two antagonists almost always divine each other's inmost thoughts and ideas. Two enemies sometimes possess a power of clear insight into mental processes, and read each other's minds as two lovers read in either soul. So when we came together, the Countess and I, I understood at once the reason of her antipathy for me, disguised though it was by the most gracious forms of politeness and civility. I had been forced to be her confidant, and a woman cannot but hate the man before whom she is compelled to blush. And she on her side knew that if I was the man in whom her husband placed confidence, that husband had not as yet given up his fortune.

"I will spare you the conversation, but it abides in my memory as one of the most dangerous encounters in my career. Nature had bestowed on her all the qualities which, combined, are irresistibly fascinating; she could be pliant and proud by turns, and confiding and coaxing in her manner; she even went so far as to try to arouse curiosity and kindle love in her effort to subjugate me. It was a failure. As I took my leave of her, I caught a gleam of hate and rage in her eyes that made me shudder. We parted enemies. She would fain have crushed me out of existence; and for my own part, I felt pity for her, and for some natures pity is the deadliest of insults. This feeling pervaded the last representations I put before her; and when I left her, I left, I think, dread in the depths of her soul, by declaring that, turn which way she would, ruin lay inevitably before her.

"'If I were to see M. le Comte, your children's property at any rate would——'

"'I should be at your mercy,' she said, breaking in upon me, disgust in her gesture.

"Now that we had spoken frankly, I made up my mind to save the family from impending destitution. I resolved to strain the law at need to gain my ends, and this was what I did. I sued the Comte de Restaud for a sum of money, ostensibly due to Gobseck, and gained judgment. The Countess, of course, did not allow him to know of this, but I had gained my point, I had a right to affix seals to everything on the death of the Count. I bribed one of the servants in the house—the man undertook to let me know at any hour of the day or night if his master should be at the point of death, so that I could intervene at once, scare the Countess with a threat of affixing seals, and so secure the counter-deed.

"I learned later on that the woman was studying the Code, with her husband's dying moans in her ears. If we could picture the thoughts of those who stand about a death-bed, what fearful sights should we not see? Money is always the motive-spring of the schemes elaborated, of all the plans that are made and the plots that are woven about it! Let us leave these details, nauseating in the nature of them; but perhaps they may have given you some insight into all that this husband and wife endured; perhaps too they may unveil much that is passing in secret in other houses.

"For two months the Comte de Restaud lay on his bed, alone, and resigned to his fate. Mortal disease was slowly sapping the strength of mind and body. Unaccountable and grotesque sick fancies preyed upon him; he would not suffer them to set his room in order, no one should nurse him, he would not even allow them to make his bed. All his surroundings bore the marks of this last degree of apathy, the furniture was out of place, the daintiest trifles were covered with dust and cobwebs. In health he had been a man of refined and expensive tastes, now he positively delighted in the comfortless look of the room. A host of objects required in illness—rows of medicine bottles, empty and full, most of them dirty; crumpled linen, and broken plates—littered the writing-table, chairs, and chimney-pieces. An open warming-pan lay on the floor before the grate; a bath, still full of mineral water, had not been taken away. The sense of coming dissolution pervaded all the details of an unsightly chaos. Signs of death appeared in things inanimate before the destroyer came to the body on the bed. The Comte de

Restaud could not bear the daylight, the Venetian shutters were closed, darkness deepened the gloom in the dismal chamber. The sick man himself had wasted greatly. All the life in him seemed to have taken refuge in the still brilliant eyes. The livid whiteness of his face was something horrible to see, enhanced as it was by the long dank locks of hair that straggled along his cheeks, for he would never suffer them to cut it. He looked like some religious fanatic in the desert. Mental suffering was extinguishing all human instincts in this man of scarce fifty years of age, whom all Paris had known as so brilliant and so successful.

"One morning at the beginning of December, 1824, he looked up at Ernest, who sat at the foot of his bed gazing at his father with wistful eyes.

"'Are you in pain?' the little Vicomte asked.

"'No,' said the Count, with a ghastly smile, 'it all lies *here and about my heart!*'

"He pointed to his forehead, and then laid his wasted fingers on his hollow chest. Ernest began to cry at the sight.

"'How is it that M. Derville does not come to me?' the Count asked his servant (he thought that Maurice was really attached to him, but the man was entirely in the Countess' interest)—'What! Maurice!' and the dying man suddenly sat upright in his bed, and seemed to recover all his presence of mind, 'I have sent for my attorney seven or eight times during the last fortnight, and he does not come!' he cried. 'Do you imagine that I am to be trifled with? Go for him, at once, this very instant, and bring him back with you. If you do not carry out my orders, I shall get up and go myself.'

"'Madame,' said the man as he came into the salon, 'you heard M. le Comte; what ought I to do?'

"'Pretend to go to the attorney, and when you come back, tell your master that his man of business is forty leagues away from Paris on an important lawsuit. Say that he is expected back at the end of the week. Sick people never know how ill they are,' thought the Countess; 'he will wait till the man comes home.'

"The doctor had said on the previous evening that the Count could scarcely live through the day. When the servant came back two hours later to give that hopeless answer, the dying man seemed to be greatly agitated.

"'O God!' he cried again and again, 'I put my trust in none but Thee.'

"For a long while he lay and gazed at his son, and spoke in a feeble voice at last.

"'Ernest, my boy, you are very young; but you have a good heart; you can understand, no doubt, that a promise given to a dying man is sacred; a promise to a father—— Do you feel that you can be trusted with a secret, and keep it so well and closely that even your mother herself shall not know that you have a secret to keep? There is no one else in this house whom I can trust to-day. You will not betray my trust, will you?'

"'No, father.'

"'Very well, then, Ernest, in a minute or two I will give you a sealed packet that belongs to M. Derville; you must take such care of it that no one can know that you have it; then you must slip out of the house and put the letter into the post-box at the corner.'

"'Yes, father.'

"'Can I depend upon you?'

"'Yes, father.'

"'Come and kiss me. You have made death less bitter to me, dear boy. In six or seven years' time you will understand the importance of this secret, and you will be well rewarded then for your quickness and obedience, you will know then how much I love you. Leave me alone for a minute, and let no one—no matter whom—come in meanwhile.'

"Ernest went out and saw his mother standing in the next room.

"'Ernest,' said she 'come here.'

"She sat down, drew her son to her knees and clasped him in her arms and held him tightly to her heart.

"'Ernest, your father said something to you just now.'

"'Yes, mamma.'

"'What did he say?'

"'I cannot repeat it, mamma.'

"'Oh, my dear child,' cried the Countess, kissing him in rapture. 'You have kept your secret; how glad that makes me! Never tell a lie; never fail to keep your word—those are two principles which should never be forgotten.'

"'Oh! mamma, how beautiful you are! *You* never told a lie, I am quite sure.'

"'Once or twice, Ernest dear, I have lied. Yes, and I have not kept my word under circumstances which speak louder than all precepts. Listen, my Ernest, you are big enough and intelligent enough to see that your father drives me away, and will not allow me to nurse him, and this is not natural, for you know how much I love him.'

"'Yes, mamma.'

"The Countess began to cry. 'Poor child!' she said, 'this misfortune is the result of treacherous insinuations. Wicked people have tried to separate me from your father to satisfy their greed. They mean to take all our money from us and to keep it for themselves. If your father were well, the division between us would soon be over; he would listen to me; he is loving and kind; he would see his mistake. But now his mind is affected, and his prejudices against me have become a fixed idea, a sort of mania with him. It is one result of his illness. Your father's fondness for you is another proof that his mind is deranged. Until he fell ill you never noticed that he loved you more than Pauline or Georges. It is all caprice with him now. In his affection for you he might take it into his head to tell you to do things for him. If you do not want to ruin us all, my darling, and to see your mother begging her bread like a pauper woman, you must tell her everything——'

"'Ah!' cried the Count. He had opened the door and stood there, a sudden, half-naked apparition, almost as thin and fleshless as a skeleton.

"His smothered cry produced a terrible effect upon the Countess; she sat motionless, as if a sudden stupor had seized her. Her husband was as white and wasted as if he had risen out of his grave.

"'You have filled my life to the full with trouble, and now you are trying to vex my death-bed, to warp my boy's mind, and make a depraved man of him!' he cried hoarsely.

"The Countess flung herself at his feet. His face, working with the last emotions of life, was almost hideous to see."

"'Mercy! mercy!' she cried aloud, shedding a torrent of tears.

"'Have you shown me any pity?' he asked. 'I allowed you to squander your own money, and now do you mean to squander my fortune, too, and ruin my son?'

"'Ah! well, yes, have no pity for me, be merciless to me!' she cried. 'But the children? Condemn your widow to live in a convent; I will obey you; I will do anything, anything that you bid me, to expiate the wrong I have done you, if that only the children may be happy! The children! Oh, the children!'

"'I have only one child,' said the Count, stretching out a wasted arm, in his despair, towards his son.

"'Pardon a penitent woman, a penitent woman! ——' wailed the Countess, her arms about her husband's damp feet. She could not speak for sobbing; vague, incoherent sounds broke from her parched throat.

"'You dare to talk of penitence after all that you said to Ernest!' exclaimed the dying man, shaking off the Countess, who lay groveling at his feet. 'You turn me to ice!' he added, and there was something appalling in the indifference

CLOTHES AND PAPERS AND RAGS LAY TOSSED ABOUT IN CONFUSION.

with which he uttered the words. 'You have been a bad daughter; you have been a bad wife; you will be a bad mother.'

"The wretched woman fainted away. The dying man reached his bed and lay down again, and a few hours later sank into unconsciousness. The priests came and administered the sacraments.

"At midnight he died; the scene that morning had exhausted his remaining strength, and on the stroke of midnight I arrived with Daddy Gobseck. The house was in confusion, and under cover of it we walked up into the little salon adjoining the death-chamber. The three children were there in tears, with two priests, who had come to watch with the dead. Ernest came over to me, and said that his mother desired to be alone in the Count's room.

"'Do not go in,' he said; and I admired the child for his tone and gesture; 'she is praying there.'

"Gobseck began to laugh that soundless laugh of his, but I felt too much touched by the feeling in Ernest's little face to join in the miser's sardonic amusement. When Ernest saw that we moved towards the door, he planted himself in front of it, crying out, 'Mamma, here are some gentlemen in black who want to see you!'

"Gobseck lifted Ernest out of the way as if the child had been a feather, and opened the door.

"What a scene it was that met our eyes! The room was in frightful disorder; clothes and papers and rags lay tossed about in a confusion horrible to see in the presence of death; and there, in the midst, stood the Countess in disheveled despair, unable to utter a word, her eyes glittering. The Count had scarcely breathed his last before his wife came in and forced open the drawers and the desk; the carpet was strewn with litter, some of the furniture and boxes were broken, the signs of violence could be seen everywhere. But if her search had at first proved fruitless, there was that in her excitement and attitude which led me to believe that she had found the mysterious documents at last. I glanced at the bed, and professional instinct told me all that had happened. The mattress had been flung contemptuously down by the bedside, and across it, face downwards, lay the body of the Count, like one of the paper envelopes that strewed the carpet—he too was nothing now but an envelope. There was something grotesquely horrible in the attitude of the stiffening, rigid limbs.

"The dying man must have hidden the counter-deed under his pillow to keep it safe so long as life should last; and his wife must have guessed his thought; indeed, it might be read plainly in his last dying gesture, in the convulsive clutch of his claw-like hands. The pillow had been flung to the floor at the foot of the bed; I could see the print of her heel upon it. At her feet lay a paper with the Count's arms on the seals; I snatched it up, and saw that it was addressed to me. I looked steadily at the Countess with the pitiless clear-sightedness of an examining magistrate confronting a guilty creature. The contents were blazing in the grate; she had flung them on the fire at the sound of our approach, imagining, from a first hasty glance at the provisions which I had suggested for her children, that she was destroying a will which disinherited them. A tormented conscience and involuntary horror of the deed which she had done had taken away all power of reflection. She had been caught in the act, and possibly the scaffold was rising before her eyes, and she already felt the felon's branding iron.

"There she stood gasping for breath, waiting for us to speak, staring at us with haggard eyes, and every feature manifesting a guilty conscience.

"I went across to the grate and pulled out an unburned fragment. 'Ah, madame!' I exclaimed, 'you have ruined your children! Those papers were their titles to their property.'

"Her mouth twitched, she looked as if she were threatened by a paralytic seizure.

"'Eh! eh!' cried Gobseck; the harsh, shrill tone grated upon our ears like the sound of a brass candlestick scratching a marble surface.

"There was a pause, then the old man turned to me and said quietly—

"'Do you intend Mme. la Comtesse to suppose that I am not the rightful owner of the property sold to me by her late husband? This house belongs to me now.'

"A sudden blow on the head from a bludgeon would have given me less pain and astonishment. The Countess saw the look of hesitation in my face.

"'Monsieur,' she cried, 'Monsieur!' She could find no other words.

"'You are a trustee, are you not?' I asked.

"'That is possible.'

"'Then do you mean to take advantage of this crime of hers?'

"'Precisely.'

"I went at that, leaving the Countess sitting by her husband's bedside, shedding hot tears. Gobseck followed me. Outside in the street I separated from him, but he came after me, flung me one of those searching glances with which he probed men's minds, and said in the husky flute-tones, pitched in a shriller key—

"'Do you take it upon yourself to judge me?'

"From that time forward we saw little of each other. Gobseck let the Count's mansion on lease; he spent the summers on the country estates. He was a lord of the manor in earnest, putting up farm buildings, repairing mills and roadways, and planting timber. I came across him one day in a walk in the Jardin des Tuileries.

"'The Countess is behaving like a heroine,' said I; 'she

gives herself up entirely to the children's education; she is giving them a perfect bringing up. The oldest boy is a charming young fellow——'

"'That is possible.'

"'But ought you not to help Ernest?' I suggested.

"'Help him!' cried Gobseck. 'Not I! Adversity is the greatest of all teachers; adversity teaches us to know the value of money and the worth of men and women. Let him set sail on the seas of Paris; when he is a qualified pilot, we will give him a ship to steer.'

"I left him without seeking to explain the meaning of his words.

"M. de Restaud's mother has prejudiced him against me, and he is very far from taking me as his legal adviser; still, I went to see Gobseck last week to tell him about Ernest's love for Mlle. Camille, and pressed him to carry out his contract, since that young Restaud is just of age.

"I found that the old-bill discounter had been kept to his bed for a long time by the complaint of which he was to die. He put me off, saying that he would give the matter his attention when he could get up again and see after his business; his idea being no doubt that he would not give up any of his possessions so long as the breath was in him; no other reason could be found for his shuffling answer. He seemed to me to be much worse than he at all suspected. I stayed with him long enough to discern the progress of a passion which age had converted into a sort of craze. He wanted to be alone in the house, and had taken the rooms one by one as they fell vacant. In his own room he had changed nothing; the furniture which I knew so well sixteen years ago looked the same as ever; it might have been kept under a glass case. Gobseck's faithful old portress, with her husband, a pensioner, who sat in the entry while she was upstairs, was still his housekeeper and charwoman, and now in addition his sick-nurse. In spite of his feebleness, Gobseck saw his clients himself as heretofore, and received sums of money; his affairs had been so simplified, that he only needed to send his pensioner out now and again on an errand, and could carry on business in his bed.

"After the treaty, by which France recognized the Haytian Republic, Gobseck was one of the members of the commission appointed to liquidate claims and assess repayments due by Hayti; his special knowledge of old fortunes in San Domingo, and the planters and their heirs and assigns to whom the indemnities were due, had led to his nomination. Gobseck's peculiar genius had then devised an agency for discounting the planters' claims on the government. The business was carried on under the names of Werbrust and Gigonnet, with whom he shared the spoil without disbursements, for his knowledge was accepted instead of capital. The agency was a sort of distillery, in which money was extracted from doubtful claims, and the claims of those who knew no better, or had no confidence in the government. As a liquidator, Gobseck could make terms with the large landed proprietors; and these, either to gain a higher percentage of their claims or to ensure prompt settlements, would send him presents in proportion to their means. In this way presents came to be a kind of percentage upon sums too large to pass through his control, while the agency bought up cheaply the small and dubious claims, or the claims of those persons who preferred a little ready money to a deferred and somewhat hazy repayment by the Republic. Gobseck was the insatiable boa-constrictor of the great business. Every morning he received his tribute, eyeing it like a Nabob's prime minister, as he considers whether he will sign a pardon. Gobseck would take anything, from the present of game sent him by some poor devil or the pound's weight of wax-candles from devout folk, to the rich man's plate and the speculator's gold snuff-box. Nobody knew what became of the presents sent to the old money-lender. Everything went in, but nothing came out.

"'On the word of an honest woman,' said the portress, an old acquaintance of mine, 'I believe he swallows it all and is none the fatter for it; he is as thin and dried up as the cuckoo in the clock.'

"At length, last Monday, Gobseck sent his pensioner for me. The man came up to my private office.

"'Be quick and come, M. Derville,' said he, 'the governor is just going to hand in his checks; he has grown as yellow as a lemon; he is fidgeting to speak with you; death has fair hold of him; the rattle is working in his throat.'

"When I entered Gobseck's room, I found the dying man kneeling before the grate. If there was no fire on the hearth, there was at any rate a monstrous heap of ashes. He had dragged himself out of bed, but his strength had failed him, and he could neither go back nor find voice to complain.

"'You felt cold, old friend,' I said, as I helped him back to his bed; 'how can you do without a fire?'

"'I am not cold at all,' he said. 'No fire here! no fire! I am going, I know not where, lad,' he went on, glancing at me with blank, lightless eyes, 'but I am going away from this. I have *carpology*,' said he (the use of the technical term showing how clear and accurate his mental processes were even now). 'I thought the room was full of live gold, and I got up to catch some of it. To whom will all mine go, I wonder? Not to the Crown; I have left a will, look for it, Grotius. "The Holland Belle" had a daughter; I once saw the girl somewhere or other, in the Rue Vivienne, one evening. They call her "La Torpille," I believe; she is as pretty as pretty can be; look her up, Grotius. You are my executor; take what you like; help yourself. There are Strasbourg pies there, and bags of coffee, and sugar, and gold spoons. Give the Odiot service to your wife. But who is to have the diamonds? Are you going to take them, lad? There is snuff too—sell it at Hamburg, tobaccos are worth half as much again at Hamburg. All sorts of things I have, in fact, and now I must go and leave them all. Come, Papa Gobseck, no weakness, be yourself!'

"He raised himself in bed, the lines of his face standing out as sharply against the pillow as if the profile had been cast in bronze; he stretched out a lean arm and bony hand along the coverlet and clutched it, as if so he would fain keep his hold on life, then he gazed hard at the grate, cold as his own metallic eyes, and died in full consciousness of death. To us —the portress, the old pensioner, and myself—he looked like one of the old Romans standing behind the consuls in Lethière's picture of the 'Death of the Sons Brutus.'

"'He was a good-plucked one, the old Lascar!' said the pensioner in his soldierly fashion.

"But as for me, the dying man's fantastical enumeration of his riches was still sounding in my ears, and my eyes, following the direction of his, rested on that heap of ashes. It struck me that it was very large. I took the tongs, and, as soon as I stirred the cinders, I felt the metal underneath, a mass of gold and silver coins, receipts taken during his illness, doubtless, after he grew too feeble to lock the money up, and could trust no one to take it to the bank for him.

"'Run for the justice of the peace,' said I, turning to the old pensioner, 'so that everything can be sealed here at once.'

"Gobseck's last words and the old portress' remarks had struck me. I took the keys of the rooms on the first and second floor to make a visitation. The first door that I opened revealed the meaning of the phrases which I took for mad ravings; and I saw the length to which covetousness goes when it survives only as an illogical instinct, the last stage of greed of which you find so many examples among misers in country towns.

"In the room next to the one in which Gobseck had died, a quantity of eatables of all kinds were stored—putrid pies, moldy fish, nay, even shell-fish; the stench almost choked me. Maggots and insects swarmed. These comparatively recent presents were put down, pell-mell, among chests of tea, bags of coffee, and packing-cases of every shape. A silver soup tureen on the chimney-piece was full of advices of the arrival of goods consigned to his order at Havre, bales of cotton, hogsheads of sugar, barrels of rum, coffees, indigo, tobaccos, a perfect bazaar of colonial produce. The room itself was crammed with furniture, and silver-plate, and lamps, and vases, and pictures; there were books, and curiosities, and fine engravings lying rolled up, unframed. Perhaps these were not all presents, and some part of this vast quantity of stuff had been deposited with him in the shape of pledges, and had been left on his hands in default of payment. I noticed jewel-cases, with ciphers and armorial bearings stamped upon them, and sets of fine table-linen, and weapons of price; but none of the things were docketed. I opened a book which seemed to be misplaced, and found a thousand-franc note in it. I promised myself that I would go through everything thoroughly; I would try the ceilings, and floors, and walls, and cornices to discover all the gold, hoarded with such passionate greed by a Dutch miser worthy of a Rembrandt's brush. In all the course of my professional career I have never seen such impressive signs of the eccentricity of avarice.

"I went back to his room, and found an explanation of this chaos and accumulation of riches in a pile of letters lying under the paper-weights on his desk—Gobseck's correspondence with the various dealers to whom doubtless he usually sold his presents. These persons had, perhaps, fallen victims to Gobseck's cleverness, or Gobseck may have wanted fancy prices for his goods; at any rate, every bargain hung in suspense. He had not disposed of the eatables to Chevet, because Chevet would only take them of him at a loss of thirty per cent. Gobseck haggled for a few francs between the prices, and while they wrangled the goods became unsalable. Again,

Gobseck had refused free delivery of his silver-plate, and declined to guarantee the weights of his coffees. There had been a dispute over each article, the first indication in Gobseck of the childishness and incomprehensible obstinacy of age, a condition of mind reached at last by all men in whom a strong passion survives the intellect.

"I said to myself, as he had said, 'To whom will all these riches go?'—— And when I think of the grotesque information he gave me as to the present address of his heiress, I foresee that it will be my duty to search all the houses of ill-fame in Paris to pour out an immense fortune on some worthless jade. But, in the first place, know this—that in a few days' time Ernest de Restaud will come into a fortune to which his title is unquestionable, a fortune which will put him in a position to marry Mlle. Camille, even after adequate provision has been made for his mother the Comtesse de Restaud, and his sister and brother."

"Well, dear M. Derville, we will think about it," said Mme. de Grandlieu. "M. Ernest ought to be very wealthy indeed if such a family as ours must accept that mother of his. Bear in mind that my son will be the Duc de Grandlieu one day; he will unite the estates of both the houses that bear our name, and I wish him to have a brother-in-law to his mind."

"But Restaud bears *gules, a traverse argent, on four scutcheons or, a cross sable*, and that is a very pretty coat of arms."

"That is true," said the Vicomtesse; "and, besides, Camille need not see her mother-in-law."

"Mme. de Beauséant used to receive Mme. de Restaud," said the gray-haired uncle.

"Oh! that was at her great crushes," replied the Vicomtesse.

PARIS, *January*, 1830.

www.ingramcontent.com/pod-product-compliance
Lightning Source LLC
Chambersburg PA
CBHW051248300426
44114CB00011B/936